Rebellion as Genre in
the Novels of Scott,
Dickens and Stevenson

Rebellion as Genre in the Novels of Scott, Dickens and Stevenson

ANNA FAKTOROVICH

McFarland & Company, Inc., Publishers
Jefferson, North Carolina, and London

LIBRARY OF CONGRESS CATALOGUING-IN-PUBLICATION DATA

Faktorovich, Anna, 1981–
    Rebellion as genre in the novels of Scott, Dickens and Stevenson / Anna Faktorovich.
       p.   cm.
    Includes bibliographical references and index.

    ISBN 978-0-7864-7149-2
    softcover : acid free paper ∞

    1. Scott, Walter, Sir, 1771–1832—Criticism and interpretation. 2. Dickens, Charles, 1812–1870—Criticism and interpretation. 3. Stevenson, Robert Louis, 1850–1894—Criticism and interpretation. 4. Social change in literature. 5. Revolutions in literature. I. Title.
PR5345.F35 2013
823'.7—dc23
                                                  2013005164

BRITISH LIBRARY CATALOGUING DATA ARE AVAILABLE

© 2013 Anna Faktorovich. All rights reserved

No part of this book may be reproduced or transmitted in any form or by any means, electronic or mechanical, including photocopying or recording, or by any information storage and retrieval system, without permission in writing from the publisher.

On the cover: "True reform of Parliament: patriots lighting a revolutionary-bonfire in new Palace Yard," Js. Gillray, inv. & fect. [London]: H. Humphrey, 27 St. James's Street, 1809. British Cartoon Prints Collection (Library of Congress)

Manufactured in the United States of America

McFarland & Company, Inc., Publishers
   Box 611, Jefferson, North Carolina 28640
   www.mcfarlandpub.com

Contents

Chronology	vii
Abbreviations Used for Sources	xi
Introduction	1

PART I: A GENRE UNDER A MICROSCOPE

1. Rebellions and Reforms in Britain	9
2. Genre Theory and the Rebellion Novel	15
3. Criteria for Selecting Rebellion Novels	25
4. Readers of Rebellion Novels	31
5. Censorship, the Publishing Business, and Subversive Literary Warfare	37
6. The Elements of Rebellion Novels	48

PART II: SIR WALTER SCOTT AND THE INVENTION OF THE REBELLION GENRE

7. Scott's Scottish Nationalism	63
8. Scott's Structural Features	80
9. Scott's Linguistic Features	97

PART III: CHARLES DICKENS: THE RADICAL SOCIALIST

10. Dickens' Socialist Purpose	113
11. Dickens' Structural Features	136
12. Dickens' Linguistic Features	152

Part IV: Robert Louis Stevenson: Patronage and Rebellion

13. Stevenson's Radical Purpose — 165
14. Stevenson's Structural Features — 187
15. Stevenson's Linguistic Features — 208

Conclusion — 219
Chapter Notes — 227
Bibliography — 240
Index — 247

Chronology

1296	England invades Scotland
1296–1328	First War of Scottish Independence
1332–57	Second War of Scottish Independence (Scotland wins)
1370s	John Barbour's *The Bruce* published (Wars of Scottish Independence)
1471–79	Blind Harry's *Wallace* published (Wars of Scottish Independence)
1689	Glorious Revolution (King James II's overthrow)
1707	Acts of Union of 1707 (Kingdoms of England and Scotland join into the kingdom of Great Britain)
1715	Jacobite Rising of 1715 (Scotland)
1719	Jacobite Rising of 1719 (Scotland)
1745	Jacobite Rising of 1745 (Scotland)
1750–1850	Industrial Revolution (Europe)
1775–83	American Revolutionary War
1780	Gordon Riots (London)
1789–99	French Revolution
1801	The Kingdoms of Great Britain and Ireland merge into the United Kingdom
1803–15	Napoleonic Wars
1803	Robert Emmet's rebellion in Dublin, Ireland
1807	Slave Trade Act abolishes the slave trade within England
1814	Scott publishes *Waverley*
1816	Scott publishes *The Black Dwarf*
1816	Scott publishes *The Tale of Old Mortality*
1817	Scott publishes *Rob Roy*
1817	Pentrich Revolution in England
1817	Gagging Acts pass, against seditious libel

1817	Repressions: 26 prosecutions for seditious and blasphemous libel in England
1818	Scott publishes *The Heart of Mid-Lothian*
1819	Peterloo Massacre in Manchester, England
1819	Six Acts pass (antilibel/sedition/reform agitation)
1819	Richard Carlile imprisoned for blasphemy and seditious libel
1820	Cato Street conspiracy in England
1820	Scottish Insurrection in Scotland
1821	Jane Carlile, Richard's wife, imprisoned for seditious libel
1821	Mary Carlile, Jane's sister, imprisoned for publishing the radical *Republican*
1821	150 people imprisoned for selling the *Republican* (England)
1822	King George IV visits Edinburgh, Scotland
1824	Scott publishes *Redgauntlet*
1828	Scott publishes "My Aunt Margaret's Mirror"
1828	Bray publishes *The White Hoods*
1830	July Revolution in France
1830	Richard Carlile imprisoned for writing against agricultural laborer wage cuts
1831–32	Reform Crisis of 1832 (a revolution barely avoided)
1831	Barrow publishes *Account of the Mutiny of the Ship Bounty*
1831	Thomas Carlyle publishes *Cruthers and Jonson*
1833	Slavery Abolition Act abolished the trade with all nations
1837–1901	Victorian Era (Queen Victoria reigns in England)
1837	Carlyle publishes *The French Revolution: A History*
1838	Lockhart publishes *Memoirs of the Life of Sir Walter Scott*
1838	Carlyle publishes "On Sir Walter Scott (1771–1832)."
1838	Affair of Blean Wood (last peasant revolt—11 rebels die)
1840	Ainsworth publishes *Guy Fawkes*
1841	Dickens publishes *Barnaby Rudge*
1841–2	Afghan Uprising
1842	Carlyle publishes *Chartism*
1845–57	European potato famine (Ireland's Great Famine & Highland potato famine)
1845	Disraeli publishes *Sybil, the Two Nations*
1847	LeFanu publishes *The Fortunes of Colonel Torlogh O'Brien*
1848	1848 revolutions
1848	Marx publishes *Communist Manifesto* in Germany
1851	The Great Exhibition (London: industrial research displayed)
1852	Dickens publishes *Bleak House*
1852	Stowe publishes *Uncle Tom's Cabin* in America

1853–6	Crimean War (Russian Empire vs. British, French, Ottoman, and Sardinian Empires)
1857–9	Indian Mutiny
1857–9	Thackeray publishes *The Virginians*
1859	Dickens publishes *A Tale of Two Cities*
1859	Darwin publishes *On the Origin of Species*
1865	Kingsley publishes *Hereward the Wake*
1866	Eliot publishes *Felix Holt*
1867	1867 Reform Act
1867	Marx publishes *Capital* in Germany
1867	Fenian Rebellion
1868	Disraeli's first term as Prime Minister
1874–80	Disraeli's second term as Prime Minister
1884	Reform Act
1885	Stevensons publish *The Dynamiter*
1885	Stevenson publishes *Prince Otto*
1886	Stevenson publishes *Kidnapped*
1888	Stevenson publishes *The Black Arrow*
1892	Stevenson writes "The Young Chevalier"
1893	Stevenson publishes *David Balfour*
1895	Stevenson publishes *A Footnote to History*
1895	Stevenson publishes *The Pentland Rising*

Abbreviations Used for Sources

"Aunt Margaret"   Sir Walter Scott, "My Aunt Margaret's Mirror" (London: *The Keepsake Annual* (Volume I), 1828. Project Gutenberg. Accessed May 27, 2011).
Balfour   Robert L. Stevenson, *David Balfour: Being Memoirs of the Further Adventures of David Balfour at Home and Abroad* (1893) (New York: Charles Scribner's Sons, 1994).
Barnaby   Charles Dickens, *Barnaby Rudge* (1841) (Oxford: Oxford University Press, 2008).
Black Arrow   Robert L. Stevenson, *The Black Arrow: A Tale of the Two Roses* (1888) (New York: Penguin, 2007).
Black Dwarf   Sir Walter Scott, *The Black Dwarf* (1816) (Edinburgh: Edinburgh University Press, 1993).
Bleak House   Charles Dickens, *Bleak House* (1852) (New York: Bantam, 1985).
Colonel Torlogh   Sheridan LeFanu, *The Fortunes of Colonel Torlogh O'Brien: A Tale of the Wars of King James* (1847) (India: Nabu Press, 2010).
Copperfield   Charles Dickens, *The Personal History of David Copperfield* (1849) (London: Bradbury & Evans, 1850, Google Books).
D'Arcy   Julian Meldon D'Arcy, *Subversive Scott: The Waverley Novels and Scottish Nationalism* (Hagatorgi: University of Iceland Press, 2005).
Dynamiter   Robert L. Stevenson and Fanny Van de Grift Stevenson, *The Dynamiter* (London: Longmans, Green, and Co., 1885. Google Books. Accessed November 15, 2010).
Felix Holt   George Eliot, *Felix Holt, the Radical* (1866) (Orchard Park, N.Y.: Broadview Press, 2000).
Footnote   Robert L. Stevenson, *A Footnote to History: Eight Years of Trouble in Samoa* (New York: Charles Scribner's Sons, 1895).
Guy Fawkes   Harrison Ainsworth, *Historical Romances of William Harrison*

Ainsworth: Guy Fawkes, Volume XIX (1840) (Philadelphia: Barrie, 1901. LaVergne, Tenn.: Kessinger Press, 2010).
Hard Times   Charles Dickens, *Hard Times: For These Times* (1854) (London: Bradbury & Evans, 1854, Google Books).
Hereward   Charles Kingsley, *Hereward the Wake* (1865) (New York: Dutton, 1961).
Kidnapped   Robert L. Stevenson, *Kidnapped* (1886) (New York: Pocket Books, 2007).
Little Dorrit   Charles Dickens, *Little Dorrit* (1855), *The Writings of Charles Dickens* (Boston: Houghton, Mifflin, 1894, Google Books).
Lockhart   Sir Walter Scott and John G. Lockhart, *Memoirs of the Life of Sir Walter Scott*, Volume I. *Collection of Ancient and Modern English Authors*, Vol. CLXXV (Paris: Baudry's European Library, 1838. Google Books. Accessed November 15, 2010).
Mid-Lothian   Sir Walter Scott, *The Heart of Mid-Lothian* (1818). *Tales of My Landlord, Second Series, Collected and Arranged by Jedediah Cleishbotham, in Four Volumes*, Vol. II (Edinburgh: Constable, 1818. Google Books. Accessed May 29, 2011).
Mutiny   Sir John Barrow, *A Description of Pitcairn's Island and Its Inhabitants with an Authentic Account of the Mutiny of the Ship Bounty and the Subsequent Fortunes of the Mutineers* (1831) (New York: Haskell, 1972).
Old Mortality   Sir Walter Scott, *The Tale of Old Mortality* (1816) (New York: Penguin, 1999).
Pentland   Robert L. Stevenson, *The Pentland Rising: The Novels and Tales of Robert Louis Stevenson, Volume 14* (New York: Charles Scribner's Sons, 1895 Google Books. Accessed November 15, 2010).
Prince Otto   Robert L. Stevenson, *Prince Otto: A Romance* (London: Chatto & Windus, Piccadilly, 1885. Google Books. Accessed November 15, 2010).
Redgauntlet   Sir Walter Scott, *Redgauntlet* (1824) (New York: Penguin, 2000).
Rob Roy   Sir Walter Scott, *Rob Roy* (1817) (New York: Penguin, 2007).
Sybil   Benjamin Disraeli, *Sybil, the Two Nations* (1845) (London: Oxford University Press, 1925).
Tale   Charles Dickens, *A Tale of Two Cities* (1859) (New York: Signet, 2007).
Virginians   W. M. Thackeray, *The Complete Works of William M. Thackery: The Virginians: A Tale of the Last Century*, Volume 7 (1857-59) (New York: Thomas Crowell, 1881).
Waverley   Sir Walter Scott, *Waverley* (1814) (New York: Penguin, 1994).
White Hoods   Anna E. Bray, *The White Hoods: An Historical Romance* (1828) (BiblioBazaar, 2009).
"Young Chevalier"   Robert L. Stevenson, "The Young Chevalier" (1892) (Unpublished. Goggle Books, accessed November 15, 2010).

Introduction

This book identifies, classifies and defines the previously unexplored rebellion novel genre in nineteenth-century British literature. Novels with similar historical rebellion plotlines can be found in other national literatures and in other centuries, but there are numerous elements that unite the rebellion novels in this study into an especially compact genre. These authors share a similar political purpose, as well as similar linguistic and structural techniques. The rebellions in these novels include political attacks against the established government by only a few rebels (assassinations), rebellions that stretch across the centuries (Jacobite risings), and briefer rebellions of enormous violence and political impact (the French Revolution). The authors who wrote these works were influenced by nationalist, socialist and radical movements that swept Britain during the nineteenth century. The three focal authors, Sir Walter Scott, Charles Dickens and Robert Louis Stevenson, all participated in radical political campaigns and movements and sympathized with residents in the periphery and with the poor. They were united by their judicial degrees, by their shared literary connections, and by the Tory Party. There is substantial proof that they read their predecessors' rebellion novels and intentionally mimicked previously utilized rebellion genre techniques, including imitating prior plotlines, character types, and linguistic tricks. An analysis of Scott's, Dickens' and Stevenson's letters, diaries, and biographies provides ample proof for how and why the rebellion novel genre was invented and maintained in this elite circle of rebellion writers. Scott and Stevenson both wrote half a dozen rebellion novels and Dickens wrote two, as well as four realistic, socialist novels. Thus, writing rebellion novels was not a passing hobby, but a lifelong passion for these writers. And they were not alone — Prime Minister Benjamin Disraeli wrote *Sybil, the Two Nations* a decade before Charles Dickens' *A Tale of Two Cities*, and two decades before George Eliot's *Felix Holt*. Nearly a hundred rebellion novels were written during the nineteenth century in Britain, and they were written by some of the best-known and most popular British writers.

Many dusty literary mysteries are solved by identifying the rebellion genre. Numerous literary critics have been baffled by the fact that many novels centered on political themes fall into not only the historical novel genre but also into a range of apparently unrelated genres, such as the gothic or the epic. Dozens of hard-to-classify nineteenth-century novels, including those by Scott, Dickens and Stevenson, find a firm home when they are measured against the elements of the rebellion novel genre.

This step in the examination of propagandistic politics in literature would not have been possible without one recent groundbreaking study that altered my perception of nineteenth-century British authors—Julian Meldon D'Arcy's, *Subversive Scott: The Waverley Novels and Scottish Nationalism* (2005). D'Arcy separates Scott from the pack of earlier Whig and anticommunist critics, dating back to the first reviewers of the Waverley novels, who called Scott a "waverer." Instead, D'Arcy labels Scott as a strong believer in the Scottish nationalist cause, who subversively criticized the British Empire with his novels. Relating stories of rebellions against the empire was a major part of Scott's and the other rebellion writers' subversive raids against unification, colonialism and exploitation. D'Arcy's argument for the presence of subversive radicalism, socialism and nationalism can be extended to Dickens, Stevenson and to other rebellion novelists, most of whom have also been erroneously called political waverers.

While no known critic has previously gathered rebellion novels together into a genre, at least one, John Farrell, studied revolutions as a fictional theme, in his *Revolution as Tragedy: The Dilemma of the Moderate from Scott to Arnold*. My objection to this study is perhaps apparent from its title; Farrell calls those who wrote about revolutions "moderates," a concept that I rebuke, providing proof of the rebellion novelists' radicalism, socialism and nationalism. In addition, I point out that not only the theme but also the plot structures, the characters, and the linguistic patterns are similar among the rebellion novels.

Misrepresenting Scott, Dickens and Stevenson as moderates and waverers is a practice that was uniquely popularized at the beginning of the Cold War. Within a year after the end of World War II, Western critics changed their tune: They went from calling Dickens a "socialist" and a "radical" to being so threatened by the communist bloc that they began labeling Dickens as a "moderate." As I will explain in greater detail in the Dickens chapter, Dickens' political standing fluctuated dramatically over the decades with the changes in Western politically acceptable norms. As the seeds of socialism spread across the globe, in 1903, Louis Cazamian first directly called Dickens a "socialist."[1] By 1908, both Edwin Pugh and Bernard Shaw were calling Dickens a "revolutionary."[2] T. A. Jackson speaks most vehemently about Dickens as a "socialist" in 1937.[3] The change in the critical perspective of Dickens' political view was an extremely sharp one, when in 1946, immediately at the start of the Cold War and of the McCarthy era, Orwell wrote that Dickens was not a socialist but rather "pro-capitalist," and that his depiction of the French Revolution shows a terror of revolutionary violence, rather than expressing support for rebellious activities.[4] The existence of D'Arcy's 2005 study on political subversion shows that critical opinion is starting to turn away from Cold War paranoia, and that critics are starting to once more see the rebellious novelists in their true radical light.

For the purposes of this book, the term "subversive" denotes disguised rebellious meanings behind linguistic and structural techniques. "Direct" rebellious statements and meanings are those where the author clearly makes radical points with any given part of the narrative. Subversive techniques were necessary to carry an extremist radical, socialist or rebellious message because the reality was that some rebellious novels were censored or otherwise blocked from going into popular production. The works that were censored were either never published or were not widely distributed, and therefore are not widely known today.

What prevented the rebellion novel genre from being identified as such by Scott's first critics, who easily spotted and defined Scott's historical novel genre? Why did they separate Scott's mixture of history and fiction as a unique literary creation but fail to see Scott's unique depictions of rebellions in those same fictional works as a genre in its own right? Perhaps they saw the rebellions as the theme of the works rather than the genre, but it is more likely that censors made it difficult for both writers and critics to talk directly about rebellion. Scott published essays defining the parameters of his own historical novel, but did not openly give the formula for the rebellious elements of his historical novels. There were numerous imprisonments in the nineteenth century for treasonous statements in newspapers and nonfiction books. The publishing industry was responsible for censoring its authors, and did prevent a lot of radical and rebellious fictional works from going into print.

A couple of examples help to explain the type of censorship that Scott, Dickens and Stevenson encountered that might have caused them to use more "subversive," rather than "direct" rebellious elements in their novels. In 1890, William Black's *Donald Ross of Heimra* was contracted by *Lloyd's Weekly*, but then the publisher "refused to publish," when the "proprietor complained that the work contained too much Scots vernacular."[5] *Donald Ross of Heimra* is not on my list of rebellion novels because the rebellion is not a central plot. But *Donald Ross of Heimra* does have rebellious elements, such as a chapter called "A Revolution That Failed," where one of the characters, Fred Stanley, says, "Indeed the meeting should be suppressed all together: it is a clear instigation to riot. I don't see how a riot can be avoided — if those howlers are allowed to rave."[6] Far more inciting rebellious speeches can be found in the rebellion novels of Scott, Dickens and Stevenson. There are a few possible explanations for why Black was censored for his use of the Scottish language, while Scott and Stevenson published novels with a significantly higher percentage of the Scots language, and were not censored. First, Black primarily used Gaelic, as opposed to Highland or Lowland Scottish or Scots. "Cha 'n 'eil beurla agam," one of the characters says in Gaelic.[7] This sentence can be translated with an English-Scottish Gaelic dictionary, such as the online *Lexilogos: Scottish Gaelic Dictionary*, as "Don't speak the English language." This sentence might have been more problematic for the publisher of *Lloyd's Weekly* than the Scots or other regional Scottish languages that Scott and Stevenson typically used because "cha" is farther from the English "no" than something like Scott and Stevenson's "hae" is from the English "have." The Gaelic cannot be comprehended by non–Gaelic-speaking English readers without looking up every word in the dictionary, while Scots is somewhat comprehensible. However, the idea that the above Gaelic sentence turned off the publisher from the manuscript is unlikely, as immediately after this statement it is translated by another character into English — the Scot said, "He has no English."[8] It is also difficult to believe that the publisher thought readers would have difficulty comprehending the Gaelic because the use of Gaelic is far more infrequent in Black than in Scott or Stevenson, as the narrator typically summarizes that characters use "rapid speech"[9] in Gaelic, rather than quoting exactly what they are saying.

One of the more convincing explanations for the publisher's refusal of Black's manuscript is the numerous scenes that involve Miss Stanley's troubles with Gaelic and with adapting to the Scottish culture as an Englishwoman. Translation between English and Gaelic is a major concern for Miss Stanley, as she tries to make claim of being a "laird" in a Gaelic-speaking region. After a few difficult encounters she wants to know how to say, "Am I welcome" in Gaelic.[10] In this scenario, Miss Stanley is a symbolic representation of the English people's occupation of Scotland. Miss Stanley and the English at large have difficulty governing the Scots, in part because of the obvious linguistic barriers between the two peoples. For Miss Stanley, the technique of asking before entering a Scottish home backfires, and soon Miss Stanley is complaining, "I want to lower their rents, and better the conditions of the people in every way, and be their friend — well, I'm kept outside of the door, and if I say, 'Am I welcome?' there is no answer."[11] There is a subversive message in this linguistic interaction — the English are seen as foreigners and are not "welcome" in Scotland, regardless of their intentions. The publisher of *Lloyd's*

Weekly might have found this anti–English sentiment and other radical and subversive messages in the book offensive or possibly treasonous. Lastly, it is likely that after Stevenson published a couple more Scots-rich rebellion novels, censoring publishers caughton and were more vigilant of new attempts at subversive anti–English messages packaged in the Scots language. As I explain in the Stevenson chapter, many earlier reviews of Stevenson's rebellion novels not only observed a similarity between the structure of Scott and Stevenson's rebellion novels but also stressed that both used enormous quantities of Scots vocabulary. After Scott's Jacobite rebellion novels and the Scottish Insurrection that followed them, for Stevenson and other rebellious Scottish writers, even the use of the Scots language became a potentially seditious activity, which could be censored by publishers and periodical owners.

As I discuss in the Dickens chapter, these three writers were pioneers in the field of subversive and dialectic linguistics. Some of the subversive techniques they used were so far ahead of their time that censors did not start checking for subversive propaganda until the end of the nineteenth century, after most of the studied rebellion novels were already in print. My argument is not that Scott, Dickens and Stevenson were censored for their subversive linguistics and structural features, or for the radical political beliefs that these techniques were veiling, but that they were not heavily censored because they successfully used subversive tools. Looking at the British censorship of radical political writers is helpful to see what these writers were working to avoid with subversive techniques.

Despite their powers as lawyers and linguists, Scott, Dickens and Stevenson still faced some censorship, but they typically overcame these obstacles at a profit. One example that portrays the importance of networking with other radicals and learning from prior rebellion novelists is the story of an interaction between one of the minor rebellion novelists, Harrison Ainsworth, and Scott. Ainsworth traveled all the way to Edinburgh in 1828 in order to solicit Scott to edit *The Annual Keepsake* magazine (one of the first English annuals, of which this was the first volume) for £800. Scott refused, but instead asked for and won £500 for publishing a single story in the *Keepsake*, which had previously been "rejected" by his own publisher. Scott wrote that he could not "afford to have my goods thrown back upon my hands."[12] The amount that Ainsworth paid Scott for one story might seem enormous until one realizes that Ainsworth gave up his law practice and became a full-time writer after Scott wrote several positive reviews of Ainsworth's first historical romance, *Sir John Chiverton* (1826).[13] We can be certain that Scott was definitely rejected by his publisher when he pitched "Aunt Margaret's Mirror," a short story, because this is not an isolated case of Scott complaining of his publisher censoring his works. In the "Peroration" part of *Old Mortality*, Scott exclaims that his "publisher ... did not approve of novels (as he injuriously called these real histories)," and then "threatened to decline the article," but was moved towards publication by the fact that the works were "anxiously demanded" by the "discerning public."[14] Only the high sales records of Scott's rebellion novels induced his publisher to run these works. However, Scott's publisher disregarded potential sales when he rejected Scott's "Aunt Margaret's Mirror," leaving it for Ainsworth to pick up. Despite these censorship problems with his own publishers, Scott made more on this one story with Ainsworth than the average hack Victorian novelist made per novel — £250.[15] "Aunt Margaret's Mirror" in its central plot concerns a murder, and is not very controversial. However it includes passages of open support for the Jacobites' cause by the narrator of the story within a story, Aunt Margaret, who states, "I am, as you know, a piece of that old-fashioned thing called a Jacobite." Scott also includes a Gaelic nationalist song, and alludes to the "Revolution."[16] Since Scott published his last historically based rebellion novel a decade earlier, in 1818, this is a significant resurfacing of the Jacobite theme. If Scott did not end up publishing this Jacobite-related story in the *Keepsake*, no record of its censorship by his publisher would have remained. It is even possible, though supporting evidence is lacking, that Scott's publisher might have directly prevented him from publishing any more Jacobite rebellion novels after 1818. One exception was that Scott published the 1824 *Redgauntlet* after the 1820 Scottish Insurrection, but this work was an invented rebellion, rather than one based on real historical events. Scott's turning away from "accurate" historical depictions of uprisings and his inability to publish the short "Aunt Margaret" Jacobite-themed story after 1820 — after the Scottish Insurrection — shows that he was asked to tone down his Jacobite radicalism in some cases, and in other cases his works were entirely censored from publication until a radical editor, like Ainsworth, came along. In addition to being a radical himself, Ainsworth was so desperate for his new annual to succeed that he was willing to pay a great deal, and certainly to overlook or even relish the Jacobite references in the story. Of course, even in these circumstances, Scott included some arguments against the Jacobite cause by another speaker in the story, and even has Aunt Margaret confess, under pressure, that she is a Jacobite in "sentiment and feeling only." Scott includes the structural subversive technique of offering the opposing point of view to a radical position, next to the radical position to soften its political impact. One can be certain that in 1840, when Ainsworth wrote *Guy Fawkes*, he reread Scott's "Aunt Margaret" story and his Jacobite novels and used similar radical rebellious techniques.

Some critics who have labeled Scott, Dickens and Stevenson as waverers might have been genuinely confused by the literary evidence. Rebellion novels look indecisive or wavering on the surface because they portray both sides of a rebellion: the rebels and the rulers of the established social order. The rebels also frequently lose. This seems politically balanced on the surface. However, the losses help to make the rebels' stories tragic, and therefore more sympathetic. And a close linguistic examination reveals that Scott and Stevenson used the Scottish dialect to hide the more incendiary views of their characters, and Dickens used lower-class dialogues with the same purpose. The fact that each successive novelist mimicked the structural, plot and character types of earlier rebellion novelists shows that they admired and strived to imitate their predecessors, not only in structure and linguistics, but also in their social and radical purposes.

This study blurs the boundaries between history, biography, politics and literary criticism because a genre like the rebellion novel genre is inseparable from all of these branches of thought, and cannot be fully understood with only linguistics or only within the historical context. Throughout, my goal is to logically define and explain the elements of the rebellion genre and prove that this key genre has been unjustly overlooked.

PART I. A GENRE UNDER A MICROSCOPE

1

Rebellions and Reforms in Britain

The rebellion novel genre that Sir Walter Scott founded with *Waverley* (1814) was intellectually revolutionary because dissent and rebellion were harshly suppressed in Britain. The aggressive suppression of dissident groups and opinions grew out of the ambitions of English kings for a unified England and their desire to suppress the endless episodes of in-fighting, violent overthrows and other forms of deadly rebellion with the Treason Act of 1351, and the various renewals and updates to this act in the following centuries.

Before 1351, political stability was hard to come by in England. Records run as far back as Julius Caesar's invasion of Britain in 55 B.C. After the decline of Roman rule, Britain experienced a steady stream of in-migration of Saxons and Angles from Germany, a tide that eventually resulted in numerous battles with the prior residents, the Britons. The memory of the bitter warfare with the Anglo-Saxons meant that by the time the Vikings attempted to settle in England, they were forced to invade the coastlines. England was divided into isolated and in-fighting small kingdoms, and both the Anglo-Saxons and the Vikings were victorious and gained a stronghold in England. English nobility became conscious of a need for unity to fortify their military strength in the region, and in the ninth century, England began a process of unification, which has kept most of the British Isles united to the present day. Despite England's unification, it was once again invaded and conquered, this time by the Danes and Normans. Just as England was recovering from the continuous rebellions and suppressions of the Norman Conquest, the wealthy regional barons rebelled against the English king and insisted that he sign the Magna Carta in 1215, a document that made the king accountable to the people and to the nobility for his actions in exchange for collecting taxes. The Magna Carta paved the way for modern British civil liberties and laws that spell out the governmental services people are entitled to in exchange for paying their taxes. It was a century after this liberating document was signed, upon seeing continued rebellions by the common people and by the nobility, that the English king signed the Treason Act in 1351.

A century later, England saw the beginning of the Tudor dynasty, which oversaw the Renaissance in England and reigned in an unprecedented century of stability, until the Stuarts dynasty took over the throne in 1603. At that time, upon the death of Queen Elizabeth, King of Scots, James VI unified the entire island of Great Britain by merging the Scottish and the English crowns into a single kingdom. Surveying this history of nonstop conquests, border disputes and overthrows of the English crown by warring aristocrats, it is awkward to call the 1685 Glorious Revolution the first major uprising in English history, unless one views the beginning of English history to be 1603, when the entire British Isles was united. It is more accurate to say that the Glorious Revolution was yet another serious threat to the British monarchy in a long list of continuous uprisings. Despite the various concessions that the British monarchy has made over the centuries (giving up on the Thirteen Colonies being one point on this long list), the British Isles have never again been divided and Britain has one of the world's last remaining monarchies, in an age when democratic elections are an essential measuring stick for just and acceptable governance.

The treason acts were an instrumental strategy for English monarchs to suppress rebellions in their country. The execution, exile, imprisonment, torture and other types of punishment inflicted on those who rose against the kings and queens of England over the centuries must have been sufficient deterrents to entirely successful antigovernmental overthrows. On the other hand, the history of England from B.C. to the present day is littered with uprisings, assassinations, revolutions and other rebellions that deprived England of some of its territories and gave some freedoms (such as the Parliament) to the people, without the monarchy's loss of control over the rest of its United Kingdom. English monarchs executed royalty, aristocrats and countless citizens to hold onto power, and yet they failed to suppress a rebellious dialogue that continued in the public stage across the nineteenth century and helped to establish many of the rights that the British people hold today.

By the end of the nineteenth century, British people gained the right to a free public education, and attained near-universal literacy, in contrast to the near-universal illiteracy at the beginning of that century. Simultaneously, the publishing industry boomed, from an institution that provided a few books to the wealthiest Britons to a machine that supplied books to nearly every household. Before the nineteenth century, writers wrote for aristocratic patrons; now suddenly they could grow wealthy by writing books that interested the poor and middle-class populace. This boom in popular reading and the success of the British publishing industry are linked with the success of Sir Walter Scott, Charles Dickens and Robert Louis Stevenson — three names that are frequently given as some of the most popular and best-selling British authors from the nineteenth century. This trio also wrote more than fourteen historical rebellion novels combined, and through the financial success of these works ensured that the rebellion novel genre would become common in the works of the nation's best novelists from this period.

Sir Walter Scott started this popular rebellion novel at the same time as he started the historical novel genre, and he became the first British author to sell incredible quantities, hundreds of thousands of copies. His Waverley series, about Jacobite rebellions in Scotland, was an engrossing topic for the nationalistic Scottish and the impoverished and hardworking British people. Jacobites are portrayed as fighting for a just cause in the Waverley novels. Despite this rebellious attitude, King George IV knighted Sir Walter Scott, rather than bringing him up on charges of treason against the monarchy. Scott, Dickens, Stevenson and many other rebellion novelists were lawyers by education or by profession and knew how to navigate the uncertain waters of libel and truth when they described historical rebellions, which could not count as attempts at inciting rebellion, as they technically depicted past events, rather than encouraging future uprisings. Thus, rebellion novels became a political and social weapon for intellectual revolt against unjust abuses of the British monarchy and government when violent revolt or direct seditious statements could be severally punished under the treason laws.

Rebellions and Reforms in the Nineteenth Century

Besides the radical political campaigns that Scott, Dickens and Stevenson openly or subversively joined, there were many major rebellions and reforms that they were aware of and might have supported. A history of these radical events and ideas helps to put these writers' radicalism into a wider context. Without this background, it is difficult to grasp why Scottish nationalism or antipoverty laws were potentially censorable topics, and simultaneously were topics that prompted the most heated open political debates of the century. While some radical and socialist beliefs had to be hidden with subversive techniques, many radical statements were openly inserted into rebellion novels because they were inspired by popular political debates from the nineteenth century. Subversive techniques were only necessary in cases that were off the discussion table and could count as treason if voiced, such as the question of Scottish independence. The three focal authors presented varied degrees of radicalism, not only because of their personal preferences and biases, but also because they wrote on varied aspects of the nineteenth century that saw vast changes in the political climate. If there is more biographical evidence that Stevenson and Dickens were socialists, it is because the beginning of the nineteenth century saw only the first boom in English social debates. Rebellion novelists frequently depicted rebellions that had happened over half a century earlier, but their radical inspirations were typically from the current rebellious events of their day. In other words, "Dickens, Eliot, Gaskel [sic] and Meredith ... are treating the past to understand the present, and it is a reflection of the mood of the present that their chosen periods are ones of agitation and revolution."[1]

The rebellion novel became popular in the nineteenth century because of several radical political changes that occurred at the turn of the century. The first rebellion novel was published in 1814, a year before Napoleon's defeat in 1815, when twenty years of warfare between France and England was finally coming to an end. Back when Scott first conceived *Waverley*, if we trust his own date, 1805, the war was at its peak and England looked like it might fall under Napoleon's sword. England's monarchy had recently recovered from the threat of the French and American revolutions. The French Revolution, while it was not waged against England, was nearby, just across a small stretch of water, unlike the Americans, who were months away by ship. Tales of the brutality of the revolutionary mob in France quickly reached English ears, and left English royalty hesitant about exploiting the poor, who had this potential violent impulse and could turn into a murderous mob.

While the eighteenth century saw more bloodshed in violent rebellions on English soil, like the 1780 Gordon Riots, which Dickens dramatized in *Barnaby Rudge*, as well as the militia riots of 1761, there were also many impactful violent uprisings in England in the nineteenth century, which kept royalty on their toes and made rebellion novels relevant to current events during the century. The year 1817 saw what is typically called "England's Last Revolution," or the Pentrich Revolution, when William Oliver attempted to overthrow the English government, but was executed instead. In 1820, the Cato Street conspiracy, led by "militant radicals," nearly succeeded in murdering "the entire Cabinet."[2] And before the Reform Bill of 1831 passed, the country suffered from the Bristol Riots, a "pro-reform agitation" that assisted in the passing of the bill.[3]

The majority of revolts against England in the 19th century occurred in distant parts of the empire, as opposed to in London or England. The century opened with the 1803 rebellion in Dublin by Robert Emmet, who protested against the union with England. At the peak of Sir Walter Scott's literary fame, 1820, Scotland saw the failed Radical War, or the "Scottish Insurrection."

Eighteen thirty-one saw the mildly impactful South Wales Merthyr Rising, and in 1837 there was the failed Upper Canada Rebellion. England occasionally responded to violent revolts with moves such as the strict 1833 Coercion Act to "combat Irish disorders" or riots.[4] England's unwilling subjects retaliated against tighter controls with enormously violent uprisings, such as the 1841–1842 Afghan Uprising, in which around "4,500 English troops and 12,000 civilians," withdrawing after negotiating a treaty, were massacred.[5] Some periphery uprisings had unusual results; for example, the Indian Rebellion of 1857 led to the dissolution of the business rights of the East Indian Company, only for India's Mughal Empire to fall and to officially become a part of England under the name, English Indian Empire. This English success did not stop another nationalist Irish rebellion, the 1867 Fenian Rebellion.

Some of the most remembered rebellions of the century are the revolutions of 1848, which began in France and spread to Germany, Austrian Empire, Italy, Denmark, Wallachia, Poland, and other European regions and countries. Karl Marx wrote his *Communist Manifesto* just before the start of the 1848 German Revolution. In it he argued in favor of violent overthrows of the bourgeoisie, capitalist, or aristocratic regimes and in favor of giving power to the working poor, the proletariat. The threat of these and other potential revolutions forced many of the reforms that followed in England, as they did elsewhere in Europe. The lack of an 1848 revolution in England has been attributed to the pacification of the middle class with the Reform Act of 1832. As a result, the major dissatisfied faction in England, the members of the Chartist movement, made a peaceful petition to Parliament in 1848, rather than revolting with violence. Of course, 1848 was not the quietest year in the history of English riots, as the Young Ireland rebels traveled across Ireland to incite rebellion against English rule over Ireland, and to express their solidarity with the 1848 revolutions, without much success or bloodshed. On a side note, 1848 also saw a rebellion in the English-ruled Ceylon.

Simultaneously, the nineteenth century saw numerous legislative or peaceful reforms. For example, the 1823 reforms in the penal code reduced the "incidence of death sentences," and otherwise modernized and simplified the legal system.[6] Slavery was abolished in 1831, after many years of campaigning by the chief originators of the bill. The most impactful reforms across the century were the 1832, 1867 and 1884–1885 Reform Acts. The 1832 act allowed for a more representative English government by enlarging the electorate in the House of Commons. The 1867 act was the work of one of the rebellion novelists on my list, Benjamin Disraeli — it made the voting system in England more democratic. The 1884 act continued this work, allowing the previously ignored agricultural workers to take part in voting.[7] Both violence and the need for more effective social reforms escalated during the 1845–

1852 potato famine, which is known to have plagued Ireland but also affected potato crops across England. Reform acts and movements were a constant element in nineteenth-century English politics.

The names of Scott, Dickens and Stevenson appear frequently in the history of English reform. There is an overwhelming amount of evidence in support of these writers' radicalism and socialism. Briefly, Scott was one of the "defenders" of the Scottish banking system, which successfully revolted against the banking reforms that England instituted after the financial panic of 1825. As a result Scott's portrait is still on the one pound note, as it was exempted from the reforms.[8] In the long term, banking and publishing reforms were enormously significant for the welfare of the poor and middle-class Scots. Scott felt secure in speaking out against England on the banking issue after hosting King George IV to Edinburgh in 1822. The king knighted Scott and otherwise showed him favor as a reputable Scottish judge, rather than as a leader of an underground artistic rebellious movement. However, this could have been an honest mistake on the king's part, as Scott did not formally acknowledge his authorship of the Waverley novels until later in his career.

Further still, Scott and Stevenson wrote an enormous quantity of rebellion novels partially because Scotland operated under mostly independent laws, despite the union, and censorship of Scottish books was more lax than of books published or originated in London. The relative size of Scotland's population was small, so England was not very threatened by independent legislation in Scotland. According to the Census Office for National Statistics, in 1801, there were 9 million people in England and Wales, versus 1.6 in Scotland and 5.2 in Ireland. By 1901, England's population grew to 32 million, versus 4.5 million in both Scotland and Ireland.

The writing of rebellion novels was one of the social protests that British intellectuals engaged in, in order to further their radical and socialist agendas, and to argue on behalf of periphery nations and on the part of the poor and the struggling lower and middle classes in the United Kingdom.

2

Genre Theory and the Rebellion Novel

There is a need for more logically divided categories of genre. To achieve this clear taxonomy, researchers should closely examine linguistic and structural patterns within existing and undiscovered novel genres. This study is a step towards identifying and classifying an unidentified or unclassified genre in a field with many holes where genre subcategories should be. Figure 1 shows where the rebellion novel genre is in relation to previously identified genres. The two sides stand for history and fiction, which are the primary components of the three genres that are the closest generic relatives to the rebellion novel: historical, political and social novels. The figure shows how these genres overlap and that the rebellion novel includes both history and fiction, and elements from all three genres. A fuller diagram might have included dozens of other genres, like the gothic, epic, and national tale. But the rebellion novel is potentially a subgenre of the historical, political or social novels, and clearly cannot be a subgenre of the gothic genre. I define the rebellion novel genre as a subgenre of the historical novel that includes only novels that center on the rebellion theme. The rebellion genre is also related to the political and social novel genre, as well as to the national tale and other genres, but Dickens and Stevenson primarily mimicked the genre techniques used by Scott, rather than by political novelists, so it fits more appropriately under the historical novel umbrella (despite other overlaps). Rebellion novels are all political and social, but it is their basis in the "real" history of past rebellions that ties them together. There is a need to add the rebellion genre to the taxonomy of the existing related genres because rebellion novels were written with a shared radical political purpose of showing the vulnerability of the empire to internal criticism and showing the internal social and cultural problems that had to be resolved. Political and social novels are distinguished from each other because one focuses on social ills, and the other on political events and characters. The rebellion novels are far more formulaic, or similar amongst themselves, than historical, political or social novels, so this category must be recognized as an individual entity, despite its overlaps with other entities or genres. Unlike a rebellion novel, a historical novel can focus on any small or large historical event, and can have highly varied structural and linguistic components and still be called a historical novel.

Why does the title of this book simplify these novels into the grouping of rebellion novels? Why not call them revolutionary or uprising novels? Why not include all of the different categories (revolutions, rebellions, assassinations, and social revolts) in the title? Under the term "rebellion," the following are included: revolutions, uprisings against local, federal and mother-country governments, assassinations, social riots, and various other forms of violent or threatening rebellions against the monarchy, aristocracy or capitalists. The following types of stories are excluded: personal rebellions against family, friends, religious icons, and the like. Rebellion novels are written with the purpose of explaining flaws in a given European empire (England, France) by depicting rebellions that were perpetrated against it. Rebellion novels are distinct from other genres because they center on a rebellion theme, use similar linguistic techniques to portray the plight of poor or regional characters, and use similar plot structures that center on a story of a rebellion. I called the genre the "rebellion genre" partially because the term "rebellion" includes the four types of rebellions that my book covers. The French, American and Russian revolutions are notorious because they were successful. The Chinese dynasties survived their genocidal rebellions (Taiping Rebellion and Lushan Revolt), but America gained its independence from England, and Russia's czars fell. My study is concerned with the portrayal of uprisings regardless of whether they were successful. If I titled the genre the "revolutionary novel genre," this would exclude all of the unsuccessful, but bloody or effective in the long run rebellions currently covered. In the common plot of a rebellion novel, at least some of the rebels (even if these "rebels" are in fact

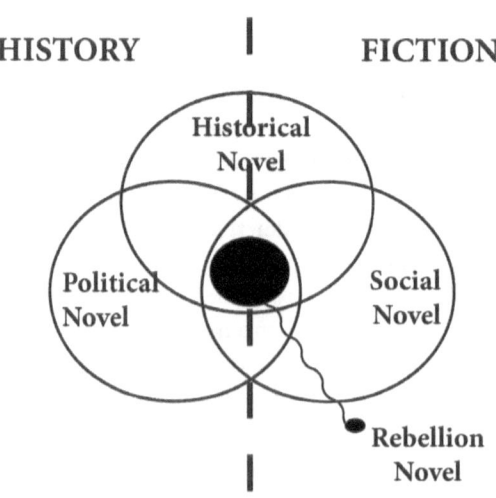

Figure 1. Intersecting Genres

anti-revolutionary rebels) are executed or otherwise come to a tragic end, before a common happy ending is reached for the main, typically wavering or apolitical, character. The tragedy of the loss of the primary rebellious cause is what makes the rebel characters in rebellion novels sympathetic. Still, the genre is not primarily defined by the presence of a tragic ending, but rather by the presence of a rebellious, anti-establishment violent action, and all four categories (revolutions, rebellions, assassinations and social revolts) include these

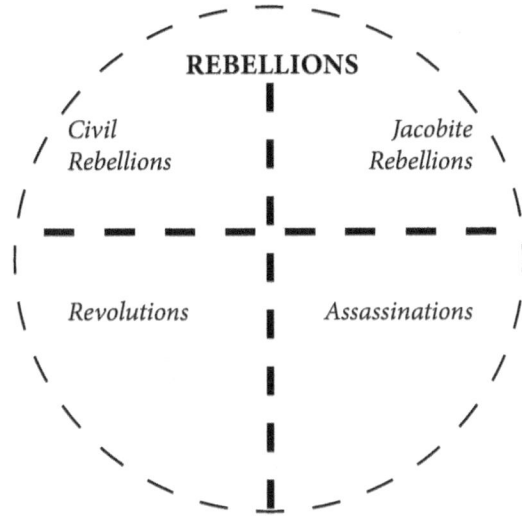

Figure 2. Four Rebellion Types

violent rebellious actions and themes. Thus, I chose the term "rebellion genre" to cover all of the discussed works. A picture explains this logic better. As you can see in Figure 2, the term "rebellion" includes all four of the main categories, listed in detail in the table in Figure 4. in Chapter 6. These are the four related rebellion themes in the novels I cover. The theme and plotlines always center on a "rebellion," but they are different kinds of rebellions.

Historical novels include various types of histories, but the general term "historical" appears by itself in the heading of the historical novel category. As you can see from Figures 2 and 4, my chosen novels fall into four categories:
1. Civil or social rebellions (typically for workers' rights)
2. Assassinations or rebellious violence directed against a few (typically a monarch or the monarch's representative, such as the murder of a Scottish-English government official in Stevenson's Appin Assassination in *Balfour*),
3. Nationalist rebellions against a core by a periphery or by a disenfranchised part of a country that desires independence or political rights
4. Nationwide revolutions or rebellions against the entire ruling order of a nation.

These four categories are the most common forms of historical rebellions depicted in 19th-century novels. These themes have also been noticed by recent critics. For example, Alan Sandison notices the dynamiter theme, a part of the assassination category.[1] Many critical books, among them John Farrell's *Revolution as Tragedy: The Dilemma of the Moderate from Scott to*

Arnold,[2] refer to the revolutionary novels. D'Arcy's *Subversive Scott* and numerous other books and articles on Scott and Stevenson discuss their Jacobite rebellions. Excluding any one of these four categories would not give a full picture of the characteristics of a rebellion novel.

These categories were also the forms of rebellion that were most threatening to the English aristocracy and the bourgeoisie. The French Revolution caused the deaths of thousands of aristocrats, just over the water from England, and many other 18th- and 19th-century revolutions led to major economic and political changes, so the English bourgeoisie were afraid of revolutions. And those in England who were not afraid of a potential revolution were at least aware of the impact prior revolutions had. "For Victorians no single event figured more prominently as 'historical' than the French Revolution.... Thus, Charles Dickens's ... *A Tale of Two Cities*" and other works about revolutions were especially significant in the minds of the English readers.[3] Jacobite rebellions, with the help of Scott and Stevenson's rebellion novels, became symbols for internal unrest within England, as Irish nationalists and nationalists in other periphery countries waged rebellions. Assassinations were a direct threat against the aristocracy and its supporters, as they were commonly the victims of these focused attacks. Lastly, civil rebellions, uprisings by the poor or workers for better working conditions or against oppressive government or religious policies, caused enormous losses in property, deaths, and prevented isolated aristocrats from feeling safe on their estates. In other words, the four categories were: national revolutions that might have overthrown the English empire; nationalist uprisings of the periphery against the core (symbolized by the Jacobite risings); assassinations of leaders or aristocrats within the English empire; and uprisings by the proletariat, the poor, against the bourgeoisie, the rich, in a given region of England. While Karl Marx argued for a proletariat "revolution," the reality was that there were frequent regional, national, and political challenges that took the shape of assassinations, civil rebellions and nationalist uprisings, instead of massive "revolutions." Because rebellion novels discussed these real historical events, rather than focusing on Marx's theoretical revolutions, all four categories have to be included within the rebellion novel genre.[4]

To further explain the reasoning behind choosing the single term "rebellion" as opposed to revolution and other possible terms, I have to define these other terms. According to the Oxford online dictionary, "revolution" is defined as "a forcible overthrow of a government or social order in favor of a new system." An "uprising" is "an act of resistance or rebellion; a revolt." To "assassinate" somebody is to "murder (an important person) in a surprise attack for political or religious reasons." "Rebellion" is defined as "an act of violent or open resistance to an established government or ruler," or as "the action or process of resisting authority, control, or convention." As you can clearly see, only the term "rebellion" fully meets the dimensions of the four categories of novels with the rebellion theme that I am discussing. "Revolution" would only apply to events such as the French and the American revolutions, and would not cover the minor worker rebellions in England that might have eventually brought social change but did not lead to the overthrow of the governing order. "Uprising" is another term for rebellion, and only leads a dictionary reader to the term "rebellion" in search for its own definition. And assassination is a narrow term that stands only for murders of individuals and does not include non violent rebellions or mass-murder revolutions.

According to the Merriam-Webster online dictionary, a "theme" is defined as the "subject ... of discourse"; while a "genre" is generally defined as a "category ... of literary composition." Thus, the unifying rebellion theme is the rebellious topic that the novels are about; but the rebellion genre includes the linguistic and structural dimensions of the category that includes all rebellion novels.

Figure 1 shows that there is an overlap between rebellion novels and not only historical novels but also political and social novels. What are the boundaries between these genres? Morris Edmund Speare defined the purpose of the political novel in his comprehensive 1966 study as, "party propaganda, public reform, or exposition of the lives of the personages who maintain government, or of the forces which constitute government."[5] Political novels are about any politician or political event; rebellion novels are always about a rebel and a rebellious event. Rebellion novels are always political. Some political novels are not rebellious. While many political novels can easily become propagandistic, it is extremely difficult for a rebellion novel to avoid slipping into propaganda, though the propaganda usually leans in support of rebellions, revolutions and other uprisings against the established order. It is simply more difficult to write a rebellion novel that is a simple "exposition of the lives of personages" or government "forces." When a rebellion novel describes the causes for rebellion or the reasons for the suppression of a rebellion, it is betraying a propagandistic or political bias. Orwell said: "Political language ... of all political parties, from Conservatives to Anarchists — is designed to make lies sound truthful and murder respectable, and to give an appearance of solidity to pure wind."[6] According to Orwell, all political novels are "propaganda," and rebellion novels are especially propagandistic.

It is also important to distinguish the rebellion novel from the genre of the social novel, which is better known as the subgenre of realism and naturalism. The term "social" refers to the focus on social or microeconomic dimensions of the novel, while the terms "natural" and "realistic" stress the factual or fact-based dimension of the works. The realistic novel is very different from the historical novel because the characters and events are typically fictitious, while in historical novels they are grounded in news clippings and history books. The "truth" behind a "realistic" novel lies in the multidimensional and true-to-life portrayal of the realities of the poor and struggling lower classes. The focus is on what the poor eat and drink and how they work and behave, rather than on the factual details of a historically recorded specific event. The rebellion novels include all of these larger categories. They are based on actual historical rebellions, but they are less realistic and are more epic and romantic in the quantity and type of their descriptive details. The writing frequently borders on propaganda, or the authors have political motivations for writing rebellion novels. Still, the characters are frequently realistically described with the details of the proletariat's daily existence. Thus, the rebellion novel blends many features from other established genres.

The rebellion genre can best be understood when its elements are broken down into structural and linguistic components, as seen in Figure 3. Primary school students learn that stories are divided into three components: setting, plot and characters. Another simplification of generic dimensions is the Aristotelian triad: mode, object, and medium, with which Aristotle separated literature into four limited genres: comedy, tragedy, epic and parody.[7] John Frow sees three "overlapping and intersecting" dimensions of genre: their organization and shape, their rhetorical structure, and their themes or topics.[8] These triads and quartets do not fully cover the various elements that I will be examining. In the sections on structural features, I look at the origins of generic features in earlier genres, structural elements that remain in the genre from other genres, and the elements of story structure. I break the examination of story structure into studies of purpose, characters, setting (time and place) and plot. In the sections on linguistic features, I examine the varieties of discourse used (sentence and speech structure, voice, perspective, tone, and borrowings), multilingual elements (the use of Scottish, French and other foreign languages and domestic dialects), and linguistic complexity (sentence/word length and structure).

The generic dimensions are used to define and classify the rebellion genre. The name "rebellion genre" is a critical decision, chosen over "rebellion subgenre." What is the difference between the labels genre, subgenre, royal, dominant, hybrid or simply motif? It was difficult for me to find support for my ideas in previously published genre theory because the logic other theorists have been using is in opposition to my own. For example, Gerard Genette defined structural and linguistic types of characteristics as "modes," as opposed to genres, because they are linguistic or "pragmatic" classifications.[9] It seems to me that linguistic classifications are the best foundations for genre definitions and analysis.

2. Genre Theory and the Rebellion Novel 21

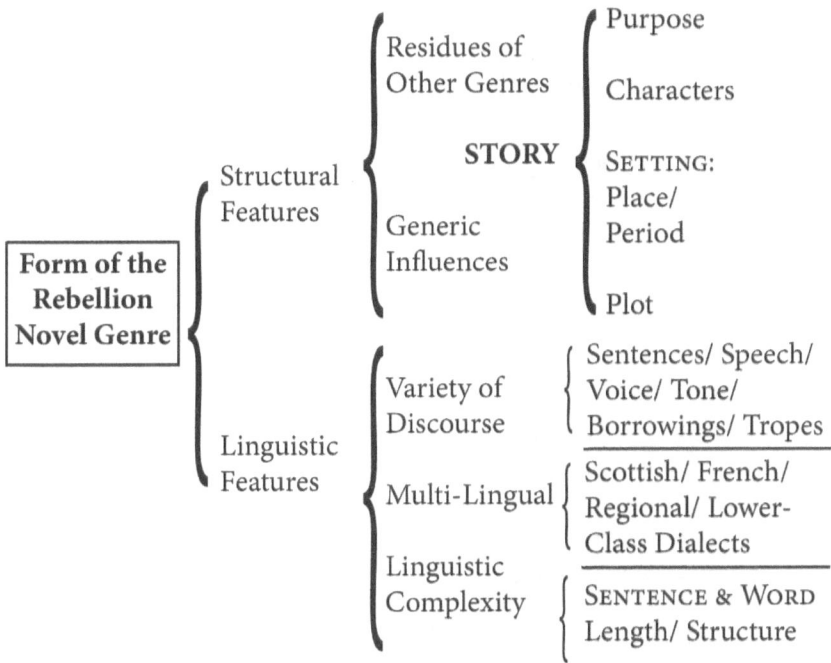

Figure 3. Structural and Linguistic Features of the Rebellion Genre

There are some useful definitions in existing genre studies. The "historical" novel genre is what Ireneusz Opacki called the "royal" or the "dominant" genre because of the quantity of historical novels that were written and because of the extensive criticism on this category. Opacki would call the rebellion novel a "genre variant," or a "hybrid," something that evolved or developed from earlier trends and into "new motifs, vocabulary, compositional devices," through merging with other genres, evolution of language and historical or literary developments. Opacki argued that a hybrid can evolve to eventually become a genre.[10]

Scott's *Waverley* was indeed a hybrid when it was created, but now it is the first example of both the historical and the rebellion novel genres. The difference between the two labels is one of use. The historical genre has been identified and examined; the rebellion genre has not been defined until this study. If the two genres were born at the same time, why is one "dominant" but the other a "hybrid?" One is dominant because critics have recognized and theorized on it; the other is hybrid because it has not been dissected and labeled by international academic consensus. Since I am dissecting and labeling the rebellion novel genre in this study, I usually refer to it as a dominant genre, and not as a hybrid or a subgenre.

Another question that has to be answered before we define a genre is, How many properties have to be similar among a group of novels for them to be labeled a "genre?" Tzvetan Todorov stresses the point that texts should not be classed as a genre simply because they have a single common property. Further still, he argues that genres are only genres if they have been "historically perceived as such." This is problematic because if literary critics base their classes and genres on the work done by previous critics, they will not be adding new insights or new theories to the field. Todorov and his supporters have retarded the growth of genre studies by putting limitations like this on generic discoveries. "Is there any virtue in calling such a combination a 'genre'?" Todorov asks.[11] I believe that this is not a rhetorical question, and that the answer to it can be yes. There is virtue in redefining and regrouping or creating new categories of genres. In addition, the rebellion novels have not only a single common property but several dimensions or properties that they hold in common. Of course, Todorov was right in arguing that works with only a single feature in common should not be labeled a genre, as statistically, a single point of similarity can be a fluke or a chance occurrence. Therefore, we need to come up with a set of several generic dimensions that would separate all novels into logical genre divisions. If evolution theory is logical and based on trees of who evolved from whom and includes the various variations, why shouldn't genre theory be just as logical or detailed? The rebellion novel genre evolved across the nineteenth century, and contains "several genres" within it.[12] Thus, *Waverley* can be both a historical and a rebellion novel without creating a problem in logical evolutionary classification.

If we assume that genres both contain other genres and that they also develop, then we should dissect the common types of development presented by Alastair Fowler in his "Transformations of Genre." The eight types of transformation Fowler offers are: "topical invention" (new topics — i.e.,: student life, love), "combination of repertoires" (Elizabethan plays, mummery, masquerade, pageant), "aggregation" ("several complete short works are grouped in an ordered collection"), "change of scale" (*macrologia* magnifies earlier genres such as the epic; *brachylogia* diminishes or reduces something like an epistle to a short poem), "change of function" (change in the standards of proper genre mechanic execution, such as changing from first to third person), "counterstatement" (doing the opposite to what the genre previously prescribed, or writing a "countergenre" work, such as *Don Quixote*), "inclusion" (one genre enclosing other genres "within it"), and "generic mixture" (some genre change and mixture is always present even when genres are prescriptive and rigid).[13] Several of the above transformations apply to the rebellion novel. The primary transformation, the thing that defines this genre, is "topical invention" of the rebellion theme. The second transformation that is applicable is "inclusion," since, as I discussed, it is a genre that includes many other genres within it (historical, political, social, etc.). A few other development patterns that can be detected in rebellion novels are: "combination" or "generic mixture," and "change of function." I will explain how Scott pulled together the features of his rebellion novels by combining features from previous genres, such as the national tale, and by adding the new topic or the rebellion theme to the old formulas.

In a perfectly logical genre theory, all texts would fall into a clearly defined genre subcategory. There would be a mathematical and logical formula that would allow a critic to calculate the percentage of linguistic and structural features that identify a work with others like it. But current literary criticism is too romantic for such pure logic. The romantic eighteenth-century theories of Benedetto Croce, that aesthetic works should not be classified into genres because art is intuitive rather than logical, are still with us. "What is art?" Croce asks in his *Guide to Aesthetics*, and he answers, "Art is vision or *intuition*."[14] Most authors in the current commercial publishing industry write according to strict, prescribed genre formulas. This means that literary critics should catch up to these fast times and should also be able to dissect generic rules. Nineteenth-century novels are already classed into various genres: historical, political, national tale, mystery, romantic, Victorian and others. The problem is that the classifications are partially based on the intuition or vision of the researchers who initially made the groupings, rather than on a logical updated division. Many modern researchers are baffled at how numerous works fail to fall into any one clear genre categorization. In fact, it is likely that nearly all great nineteenth-century English novels fall into more than one established genre category. This signals that the genres are not well defined and that there is a major problem with the current taxonomies. The task of creating a more logical structure that allows for productive classification is too large for a single researcher. On the other hand, identifying a missing or a previously unnamed genre and explaining its properties and functions is a useful step towards this goal. Proving that there is a parallel between a significant number of texts that point to a genre that has not been previously named also proves that there is a need for more research in the larger field of genre categorization.

The rebellion novel is in the middle of an overlap between at least three previously classified genres: social, political and historical. But the fact that there are characteristics that separate works in the rebellion novel genre into a category of its own proves that literary critics should not be stopped from creating a new genre category simply by the fact that it overlaps with previously identified genres. When they fail to form a new genre category among works that are more similar to each other than to the works in the large genre categories that they were previously part of the critics are left confused and uncertain about which genre the works under investigation should fall and instead place them into all of the overlapping categories. If each of the rebellion novels can be placed into the historical, social and political genres, then doing so does not help a student of literature that wants to know to which specific genre a given work belongs.

To further clarify the significance of separating the rebellion novels into an individual category, let's imagine the possibility that species categories were equally confusing. What if a duck could not be classified as a duck, as opposed to being a chicken, simply because science failed to create a distinct morphological species category for a bird with webbed feet and a differently shaped bill? Try substituting this discussion about the rebellion novel genre category with a discussion about the existence of the duck morphological species. Both the chicken and the duck fall under several overlapping categories — they are both in the same "class" or are both called "birds," and they are both within the "kingdom" of "animals," as opposed to plants or minerals. Biological taxonomy breaks life neatly into several layers of subcategories: species, genus, family, order, class, phylum, kingdom, domain, and life. Therefore, two closely related species overlap in all other subcategorizations, and are only separated from each other by a few characteristics that mean they are not of the same "species." The same should be true for fiction taxonomies. Even if the rebellion novel falls under the larger categories of social, political and historical novels, it is still a unique species that is unlike most of the other subgenres around it. Understanding that it is a different entity than, for example, a historical novel that does not discuss a rebellion, helps researchers to see the connection between the purpose, structure and linguistic characteristics of the rebellion novels' formula. Without uniting them into a single genre, we are just as lost in our understanding of rebellion novels as we would be if we were not sure whether a duck were a chicken.

3

Criteria for Selecting Rebellion Novels

Hundreds of rebellion novels were published during the 19th century in Britain. Grace Moore writes, "The number of novels set during the uprising [Indian Mutiny, 1857–59] ... runs into hundreds with Philip Meadows Taylor's *Seeta* (1872) and Flora Annie Steel's *On the Face of the Waters* (1896) representing some of the more enduring outpourings."[1] With "hundreds" of novels centering on a single rebellion, it is clear that a full search through the records would turn up many hundreds of novels published about all the other rebellions that took place prior to and in the 19th century.

However, while Taylor and Steel might have made impactful statements about the Indian Mutiny, these authors are not as popularly known as my focal writers: Scott, Dickens and Stevenson. Because these three authors were household names in the 19th century and were widely read by the impoverished public, they contributed to the structural and linguistic development of the rebellion novel genre to a greater extent than some of the other writers that joined this canon. In other words, due to the fact that a structural and linguistic comparison of hundreds of novels in a genre would simplify to mere numbers the larger political and literary issues involved in this genre, the foci of this study are only the genre-defining works by Scott, Dickens and Stevenson. Their works point to the elements that all rebellion novels have in common, and they changed or developed the rebellion genre in radical ways.

I imposed several limitations on my research that led me to pick these three authors. The works in this study would not fall into a neat generic category if dissimilar works were not excluded from examination. To be included under the umbrella of the rebellion novel genre a work had to have all of the following characteristics:

1. Plot centers on a historical rebellion, or a rebellion that is based on a historical fact
2. Written by a British author (English, Scottish, Irish, Welsh and all other parts of the British Isles) in the 19th century
3. Is a novel
4. The rebellion is at the core of the plot's structure
5. Includes social and political arguments in the dialogue or narration, which propagate for radical or social change (slogans, political or revolutionary rhetoric, etc.)
6. Focuses on any of the four major categories of rebellions under investigation: revolutions, assassinations, Jacobite rebellions and civil rebellions.

In addition, this particular study examines only novelists who wrote at least two rebellion novels. Works that fell outside of these parameters are:

1. Utopias and dystopias
2. Rebellions that are not based on historical fact
3. Works in genres other than the novel, including short stories, poems, plays, etc.
4. Works where the rebellion is a minor event that happens in a chapter or less, and does not significantly affect the rest of the plot
5. Personal rebellions, or rebellions by an isolated individual, for personal, rather than political reasons.

As demonstrated in Figure 2, the novels are divided into four main categories by rebellion type: civil rebellions, assassinations or violence directed against a few privileged people, nationwide revolutions or rebellions, and Jacobite rebellions. The goals of the rebels range from desiring better working conditions, to wanting a Jacobite monarchic ruler, to clan vengeance, to political maneuverings, to the overthrow of an entire government. Novels by Scott and Stevenson are overrepresented, as there are at least five from each. I am not counting the two dystopian and non-historically-based rebellion fictions that Stevenson and Scott wrote. While More's *Utopia*[2] and Swift's *Gulliver's Travels*[3] are great ways to show the underlying problems in a society, including works like Stevenson's *Prince Otto* and Scott's non-historically-based Jacobite stirrings would have significantly altered the formula of a rebellion novel, and would have made the genre more difficult to identify and classify. More importantly, non-historically-based and utopian or dystopian rebellions do not fit into the historical novel genre, and therefore do not fall into the subcategory of the rebellion novel that I am creating within the larger umbrella of the historical novel. Utopias and nonhistorical rebellions should be studied as separate subgenres.

The novels in this study come from the nineteenth century to show that most of the patterns in genre structure and linguistics remained stable across the century. As Figure 5 shows, the peaks in rebellion novel publication are the 1800s, 1850s, 1880s, and 1890s because those are the decades when the three focal novelists experienced creative peaks. You can clearly see that most rebellion novels are set in the 18th century. The eighteenth century was chosen by all three as the primary time for rebellions because it was the century that saw the bloodiest rebellions and revolutions in European history. Scott set most of his novel sixty years in the past, the early half of the eighteenth century and the Jacobite rebellions. Dickens mimicked this timing, also turning the clock back by sixty years to the Gordon Riots and the French Revolution. Stevenson broke from this pattern and primarily looked back to the eighteenth century. If one steps back and looks at rebellion novels by other writers one notices that they were conscious of the sixty-years rule, but felt a need to create a more innovative time setting; thus, Ainsworth writes that the actions of Fawkes took place "More than two hundred and thirty-five years ago."[4]

Because Scott and Stevenson were from Scotland, it is the most frequent setting for their rebellion novels, as seen in Figure 7. England is the next most frequent setting, which is only natural, as it is the home country of most of these British novelists. France and Ireland are the two countries with double appearances, as France underwent a major revolution and Ireland's struggle for independence from England began long before it joined the union.

The character list typically includes a group of rebels, a group or militia that is defending the empire, and a few "idiots," wavering characters who are in the fight accidentally and either wish they could escape the fighting or are ignorant of the nature or danger of the fight.

This study is limited to England and Scotland because it is easier to isolate patterns in genre in isolated geographical boundaries. It focuses on the nineteenth century because Fleishman pegs the founding of the historical novel to the beginning of the nineteenth century with Sir Walter Scott's work,[5] and Speare pegs the founding of the political novel to the middle of the nineteenth century with Benjamin Disraeli's novels.[6] In fact, both the realist and naturalist novels also bloomed in the nineteenth century. Therefore, it is logical to conclude that the rebellion novel, as a subgenre of the historical and political novels, could not have been founded before the beginning of the nineteenth century.

Scott, Dickens and Stevenson occupied diverse periods, as one wrote at the beginning of the nineteenth century, the second in the middle and the third at the end. I chose writers who did not just dabble in this genre but returned to it at least once with evolved tricks and techniques. Scott and Stevenson, in fact, wrote at least five rebellion novels each. Since five novels is a significant part of Scott and Stevenson's total published works, a dominating passion for the rebellion genre can be seen in both novelists. The fact that Scott, Dickens and Stevenson were some of the most popular, best-selling and critically acclaimed writers of the century in England also means that studying their techniques involves studying masterly linguistic and structural efforts, as opposed to amateur attempts. Because of the financial and popular success of the novels on my list, the rebellion novel genre can be seen as an example of superior literary craft, and not a case of simple formulaic fiction, mimicry, plagiarism, and the like. The use of strict formulas, when done by a crafty hand, can be a tool for greatness, rather than simply a makeshift device for quicker returns on artistic investments.

The chapters on Scott begin with an explanation of what came before Scott's "discovery" of the rebellion genre, and the building blocks that Scott used in its construction. Scott's six rebellion novels are: *Waverley* (1745 Jacobite rebellion), *The Black Dwarf* (Jacobite rebellion), *The Tale of Old Mortality* (1679 Scottish Covenanters' rebellion), *Rob Roy* (1715 Jacobite rebellion), *The Heart of Mid-Lothian* (1720–1750 Edinburgh Porteous riot), and *Redgauntlet* (1765 "imagined" Jacobite rising). You might have noticed from the above that every single rebellion on Scott's list occurs in Scotland. Of course, one might disregard the pattern by claiming that Scott spent most of his life in Scotland and probably chose a familiar setting. But it is more likely that Scott expressed subversive fervor for Scottish independence from the English empire.

In the chapters on Dickens, I leap temporarily away from Scottish nationalism to study the mid-century concerns for the poor and disenfranchised of England's mainland. Without a look at Dickens or one of the other London writers of rebellion novels, this study might otherwise be dismissed as a study of two ultra-nationalist Scotsmen: Scott and Stevenson. By sandwiching Dickens in between, we can see how Dickens utilized the techniques that Scott developed in his numerous Scottish rebellions to project the same formula onto uprisings in France and England. *Barnaby Rudge* was published in 1841, a few years before the beginning of the great Irish potato famine, and *A Tale of Two Cities* was published in 1859, several years after the end of the same. Starvation and other extraordinary social ills in this period redirected Dickens to writing social novels like *David Copperfield* (1849), *Bleak House* (1852), *Hard Times* (1854), and *Little Dorrit* (1855). The large gap of time, in terms of Dickens' maturity as a novelist, between *Barnaby Rudge* and *A Tale of Two Cities* helps us to see the radical changes and innovations that Dickens made in the latter work. *Tale* was one of Dickens' best-selling books, while *Rudge* killed one of his earliest magazines due to an extreme drop in circulation.

Closing with Stevenson is appropriate, as he is a great example of late nineteenth century radicalism, socialism and Marxism. Stevenson echoed Scott by publishing a few novels about Scottish uprisings: *Kidnapped* (1886), *David Balfour* (1893), *The Young Chevalier* (1892), and *Pentland Rising* (1895). However, because he spent a lot of time in England's mainland, or perhaps because of Dickens' precedents, Stevenson did not confine his rebellion novels to the periphery, writing two unique works in 1885: the Irish nationalist *Dynamiter* and the dystopian *Prince Otto*. Caroline McCracken-Flesher claimed that Stevenson and Scott fell into the group of Scottish writers who were waging a "literary battle with England."[7] Stevenson was far more radical and revolutionary in his beliefs and purposes than he publicly acknowledged, and his socialist views sharpened rather than waned in his later years. Looking at the works of a writer who was honored with flags in communist parades in the twentieth century will show a contrast between him and the comparatively more moderate Scott and Dickens.

By choosing novels that use a specific structural formula, I am deliberately choosing works that "mimic" their predecessors. Edwin Eigner claimed that in Stevenson, "characters from the Walter Scott–derived tradition of romance are thinly conceived and executed."[8] The term "Walter Scott–derived tradition" appears in other phrasings in several other critical studies, and it is taken as a fact that even great writers like Dickens and Stevenson frequently wrote works that were "derivative" of Scott. One can also conclude that the parallels between *Kidnapped* and *Rob Roy* partially stem from the fact that Scott mentioned Allan Stewart, or Rob Roy, and the Appin murder in the introduction to *Rob Roy*. There have not been any studies that prove that Stevenson "plagiarized" Scott, so the borrowing is not a loss. And my goal is not to make a case for plagiarism, but rather for "mimicry," which I do by using Stevenson's own confessions that he blatantly and with pleasure mimicked Scott, whom he greatly admired. I am going to work to prove a case for mimicry in order to establish parallels among these novels, to show that they are a single genre. It would be absurd to write that Dickens *only* "mimicked" Scott when he wrote *A Tale of Two Cities*. As early as 1826, Scott was conscious of his imitators, and he wrote in his journal that Ainsworth's *Sir John Chiverton*[9] and *Brambletye House*[10] are imitations of his work, and that his "contemporaries steal too openly," but that he hopes to persevere by consciously working on "new devices to throw them off, and have a mile or two of free ground."[11] Scott wrote more than one sanguine comment about Ainsworth's imitation of him, and his biographer John G. Lockhart even included a note about the imitation in the *Memoirs of the Life of Sir Walter Scott*.[12] Scott admired *Sir John Chiverton*, and thought that the imitation was well executed and that it mimicked his historical genre and classical chivalry romances. An early critic wrote about Ainsworth's *Chiverton*, "The characters, indeed, which he has introduced into his romance are not remarkable for novelty, though they are free from the charge of being servile imitations of any particular originals."[13]

Brambletye is another interesting example of mimicry. This historical novel by Horace Smith touches on the rebellion theme, with side commentary like these lines the lead character finds in a paper: "An Impeachment of High Treason against Oliver Cromwell and his son-in-law Henry Ireton, and other similar attacks upon the Protector, for which he was at that moment in prison."[14] Scott must have noticed hundreds of similarities like this to his own novels when he read these books. The historical novel genre formed through a series of mimicries, among which Ainsworth wasn't the first, of Scott's novels. After the financial and public success of Scott's novels, new novelists must have felt that following Scott's formula was a way to assure literary success. The same type of mimicry also applies to the rebellion novels that followed Scott's novels.

This book covers a mixture of structural and linguistics features of rebellion novels because one of these dimensions cannot be explained without offering evidence in the other field. For example, the use of subversive linguistics in Scott, Dickens and Stevenson cannot be explained without showing evidence that these three authors had a common political, or financial/authorial, purpose for utilizing such subversive techniques. If Scott did not believe in the Scottish nationalist cause, why would he hide an anti-union message in a heavy Scottish accent that would be unintelligible to Londoners? The multidimensional approach is appropriate because generic formulas cannot be studied from only one dimension. The genre evolved across the century through various innovations, improvements and experimentations on the part of the rebellion novelists. There will be a description of how the rebellion genre changed over time, through the comparative differences and similarities between Scott's, Dickens' and Stevenson's rebellion novels.

4

Readers of Rebellion Novels

Were rebellion novels primarily bought by and written for poor or lower-middle-class readers? What was the effect of rebellion novels on 19th-century culture and social views? There is a close correlation between the rebellious message in these novels, the desire of the poor to buy books that helped or sympathized with their plight, and the wider literacy movement. Thompson noted: "The books or instructors were very often those sanctioned by reforming opinion."[1] Scott, Dickens and Stevenson were all members of this "reforming opinion" and their rebellion novels were "sanctioned" as pro-reform. As a result, they outsold most of their literary competitors.

The link between politics and literature can best be seen in the biography and literary technique of Benjamin Disraeli. Despite several unsuccessful early political runs on a radical ballot, by his thirties he was a Conservative MP for Maidstone. A decade later, in 1845, he published the acclaimed, *Two Nations: Sybil*, considered as the first "Condition of England" novel, and two decades after this he served as the first "Jewish," by origin, prime minister in 1868 and then in the period 1874–1880. While he had to switch to the Conservative Party to win elections, his socially conscious or radical novels sold very well with the poor public. Disraeli managed to win elections by appealing to the tastes and manners of the rich nation, and he also managed to sell books by appealing to the beliefs and values of the poor in the United Kingdom. St. John wrote: "In *Coningsby*[2] and *Sybil*, he called for a restoration of monarchical authority from the subservient position it had occupied since the Whigs had brought George I from Hanover, while in those same novels he drew attention to the just claims of the poor."[3] Critics have noticed that Disraeli makes rhetorical arguments in his novels for both the monarchy and the poor. Coming from a middle-class background, with aspirations to the upper class, he sympathized with both the rich and the poor. But the poor needed his help more than the rich, and Disraeli frequently betrays his bias towards the lower class. The fact that Disraeli makes various pro-poor arguments in his novels is the reason poor and middle-class readers bought his books. St. John wrote: "Disraeli had a genuine sympathy for the common people. He knew how they suffered in the process of industrialization and urbanization. In *Sybil* he described the desperate log of the handloom weavers."[4] As St John looks at more and more evidence from *Sybil*, he seems to be convincing himself of Disraeli's radicalism. *Sybil*, he writes, was "essentially antiaristocratic" because in it "great territorial magnates are satirized."[5] In other words, "It is impossible to deny that with the author of *Sybil* social reform was a matter of longstanding conviction and genuine enthusiasm."[6] Publishing novels that supported the poor was not an easy task because to publish a work that appealed to the poor, he first had to argue against the objections that conservative or pro-bourgeoisie publishers had. According to St. John: "Traditionally publishing had proved itself to be a notoriously conservative profession." Thus, for example, John Murray declined Disraeli's *The Young Duke*[7] "because of 'his fears for the future of the country owing to the passing of the Reform Bill.'"[8] *The Young Duke* was published a bit later, in 1853, by G. Routledge; this publishing house is a major academic publisher today. It was started in 1836 by George Routledge. Disraeli found a friendly ear in Routledge because the publisher had just incorporated the company in 1851, and was probably looking to make political and cultural connections.

Social novels were most likely to be accepted by publishers who were sympathetic to socialist politics, or were desperate for money or connections. At the same time, because the spike in readership occurred when the poor started buying books, writers who subversively or openly resisted censors and conservative publishers by publishing rebellion novels sold a lot of copies to this new poor reader market. The high sales records are apparent from the numbers of how much these authors made from selling rebellion novels; for example, £10,000 for Disraeli's *Endymion*,[9] £4,000 for Dickens' *Barnaby Rudge*, and £6,000 for Thackeray's *Virginians*. In fact, these rebellion novels paid these authors more than any other novel from their long literary careers. They would not have been paid so well if the publishers were not certain that they would recoup their investments.

While it became easier to make a living as an author in the nineteenth century than previously, most writers needed a supplementary income from a job that only the English aristocracy and upper class could offer. It is reasonable to assume that most radicals, like Disraeli and Stevenson, were forced to conform and join the Conservative Party in public. Therefore, statements by these radical novelists about their conservative sentiments should be judged as compromised statements, without which they would not have been able to maintain their positions of social, cultural, political and financial prestige. This pattern is best exemplified by Stevenson, who joined the Samoan Civil

War and the Irish nationalist movement, while publicly claiming to have changed his ways and to have become a conservative.

Because most rebellion novelists frequently contradicted the radical nature of their fiction with public statements against radicalism, proving that they were radicals requires a study of the microscopic elements of their writing style. In addition, when these novelists express what appear to be pro-rebellion or pro-poor sentiments, a critic faces uncertainty as to the political or social purpose or personal opinion of the author, as opposed to the common opinions of the time that the author might simply be recording. For example, when Disraeli has Lady Marney say in *Sybil* that she fears that somebody will take office who will be "preaching reform and practicing corruption,"[10] it is a long stretch to extend this to Disraeli himself, or even to the current government. If Lady Marney announces "that a revolution was inevitable, that all property would be instantly confiscated, the poor deluded king led to the block or sent over to Hanover at best, and the whole of the nobility and principal gentry, and every one who possessed anything, guillotined without remorse"[11]— should we project these views onto Disraeli? The answer appears to be a clear "no" for literary critics who are used to reading satire and irony in overstatements of this kind, or to separating authorial purpose from characters' opinions. But why do antiaristocratic statements saturate rebellion novels at a rate that was likely to be alarming to readers who "possessed anything"? And what about when Disraeli and others describe the scenes of impoverished neighborhoods in sympathetic terms, writing about the "Beautiful illusion!" that veils "penury and disease fed upon the vitals of a miserable population?"[12] How should we evaluate what an author's social criticisms or conclusions in a work of fiction imply? The answer lies in the linguistic and structural subversive hints to authorial intent and purpose that Scott, Dickens, Stevenson, and Disraeli have left behind.

Like Disraeli, other rebellion novelists were also running in two different elections. Dickens, for example, had to appeal to the rich to maintain his paying editorial day jobs, and had to appeal to the poor or the middle class in his novels, which primarily had a buying market of the poor. Dickens "spoke directly to the workers, for they repeatedly called upon him to describe their own life experiences."[13] According to reader surveys and studies on readership published by the Statistical Society of London, which surveyed "book ownership and readership among the working classes," "Dickens was the favorite author..., with Scott not far behind."[14] Dickens is especially relevant in a discussion of rebellion novelists as salesmen, because he was also the publisher of many of his ventures. "Dickens's career, viewed from one aspect, emerges as a successful exercise in elbowing aside the booksellers who stood between him and the reader.... His usual 75–25 percent split,"—in other words, 75 percent of profits — went into Dickens' pocket, meaning that "Dickens reduced the publisher to the purely functionary status of printer."[15] As was shown with Black, Disraeli and Scott, and due in part to the Seditious Societies Act, nineteenth-century publishers frequently prevented the publication of projects when they objected to the politics behind them. Only by achieving independence from the publishers, or by working with a publisher who was sympathetic to one's political causes, could a novelist publish a radical rebellion novel. Thus, by wielding the power to publish what they pleased through their independence or prior sales success, writers like Scott, Dickens and Stevenson could disregard worries about censorship from publishers who might have otherwise worried about aristocratic reactions, and could focus on selling works that appealed to the larger poor and middle-class markets.

Both Dickens and Scott were selling their books deliberately to lower- and middle-class readers by lowering the price of these books and making them available to circulating libraries. The sheer number of copies that Dickens sold shows that he had to have had popular, rather than only upper-class, appeal. Dickens became especially popular when his independent magazine *All the Year Round* became a best-seller among magazines, and caused an explosion in serialized fiction in the "closing years of the 1850s ... Dickens's rivals might occasionally attain these figures [120,000 per issue] as a sales peak but none could boast it as a steady current circulation."[16]

The reason Scott became enormously popular is not only the fact that his publisher, Constable, made the price of his books very low to begin with and went bankrupt due to this bargain, but also due to the fact that then, "seeking to sell Scott to every willing buyer in order to rescue him from bankruptcy, Cadell began the cheap reprinting of novels for readers in earnest by reissuing the Waverley novels in a small format in June 1829 ... [at] less than one-third of their original price." This second lowering of the price actually started to make a profit (or at least started to pay off some of the publisher's debts from prior ventures with Scott), and made Scott even more popular with lower-class readers than he was prior to this drop in price.[17]

Thus, Scott was partially the cause of the enormous new lower-class reading public. Other publishers started printing cheaper books, seeing Scott's success, and many of these books were marketed for the poor. When the poor saw that they could suddenly afford to buy books, they saw a motivation to improve their reading skills, and literacy began expanding.

At the same time, Scott also partially increased the conservative character of the publishing industry in the decades after the 1820s. Scott's sales records "inaugurated the new era of huge readership." But the bankruptcy of his publisher Constable and Ballantyne, after making an attempt to create "a 'total revolution' in bookselling, by which was meant, *among other things* [my italics], offering fiction to the 'millions' at a price that could be generally afforded,"[18] made the publication of fiction for the poor into a risky venture. The publishing business still has similar risks today, as a publisher has to predict total sales and the price at which this goal will be achieved prior to printing. If the book's price is too high, the book might not sell and the investment that was made into the printing is lost.

The strategy of writing socially conscious or pro-rebellion novels that were bought by the poor worked so well that these works were indirectly or directly (as a propaganda tool) responsible for some of the century's political crisis, such as the Scottish Insurrection, which was one of the bloodiest Scottish rebellions that occurred at the peak of Scott's literary fame. To prevent these types of risings, cheap novels written for a poor readership were censored by the profit-seeking bourgeoisie, as well as by the politically conservative censorship laws. In the next chapter, on censorship, I will explain the severity of these laws, which led to the imprisonment of hundreds at the beginning of the nineteenth century. In general, rebellion novelists, after Scott, had to keep the price of their books high enough to make a profit, but still low enough for them to be affordable for the poor. They also had to juggle between offering topics that the poor would enjoy reading about and staying clear from being seditious or libelous. It was a complex dance, so most rebellion novelists were lawyers, as only lawyers could feel confident treading on this unstable ground.

The failure of Ballantyne was particularly surprising, as Scott's books were enormously popular. On the survey list of "working class" readers' favorite books in 1888, Scott's historical novel *Ivanhoe*[19] is fourth among boys, even before the Bible; *Ivanhoe* is eighth on the girls' list, after the Bible.[20] Scott won a barony from King George IV, but this didn't negatively affect his popularity with his Scots and the poorer reading public. The fact that Scott expected that most of his readers would be Scots in the lower and middle class is clearly seen in his use of the Scottish dialects, which he could have avoided if he expected that all of his readers would be English.

There is witness evidence that Scott and Dickens were read by members of all classes, and with a concentration of readers in the expanding lower and middle classes. Richard Altick relates stories of Scott's "fame among all classes of society," such as a London workman recognizing Scott on the street, as well as subscriptions to his works by an "old charwoman," as well as "three hundred soldiers in the Boer War," all avid Scott readers. Altick finds records of similar admiration for Dickens.[21] Working-class people could purchase Scott's and Dickens' rebellion novels at a low price and must have sympathized with the social causes that the rebel characters in these works struggled for.

One important similarity between Disraeli and Scott is their publisher, Longman (the full name was, Longman, Rees, Orme, Brown, Green and Longman), "who," Sutherland wrote, " offered the novel its highest reward of the century — £10,000 for Disraeli's *Endymion*," and also published Scott's *Waverley*.[22] According to Sutherland, Longman avoided publishing novels, with a few exceptions like the above, which shows that they only swayed into novels when the works were political — Disraeli was the Prime Minister of England and Scott was a Scottish judicial clerk and baron. This supports the conclusion that novelists had to find the rare publishers who had radical political motivations for going to press, or had to nearly publish the rebellion novels themselves, or with the help of their friends.

The relationship between rebellion readers and writers was not a one-way stream. There is proof that working-class readers who read Scott, Dickens and Stevenson became more politically active. "Reader surveys conducted by the *Review of Reviews* and Arnold Freeman, along with Robert Roberts's memoir *The Classic Slum* and David Vincent's investigations, all confirm that the workers who were most active politically were usually those who had read Dickens, Carlyle, Ruskin, and even that arch–Tory Sir Walter Scott."[23] This list of politically affecting writers includes two of my focal authors — Dickens and Scott — and Carlyle, who also wrote a Jacobite rebellion story. The fact that readers were stirred by the politics in these writers' works, so much so that they took political actions after reading them, means that reading these writers' rebellion novels inspired rebellious feelings in oppressed readers.

Disraeli, Scott, Dickens and Stevenson's readership was comprised of "two nations," or of the upper and of the lower classes. The upper class might have seen fanciful romances and skillfully executed histories in rebellion novels. The lower and lower middle class was attracted to the cheap price of these novels, and to the social message in these books that appealed to their budding class consciousness. The poignant political nature of rebellion novels can be vividly seen in Disraeli's mixing of politics and literature in life and art. Disraeli was one of the most skillful English politicians of the century, and poor readers responded to his socially conscious message not only by helping to get him elected to office but also by buying his Condition of England novels. The poor started reading when public education became available to them, and they read rebellion novels because they found a sympathetic radical voice behind the subversive language and messages. The poor also read rebellion novels because Scott and Dickens were pioneers in lowering the price of the printed book and serial, and directly helped to make their books affordable, and therefore desirable, to poorer readers. Lastly, there is evidence that reading novels by Dickens, Scott and Carlyle correlated with workers becoming more politically active. Rebellion novels were a form of popularly read radical political propaganda.

5

Censorship, the Publishing Business, and Subversive Literary Warfare

There are three major techniques for repression of the press that were used in the nineteenth century, according to Robert Justin Goldstein:
1. Prepublication repression imposed licensing, a system where nobody could publish any printed matter without first receiving a permit from the government, meaning that only "reliable" individuals could publish. This was abolished in Britain in 1695.[1]
2. Post-publication censorship meant that the government could ban a book it considered to be in opposition to church or state; this was enforced by requiring that books be submitted for governmental review after they were in print.[2]
3. "Caution money" from publishers and special taxation from newspapers — high taxes that made the cost of publications prohibitive to the poor.[3]

Being charged with sedition and libel was a real threat for authors at the beginning of the nineteenth century. Scott's popular rebellion novels played a role in this sudden spike in censorship, and he was one of the victims of this period. One of the most dangerous times to be writing antigovernmental propaganda, pamphlets and satirical or critical fiction was between 1817 and 1823, when there were numerous libel trials and imprisonments, in reaction to several violent uprisings and revolutions across the United Kingdom. Thompson wrote: "The first round of the battle was fought in 1817, when there were twenty-six prosecutions for seditious and blasphemous libel and sixteen *ex officio* informations filed by the law officers of the Crown."[4]

The battle raged on until 1836, by which time "the struggle was substantially over, and the way had been opened for the Chartist press."⁵ Thompson explains that the working class was developing its agenda before 1836, and was solidified and "made" into a coherent social unit under the Chartist movement. In the volatile years between 1792 and 1836, "perhaps 500 people were prosecuted for the production and sale of the 'unstamped,'" or radical, publications, including "editors booksellers, and printers ... newsvendors, hawkers, and voluntary agents."⁶ The longest sentence given to a news vendor was five and a half years to Joseph Swann in 1819 for selling unstamped pamphlets with the following poem:

> Off with your fetters; spurn the slavish joke;
> Now, now, or never, can your chain be broke;
> Swift then rise and give the fatal stroke.⁷

These lines, compared to any rebellious song in Scott or Stevenson, are a lullaby. For example, here is a "Scottish Popular Rhyme" from Scott's *Rob Roy*:

> Baron of Bucklivie,
> May the four fiend drive ye,
> And a' to pieces rive ye,
> For building sic a town,
> Where there's neither horse meat, nor man's meat,
> Nor a chair to sit down.⁸

Scott was never brought up on any sedition charges. Scott was immunized to prosecutions not only because he was a judge and wrote fiction but also because of the distinct Scottish, as opposed to English, publication laws. In the 1707 Acts of Union, the Parliament finalized the union between the Scottish and English kingdoms, which had actually been housed under a single crown since 1603, when a Scottish king sat on the English throne. During the intervening "104 years [when] the booksellers in Scotland had no relationship to the formal structure of the English trade,"⁹ this long separation caused the eighteenth-century Jacobite struggles depicted by Scott, Stevenson and other rebellion novelists, and the tendency of Edinburgh publishers to be subversively rebellious against the stricter English censorship.

There would not have been a rebellion genre if the British publishing industry did not receive a boost from the Copyright Act of 1710, which granted ownership and publication rights of books to their authors, instead of their publishers.¹⁰ This act was further confirmed and strengthened with the later 1814 and 1842 Copyright Acts. The 1710 Copyright Act meant the birth, by 1750s, of the "professional" author, one who could make a living from writing.¹¹ The existence of writers who could pay for their own room and board was an unprecedented concept. For example, Shakespeare relied entirely on royal patronage. Royal patronage remained as an important funding source for writers, but was no longer central in the 19th century. Royal funding was

5. Censorship, Publishing and Subversive Literary Warfare   39

formalized with moves such as the 1790 foundation of the Royal Literary Fund and then the 1820 Royal Society of Literature, both of which funded only the most gifted writers.[12] Because by the 1750s writers could survive on their own efforts, there was now a financial incentive for publishing works that opposed the Crown and addressed the more numerous populace. Among the writers who benefited from the Copyright Act was the author who fueled the fire of the American Revolution, Thomas Paine, with his 1776 pamphlet *Common Sense*[13] and his later revolutionary writings from the front, where he served as a reporter. His rousing, rebellious words inspired Americans to see their struggle as a revolution, and not just a fight about taxes.

While authors gained copyrights, and pre-publication censorship was abolished by the beginning of the nineteenth century, the turn of the century also saw a major blow to post-publication rights for both publishers and authors. The Seditious Societies Act of 1799 forced publishers to censor themselves in order to avoid publishing a work that would be censored or prevented from being distributed after publication. The Seditious Act required, inter alia, the registration of all presses and printing type, the inclusion of the printer's name on all printed matter, and the maintenance by each printer of a complete file of all his products which the justice of the peace could inspect on demand. Unlike so many previous attempts it did actually succeed in controlling the press to a very considerable extent. Indeed, the opposition newspaper press, at least in London, was virtually eliminated by the end of the [18th] century.[14]

The act was not titled the "Seditious Act" at random, but because it intended to suppress radicalism in the press. While before, radical presses or editors could function incognito, now they were directly responsible for the content they published, and could be prosecuted if they published seditious content. Before long, publishers had to send at least one copy of every book they published to the justice of the peace, and were likely to look at radical material as potentially dangerous for their business. Scott dodged this problem by publishing with his close friends in Edinburgh, a city that was not entirely under the control of the Seditious Act. Dickens published rebellion novels by working with "printers" instead of publishers, or by first publishing the works in his own journals. Lastly, Stevenson published his rebellion novels with Edinburgh or radical publishers, and was working with slightly looser censorship controls at the end of the nineteenth century. All three still used subversive techniques to hide radical or pro-rebellion sentiments to bypass the justice of the peace, who might otherwise have found them guilty of "sedition." There are no surviving detailed records of all of the books that publishers rejected with censorship or potential sedition charges in mind. But there was definitely abundant censorship, as can be deduced from examples like Black and Disraeli's rejection letters, where the publisher explains that he can't publish the book because of its censorable content.

It's likely that the Seditious Societies Act of 1799 was a response to the building radicalism in the press after the American and the French revolutions. Two key players in this publishing agitation were William Blake and his publisher Joseph Johnson. Joseph openly supported the French Revolution with numerous books on this and related topics in the 1790s. The decade of Johnson's radical publishing might have started with his arrest in 1791, as he was printing the first book of a planned seven-book poetic series by William Blake called *French Revolution*. Johnson was not formally brought up on charges for this book because he abandoned its publication after his arrest. Johnson also avoided prosecution upon publishing Thomas Paine's *Rights of Man*. But his luck ran out in 1799, because of the new Seditious Societies Act, and he was convicted and incarcerated for six months on seditious libel charges for publishing a pamphlet by Gilbert Wakefield, a Unitarian minister who went to prison on the same charge for two years. The pamphlet was *A Reply to Some Parts of the Bishop Llandaff's Address to the People of Great Britain,* an argument against raising taxation rates and for the rights of the poor, as opposed to the privileged (basically a pre-socialist tract). The criticism in this essay is blunt and accuses the bishop of no less than corruption: "Certainly, a ſyſtem with all it's corruptions muſt neceſſarily appear more eligible to men ſo ſituated, than the dangerous alternative of reformation."[15] William Blake's 1791 *French Revolution* also touched on a religious figure: "She refus'd to be whore to the Minister, and with a knife smote him."[16] Of course, this first book in the series only develops the events that led to the French Revolution, so it doesn't fully describe the crimes of the French monarchy or the way the revolutionaries executed justice. This was hardly the only sedition charge against Blake. Back in 1780, he was seen in the front ranks during the Gordon Riots, which Dickens depicts in *Barnaby Rudge*. And over a decade after the failed attempt to publish *French Revolution*, in 1803, Blake was brought up but acquitted on sedition and assault charges for violating a Dragoon Guard, John Schofield, and telling him, "Damn the king.... Damn his soldiers, they are all slaves: when Bonaparte comes it will be cut-throat for cut-throat. I will help him."[17] Many sources, including Blake's biographer, Chesterton, don't believe it was likely that Blake uttered these words, but rather that he simply escorted the dragoon out of his garden, where the soldier was trespassing. Still, if Blake did say these things to a soldier while physically handling him, this is an extremely radical antiaristocratic statement to have made at the turn of the 19th century. The period of trials and seditious unrest, which included both major actors like Blake and various minor players, during and after the American and French revolutions, planted the seeds for the early-nineteenth-century sedition trials and suppressive laws.

5. Censorship, Publishing and Subversive Literary Warfare 41

According to Thompson, "the main battle" over libel, sedition and blasphemy in the press "was over by 1823, although there were renewed prosecutions in the late Twenties and early Thirties, and blasphemy cases trickled on into Victorian times."[18] Scott had slowed his production of rebellion novels during this period, only publishing *The Heart of Mid-Lothian* in 1818, perhaps because it was already completed and accepted when the 1817 prosecutions began. As a judge, Scott would have been quick to hear about the libel cases in England, and probably felt directly threatened by potential litigation if he continued publishing novels about rebellions against the English empire.

The most repressive legislation from this period were the Six Acts of 1819. They:
1. Prohibited training in weapon use
2. Gave the government a right to search for and seize weapons
3. Prevented seditious meetings against Church and State (this Act was repealed in 1824)
4. Prevented blasphemy and libel in the press
5. Encouraged speedy trials for misdemeanors
6. The Newspaper and Stamp Duties Act raised the tax of cheap labor publications that cost less than 6d to a tax of 4d. The latter forced radical publications to go underground, refusing to pay the tax.

Among other liberty infringements, the Six Acts gave authorities "the power to banish the authors of sedition for offences far less than those which Carlile both committed and proudly admitted."[19]

Richard Carlile was a leader in the movement of newspapermen and book publishers who fought against these restrictions after authorities started enforcing the Six Acts. "By one count, before the battle had ended Carlile had received the help of 150 volunteers, who — shopmen, printers, newsvendors — had between them served 200 years of imprisonment."[20] Some of the key points of this massive prosecution were when Carlile was found guilty in 1819 of blasphemy and seditious libel and was imprisoned for three years for publishing Thomas Paine's *Age of Reason*,[21] and antigovernment pamphlets. And in 1821, Jane Carlile, Richard Carlile's wife, who helped him print radical papers, was also imprisoned for two years for seditious libel. Her sister went to jail shortly after Jane, and Richard returned to prison for a couple more years a few years later. Overall, this was a massive wave of prosecutions against anybody even remotely suspected of committing a "seditious" publishing act.

Most censorship prosecutions focused on nonfiction or newspapers after a notorious legal case. A parody led to publisher, William Hone's imprisonment for "blasphemous libels, in the form of parodies upon the Catechism, Litany, and Creed."[22] Here is a sample:

"Our Lord who art in the Treasury, whatsoever be thy name, thy power be prolonged, thy will be done throughout the empire, as it is in each session. Give us our usual sops, and forgive us our occasional absences on divisions; as we promise not to forgive those that divide against thee. Turn us not out of our places; but keep us in the House of Commons, the land of Pensions and Plenty; and deliver us from the People. Amen."[23]

During Hone's trial, as the parodies were read, the sheriff threatened to arrest "the first man I see laugh."[24] Because the author won (perhaps because the jury couldn't stop laughing), after this trial, "all parodies and squibs were immune from prosecution."[25] This was one of the precedents that made it possible for Scott, Dickens and Stevenson to criticize the government in especially satirical sections of their books, or with the broken voice of the poor, which stressed the jovial or satirical nature of the comments.

The popularity of this and other censorship trials soon prompted radical publications by publishers who hoped to be brought up on charges to attract press and, as a result, high sales for their books. The insistence of radical publishers on defending themselves at trial and on their right to a free press meant that "imprisonment as a Radical publisher brought, not odium, but honour. Once the publishers had decided that they were ready to go to prison, they outdid each other with new expedients to exhibit their opponents in the most ludicrous light."[26] Carlile was imprisoned for five years for his radical *Republican*[27] newspaper and for other offenses, and he saw a sharp spike in his profits during his first imprisonment. As they say, "There's no such thing as bad press," especially if there is scandalous news published about you, and you come out as someone who is standing up for justice and freedom of the press. When the press began competing to make the most satirical and critical depictions of the monarchy, it succeeded. "No British monarch has ever been portrayed in more ridiculous postures nor in more odious terms than George IV during the Queen Caroline agitation, and notably in Hone and Cruikshank's *Right Divine of Kings to Govern Wrong*,[28] *The Queen's Matrimonial Ladder*,[29] *Non Mi Ricordo*,[30] and *The Man in the Moon*."[31,32] The note on the title page of *Non Mi Ricordo* reads, "Printed and Sold by Geo Smeeton.... And may be bad for all Booksellers and Newsmen."[33] Many of these writers were influenced by Scott's Waverley novels; for example, Thomas Jonathan Wooler started the *Black Dwarf*,[34] a radical journal-pamphlet, in 1817, a year after Scott published his *Black Dwarf* Waverley novel.

Prosecutions for censorship did not end by 1831, as there were several scattered trials across the United Kingdom after this date. Even as late as 1977, Ngugi wa Thiong'o was detained without a trial for writing a rousing play, *I Will Marry When I Want*, which was developed with Kikuyu actors at the Kamiriithu Cultural Centre at Limuru. The play was banned. A few years

5. Censorship, Publishing and Subversive Literary Warfare 43

later, Ngugi put together in the same theater a new play, *Mother, Cry for Me*, but this time the whole Kamiriithu theatre was dismantled to prevent the production. The play's background is a labor revolt against the threat of confiscation of their land, echoing the Mau Mau Rebellion (1952–1960). Thus, it is a rebellion genre play in the social realism style. It depicts the impoverished life of a laboring family. The setting is similar to one of the shanties depicted in a 2011 film about the African slums crisis, *Dear Mandela*. The family's one-room shack is something that could have been taken out of one of Dickens' social novels, or from the poor regions of Africa today. An ongoing problem, it is one that Thiong'o must have felt compelled to speak out about, regardless of censorship and imprisonment. The ending of the play is perhaps the most censorable part, and not surprisingly Ngugi uses a song, similar to Scott and Stevenson before him, to convey the passion of the revolutionary movement. All sing:

> The trumpet of the masses has been blown.
> We are tired of being robbed
> We are tired of exploitation
> We are tired of land grabbing
> We are tired of slavery
> We are tired of charity and abuses...
>
> The trumpet of the poor has been blown.
> Let's unite and organize
> Organize in our club
> Organize is our sword
> Organize is our gun
> Organize is our shield.[35]

Back in the 19 century, the tumultuous years of trials and uncertainty ended, and the Chartist movement of reform started a few years after England nearly boiled into a revolution, during the Reform Bill crisis between 1831 and 1832. Thompson wrote: "England was without any doubt passing through a crisis in these twelve months in which revolution was possible."[36] Unlike other reform demonstrations, which frequently drew the semi-bourgeoisie or the middle class, the demonstrations in this period were massive ("above 100,000 in Birmingham and London") and were made up primarily of the "lowest class" or "artisans and working men."[37]

The failure of a revolution in England to materialize is blamed on the profit-seeking middle-class leaders, who roused the masses but pacified them when an actual revolution began forming. This is an important element to consider, as Scott, Dickens, and Stevenson were leaders among this middle-class profit-seeking radical movement. Half a century later, Marx wrote that a revolution was unlikely in England,[38] and this also became apparent during this crisis. "When Marx was still in his teens, the battle for the minds of

English trade unionists, between a capitalist and a socialist political economy, had been (at least temporarily) won."[39] Thompson continued:

> The reason is to be found in the very strength of the working-class Radical movement; the skill with which the middle-class leaders, Brougham, *The Times*, the *Leeds Mercury* both used this threat of working-class force, and negotiated a line of retreat acceptable to all but the most die-hard defenders of the ancient regime; and the awareness on the part of the Whigs and the least intransigent Tories that, while Brougham and Baines were only blackmailing them, nevertheless if a compromise was not come to, the middle-class reformers might no longer be able to hold in check the agitation at their backs.[40]

A violent revolution was likely to hurt the middle class's profits, and was likely to give a radical advantage to the poor. Therefore, the middle class frequently made arguments for violent revolt or total reform, but were quick to settle for a very conservative middle ground, and convinced the laborers there was no reason to press forward just at the times when they were prepared for a revolution.

However, the idea that the middle class or the radical press was wholly against a violent revolution is an overstatement, when one considers that the *Poor Man's Guardian* published Colonel Macerone's *Defensive Instructions for the People* (a manual in street-fighting) in 1832, during the peak of the Reform Bill Crisis, clearly providing direct support to anybody who might have needed help in staging a violent revolution in England. "The masses were not satisfied with the mere possession of arms and sought practical advice on military operations," wrote Frank Ferdinand Rosenblatt in an early review of Macerone's *Defensive Instructions*.[41] The argument that the publishers of the *Poor Man's Guardian* were representatives of the lower class, while Baines and other middle-class reformers were representing the desires of the middle class, is illogical when one considers that any successful publisher in that period would have been in the middle class, and could not have had any controlling interest besides the interests of their own class. The early reform bill focused on benefiting the middle class, rather than the poor. In a study conducted by Lord John Russell, "It appeared that of the working classes not more than one in fifty would be enfranchised by the Bill."[42]

Censorship was perpetrated not only by the publishers, but also, in a sense, in the home. Fathers shielded their children, and especially their daughters, from reading works like Scott's rebellion novel, *The Heart of Mid-Lothian*. Kate Flint writes that Dorothy McCall reflected in 1884 that *Mid-Lothian* "was the one book in her father's library which she and her siblings were forbidden to read." Flint explains that the book was off limits due to the problems in it with "sexuality and religion."[43] Rebellion novels could be banned by parents because they portrayed immoral, devilish, or irreligious rebellions against aristocratic authority. Thus, authors of rebellion novels had to use subversive techniques not only to fool the printers and censors but also to bypass parents who could potentially prevent the buying or reading of works of questionable moral character.

An important detail that explains why Scott, Dickens, Stevenson and most of the other rebellion novelists escaped censorship is that most of them were lawyers. It took not only a highly developed linguist and editor to bypass censorship but one who also had a professional knowledge of the law. Thackeray was a "failed barrister," Dickens "articled as a solicitor's clerk in Gray's Inn," Stevenson "studied law at Edinburgh," Ainsworth "studied law at the Inner Temple,"[44] and Scott practiced law first as a clerk, and later as a judge in Scotland. In a way, these writers were in part disgruntled enough with the English system to write rebellion novels because they failed at law due to the fact that, in Suterland's words, "To read for the English Bar, it is necessary to have family money, contacts, and (usually) an Oxbridge education. To practice at the Bar was, and is, a top job and one from which the working classes are generally excluded."[45] Stevenson was denied a law professorship at the Edinburgh university, Scott could not advance in the law beyond serving as a regional provincial Scottish judge, and Dickens never advanced in the law beyond office work. All three were from middle-class families, without enough family money and connections to meet their ambitions. This wall between ambitious intellectuals and the top-paying, non literary careers left highly educated lawyers with a grudge against the establishment and with the know-how to bypass censorship protocols. Disraeli is a partial exception to this rule because, unlike the others, he succeeded in politics as well as in literature, but there must have been something about his climb that left him just as bitter about the establishment to also make a contribution to the rebellion genre.

While the Copyright Act made it possible for writers to benefit from publishing, only widespread literacy allowed them to grow rich on the trade. Across the nineteenth century, England passed acts in support of the "education of the poor" (1833), for the universal education of the poor (1870), for the compulsory education of the poor (1880) and finally, for the free education of the poor (1891).[46] Widespread literacy widened the market for books from a few aristocrats to most of the English population. Sales of titles skyrocketed to hundreds of thousands and then to millions of copies. Scott and Dickens were two of the leading beneficiaries of this boom, as they were the most "popular and commercially successful."[47] Suddenly, the primary buyers of literary products were the disenfranchised poor and not English royalty. Rebellion novels sold well to a public that continually supported reforms that might better their economic and social conditions. When the masses began reading, and primarily bought novels, middle-class authors realized that they could utilize the press with the same type of propagandistic purpose as the monarchs, or to persuade the public to support their social causes. Political, social and especially rebellion novels are examples of radical social reformers using the "power of the novel to make points which were perhaps more acceptable, and certainly more forceful, by their embodiment in fictional form."[48] To put it another way, those who witnessed the French and American revolutions were probably less sympathetic towards rebellious causes than those who read rebellion novels.

The commercialization of the publishing industry also meant that the most successful authors had to produce novels quickly or on tight magazine and publishers' schedules. The sooner the next novel was in the mail, the sooner the author was paid. This push towards speeding up the production of novels was one of the primary catalysts for the birth of "formula fiction."[49] Victorian writers averaged "17.6 novels per writer" per lifetime, with 18 percent writing 100 novels or more per lifetime. After copyrights were transferred to authors, "the practice of fiction was thoroughly professionalized."[50] When viewed from this perspective, the output for the focal rebellion authors was below average: Dickens wrote 15, Thackeray wrote only 9, Eliot wrote 10, and Scott's and Stevenson's numbers were similarly under the 17.6 average. These authors stayed afloat by being paid more per novel than the average speedy, or "hack," writer of the century, who averaged £250 per novel.[51] Still, the professional novelists, who also wrote rebellion novels, felt an incredible pressure to produce novels as rapidly as they could to compete in this highly productive fiction market. The clock was an important factor in the productivity of Scott, Dickens and Stevenson. All three were acutely aware of their families' financial needs. Each of these writers mimicked their predecessors to match their financial, as well as social successes. Writing a novel in the rebellion genre also meant that an author like Dickens or Stevenson did not need to think about what would sell; they instead could rely on what previously worked for a sales giant like Scott. The fact that both Dickens and Stevenson made a lot of money from the sales of their rebellion novels and that they completed these books in record time proved that they were right in these assumptions. Of course, Scott, Dickens and Stevenson had to be sympathetic to the causes of the rebellions they depicted in order to join this market. The newly educated poor and the empowered middle class would not have bought rebellion novels that portrayed them in an unsympathetic or a negative light. Despite this, it is clear that Dickens and Stevenson made at least partially strategic business decisions by following Scott's rebellion novel formula, and did not simply follow their radical political purposes.

Rebellion novels were published despite censorship barriers because they sold well. Still, it is also clear that only the most respected and well-known writers like Scott, Dickens and Stevenson could slip a few rebellion novels through. "Reputation — which in this case means not so much personal or artistic standing as a solid record of commercial success — is an enormously influential factor in establishing authorial control; any sensible publisher will try to please an author who is a popular success and gains a great sale."[52] Some of the publishers of rebellion novels were new to the industry and only too happy to work with established writers like Stevenson. For example, McClure "was slow to take off," but the "enterprise apparently leaped ahead in 1887 after a meeting with Robert Louis Stevenson, and arrangements were made to republish *The Black Arrow*, which had been serialized in England years before."[53] This sale was one of the most profitable ventures of Stevenson's career, and allowed for his move to Samoa, among other luxuries. Stevenson was not alone in benefiting from publishing a rebellion novel. Dickens was better paid than even French writers, when he was paid £2,000 by Bentley in 1839 "for copyright in book form of *Barnaby Rudge* (1840), to pay an additional £1,000 if more than 10,000 copies were printed and to pay a final £1,000 for more than 15,000 copies."[54] Rebellion novels sold well, and publishers who were not afraid of potential reprimands from the English government or from other bodies had a lot to gain by taking the risk of publishing a rebellion novel.

Writers bypassed post-publication Seditious Act barriers and other types of publishing and domestic censorship with the help of the Copyright Acts, the unique publishing laws in Edinburgh, the popular success of best-selling novelists, a new poor reading public that wanted rebellion novels, the money-minded, hack-like formulaic, rebellion novels, and the legal experience of the majority of the rebellion novelists. Rebellion novels were published because they sold well. In turn, they sold well because they were more radical or pro-labor in their content than society fiction, the novels that focused solely on the lives of the wealthy and powerful. Writers now held copyrights to their work, so they had the freedom to write radical works as long as they could find a radical or friendly-to-financial-gain publisher and could write a novel that would not be labeled as "seditious" by the censors, with the common use of subversive techniques to hide the more radical elements of the works.

6

The Elements of Rebellion Novels

The plots are about rebellions against the government, and the characters are rebels. To understand why writing about a rebellion, in general, was a radical and potentially censorable act, one can look at an example from a May 27, 2011, incident where, according to the *Associated Press*, an American citizen who moved to Thailand faced charges for "inciting public unrest and violating Thailand's Computer Crimes Act," and possible jail time from three to fifteen years for translating an unauthorized biography of King Bhumibol Adulyadej, *The King Never Smiles*,[1] into Thai and posting a link to it on his website. Several Thai citizens had already gone to jail on comparable charges.[2] Similar biographies "insulting" to the monarch were published in 19th-century England, such as Hone.[3] Rebellion novelists found a way to criticize the monarchy by referring to past problems, rather than insulting their current administration. If the kings and queens that they ridiculed in their novels were long dead, then inciting rebellions against them could not be a punishable crime.

Generic Influences

Defining the elements of rebellion novels is both complicated and simplified by the elements from other genres that are mixed into these works. The nineteenth century was rich in the "shifting and mixing of genres," or in "textual hybridization," which was "accelerated under fast capitalism and a globalized economy."[4] There is barely an author on my list who was not the first or the best in some new strand of genre. Le Fanu is credited with making major contributions to the gothic genre.[5] Scott "invented" the historical novel.[6] Disraeli founded the "condition of England" novel.[7] Most of the rebellion novelists mixed several genres into their stories. The most frequently reappearing genres are romance, epic, satire, gothic, historical, political, social, national and bildungsroman. In *Colonel Torlogh*, Le Fanu writes that he will depict a story that includes: "history," "meanness and buffoonery of comedies" and "dire events of tragedies."[8] The genre mixing was an intentional technique by all rebellion novelists, and this is probably the reason the rebellion genre has not been pegged as such. A critic digging into an individual rebellion novel notices so many generic strands that it probably seems absurd to create a new one, but only by defining these works as rebellion novels can one make sense of why so many different genre techniques needed to be utilized in them to make them whole. The formula of mixing the above-mentioned popularly used genres includes only purposeful strands. The rebellion had to be a historically accurate event set in the past for censors not to take it as a direct threat of violence against the establishment. Nicholas Rance explains that especially after the 1848 revolutions, English writers became "detach[ed] ... from the historical process." For example, "Carlyle abstracts himself from a history [*French Revolution*] which is regarded as spectacle, madness and feverfrenzy running their course."[9] Only by appearing to be unopinionated and detached from revolutionary violence could socialist and radical writers depict rebellious violence and distribute it in pamphlets to the masses. Imagine the alternative, that Carlyle instead expressed passionate support for the violence perpetrated in the French Revolution in his historical book. He would have been put on trial for sedition and for inciting rebellions, just like the leaders of other violent rebellions. To return to why rebellion novels use a mixture of genre elements, the events of a rebellion, assassination or a revolution also had to be painted with an epic or a romantic brush for the characters, and especially the rebels, to stand larger than life and to inspire the readers with awe and admiration. Depicting the poverty of the poor and including socialist and political arguments was necessary to create sympathy for the degree of violence and mayhem that typically accompanies a rebellion. These ingredients had to be in the right proportions, and simultaneously had to vary from one novel to the next to remain original.

Structural Features

There were several changes in goals and structural formulas between the three main novelists and other rebellion novel writers. However, there are a few elements that repeat across all rebellion novels. The structural formula for a rebellion novel can be simplified as:

Structural Formula of All Rebellion Novels = **R** (Rebellion) + **T** (Travel) + **A** (Adventure).

This formula is different from the formula for national tales, which included travel to the periphery, engaging with a foreign culture and marrying in the periphery. Most of these early Irish and Scottish nationalist elements were stripped away as the rebellion novel became more and more established as a unique genre. Writers such as Stevenson deleted love from the equation because depicting women and love was not their strong point. Rebellion novels, in general, do not fit well with the marriage theme because they depict disunion and repulsion between the core and the periphery or between the poor and the rich nations, as opposed to a union between the two. What is left is the repeating rebellion plot structure, with the bulk of rebellion novels dedicated to depicting the reasons for a given rebellion, then portraying the details of the rebellion, and then offering a tragic end for some of the rebels, and typically, supplying a happy ending for the main character. This plot is always supported with some travel to new, exotic, picturesque or strikingly impoverished places. Another crucial element of all rebellion novels is that in all parts of the book, including the times when the rebellion is building or declining, the characters are always engaged in adventures, which keep readers captivated by brave, cowardly, amusing and otherwise enthralling acts. Rebellion novels are spectacular and epic in the quantity of scenes and plot twists they relate.

The patterns between rebellion novels in terms of their setting, participants and type of rebellion can best be seen in the following table and graphs, based on a few rebellion novels that were published by a few other novelists besides Scott, Dickens and Stevenson.

Mimicry of Scott

Mikhail Bakhtin wrote in "Epic and Novel," "In general any strict adherence to a genre begins to feel like stylization, a stylization taken to the point of parody, despite the artistic intent of the author."[10] Bakhtin goes on to explain that the novel is in flux as a genre because "there is a constant parodying or travestying of dominant or fashionable novels that attempt to become models for the genre."[11] He concludes that genres such as the baroque, pastoral, and sentimental novels were all a series of parodies of successful novels. From this perspective, the rebellion novel genre is a parody of the initial profitable novels of their kind: Sir Walter Scott's Waverley novels.

In the introductions to a significant number of rebellion novels, the writers who followed Scott directly credit him as their inspiration or as the linguistic and structural teacher for their own projects. By 1890, Charles Kingsley

6. The Elements of Rebellion Novels

Novel	Event Dates	Rebellion	Participants	Locations
		CIVIL REBELLIONS		
White Hoods	1576	Civil Uprising in Ghent	Rebels vs. state	Ghent, Flanders
Pentland Rising	1666	Pentland Rising	Scot poor vs. rich	Edinburgh, Scotland
Old Mortality	1679	Covenanters' Rebellion	Covenanters vs. establishment	Southwest Scotland
Colonel Torlogh	1686-1700	Williamite War	Protestant vs. Catholic, James	England, Ireland
Mid-Lothian	1736, 1720-60	Porteous Riot	Porteous vs. establishment	Edinburgh
Sybil	1837-44	Chartist Agitation	Workers vs. rich	England
		ASSASSINATIONS OR VIOLENCE DIRECTED AGAINST A FEW		
Guy Fawkes	1604-05	Gunpowder Plot	Rebels vs. King James	England
Mutiny	1768-69	Munity on the ship, Bounty	Tahitians, English	Tahiti, England
Barnaby Rudge	1775, 1780	Gordon Riots of 1780	Assassinators vs. aristocracy/Catholic	England
Felix Holt	1832	1832 Reform Bill violence	Felix, aristocrats	England
Dynamiter	1885	Act of Irish anti-union terrorism	Irish rebels vs. Irish unionists and English	Ireland
		NATIONWIDE REVOLUTIONS OR REBELLIONS		
Hereward	1067-71	Rebellion vs. Norman conquest of England	Hereward, English, Normans	England
Virginians	1774-76	American Revolution	English, Americans	America, England
Two Cities	1775, 1789	French Revolution	Aristocrats vs. poor	England, France
		JACOBITE REBELLIONS		
Black Dwarf	1707+	Attempted rebellion	Scots vs. English	Scotland, England
Rob Roy	1715	1715 Jacobite Rebellion	Jacobites vs. English aristocracy	Scotland; England
Waverley	1745	1745 Jacobite Rebellion	Jacobites vs. English aristocracy	Scotland, England
Young Chevalier	1749	Prince Charlie's rebellion	Prince Charlie vs. England, unionists	Scotland
Kidnapped	1752	Appin Assassination	Jacobites vs. English aristocrats	Scotland, sea, England
David Balfour	1751-53	Exoneration for Appin	Jacobites vs. English aristocrats	Scotland, sea, England

Figure 4. Rebellion Novels by Categories

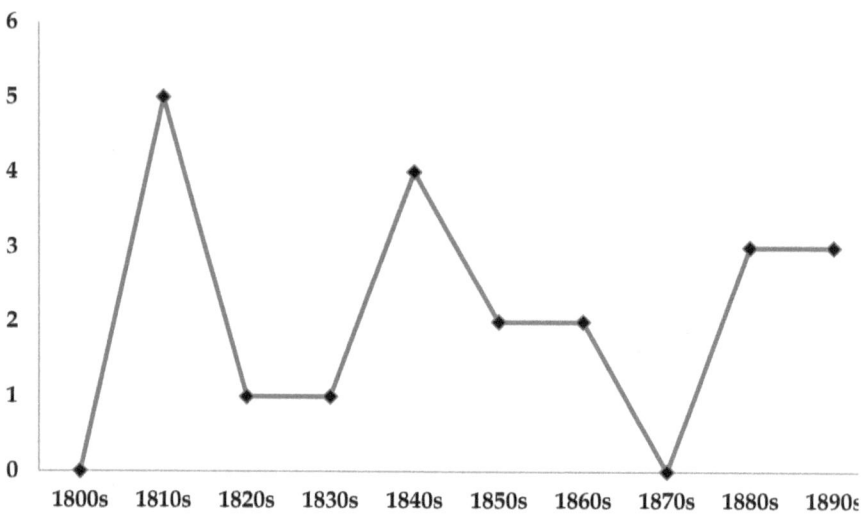

Figure 5. Rebellion Novels by Publication Decade

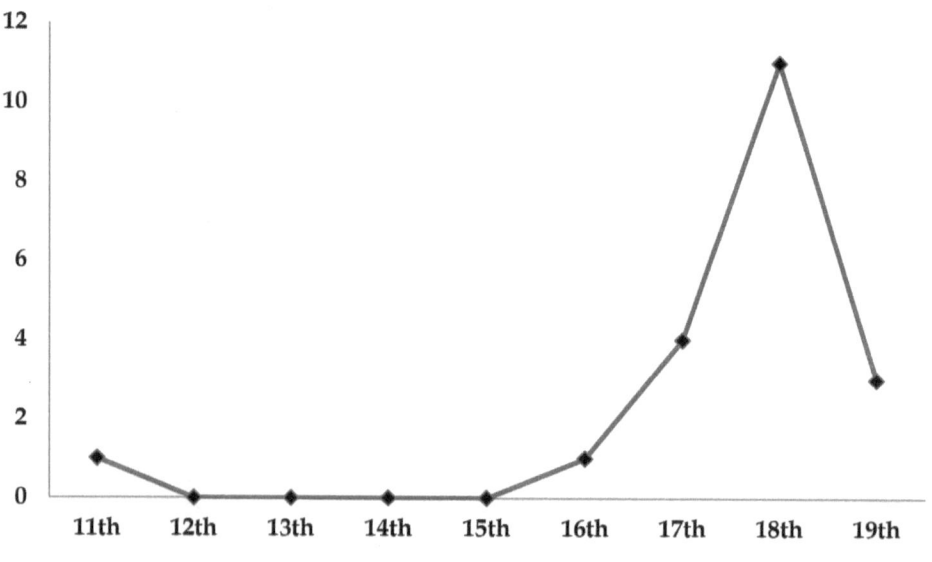

Figure 6. Novels by Century of Event

even begins *Hereward the Wake: "Last of the English"* with a prelude that explains that the "Scottish highlands" are far richer in "romance and wild adventure" than the lowlands could be, as was made clear in the "pages of Walter Scott."[12] The remainder of the prelude is spent in defending or explaining the richness of lowland history, and ends in approximately 1054, with the

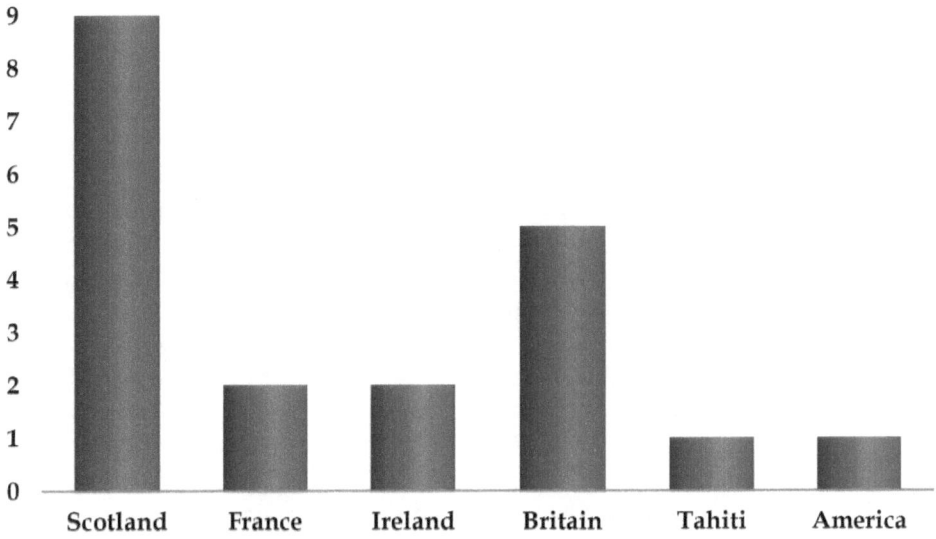

Figure 7. Novels by Country of Rebellion

introduction of the hero, Hereward, who took "undisputed command" of an aristocratic rebellion because he had a "natural right of birth" to the "ancient royal, and therefore God-descended, blood" similar to the claims of the Jacobites that Scott explored.[13] It can clearly be concluded that all historical rebellion novelists at least read Sir Walter Scott and a few of the other well-known novelists' rebellion novels before setting out to write their versions on the rebellion theme. I will offer concrete proof throughout the Dickens and Stevenson chapters that these writers studied their rebellion genre predecessors closely. This intermingling of structural and linguistic techniques is what unifies and solidifies the definitions and properties of the rebellion novel genre.

Plot

The plot of nearly all rebellion novels typically follows five major movements. There are some exceptions to this rule, such as Dickens splitting his plots in two and incorporating a mystery with a rebellion plot, which complicates the far more common single rebellion plotline with five movements, which is discussed in this section. Since, as I will discuss in the Stevenson chapter, Stevenson was the author among my main authors who was most frequently accused of mimicry, he naturally follows the five rebellion plot movements very closely in his five rebellion novels. Here is the formula for these five movements. You will notice that if you look across at any one of the rows in the table that follows, there are many repeating elements, and the five plot movements are clearly present in all eight of these rebellion novels.

> Five Plot Movements: 1) Exposition + 2) Threat or Conflict Begins + 3) Rebellious Attack + 4) Rebels are Defeated, Run or Escape + 5) Varying Resolution for the Main Character (marriage/inheritance/death).

The plot of a rebellion novel is defined by the limitations of its theme. The climax is the rebellion and the aftermath of the rebellion is the resolution, but these elements fall on varied parts of a given novel. The exposition is usually a social commentary on the poor conditions of the central country, with a panoramic and historic perspective on the landscape and on the main characters. The rising action frequently comprises violence by either the rebels or the party that they are rebelling against, and most typically the violence comes from both sides. In *The White Hoods*, for example, Sir Simon and Peter and Gilbert Matthews have a "fray" at the Moon lounging house, where Peter is killed when he is pushed down a flight of stairs with too much force.[14] The early violence typically leads to one of two and usually both of these two outcomes: the villain (rebel or not) quietly slips out, as John Lyon does, or otherwise runs away, or the villain or the friends of the person who is hurt gather and plan a rebellion. The bulk of most rebellion novels consists of the hero, such as Waverley, Frank, David Balfour and others, running away through the marshes, forests, or across countries, away from their pursuers either before, after or even during the main battles of a given rebellion. In parallel, troops of men frequently spend long chapters marching "Up the Hill and Down Again" (Chapter 13 title), as they do in the maneuvers in the American Revolution in Thackeray's *Virginians*. Walking, transport, or motion from one city to another, or from one battle to the next, is the force that moves the actions and plots of rebellion novels. Rebellion novels sold well because they are filled with nonstop action, frequent outbursts of violence, and constant scheming and planning — all ingredients necessary for a suspenseful and unpredictable twisting plot. The main plot points are similar in different rebellion novels, but the roads to these points are richly diverse.

Characters

The characters in rebellion novels are frequently binary, epic exaggerations, with sympathetic or outrageous rebels and corrupt, sinning imperialists, aristocrats or capitalists. One of the best examples of a hyper-sympathetic rebel is Disraeli's Devilsdust, who defied "starvation and poison," saw his family die of diseases, was homeless, then found a children's shelter, where soon everybody died, and he "slept on the same bed of straw with a corpse," only to begin factory work while at age five or six, and finally joined the

6. The Elements of Rebellion Novels   55

	White Hoods	Mutiny	Fawkes	Sybil	O'Brien	Virginians	Wake	Felix
Plot:	White Hoods vs. rulers	Mutiny on a ship	Gunpowder Plot	Social uprising/ riots	Jacobite stirrings	American Revolution	Resistance to Norman conquest of England	Post-Reform Act tensions
1st Movement	Tensions between classes	Mutiny sails for the South Seas	Tensions between classes	Tensions between classes	Tensions between Ireland & England	Tensions between England & America	Tension that led to Hereward being out-lawed	Tension between classes
2nd Movement	John Lyon, by accident, kills a political rival	Tensions start after years at sea	Radcliffe family's home burned because they support priests	Rioting start in Lancashire	A few assaults, executions and other military moves	The Prince and army begin marching	Hero begins a war with the invader	A radical political campaign excites locals
3rd Movement	Civil War	Mutiny–captain and supporters forced out in an open boat	Attempt to blow up the House of Parliament	Riots intensify and spread to other regions	Assassination and other battles	Battles in the American Revolution	Hero fights several battles for England	Felix kills an official by accident while campaigning
4th Movement	Rebels are defeated by the Earl	Mutineers take Tahiti wives and live on an island for 20 years	Rebels, including Fawkes, defeated & executed	Rioters disperse	Rebels, mostly, disperse	Lead characters on both sides run away after fighting	Lead rebel is made into a knight by the grateful English	Felix is put on trial
5th Movement	Anna marries Earl after stopping an assassin	Captain survives, leading his boat to shore	Fawkes repents before his execution (tragedy)	Charles and Sybil marry	Garrett, a Lead outlaw, tries new rebellion and dies	Brothers survive, see England agree to free America	Hero fights many other battles for England	Felix is freed and marries
Time/ Place	1576/ Flanders & travel	1787-89/ South Seas & travel	1605/ England & travel	1837/ England & travel	1689-90/ Ireland & travel	1789 app/ England, America & travel	1035-72/ England & travel	1832/ England & travel
Characters	Varied classes	Seamen vs captain	Catholics vs Protestants	Aristocrats & rich vs workers	Irish rebels vs rulers	Brothers: America vs England	Hereward (English) vs Invader	Felix; rich vs poor

Figure 8. Plot Movements of Other Rebellion Novels

Chartist rebellion against poor factory work conditions.[15] Even the most workaholic capitalist or the most heartless aristocrat would sympathize with this enormous heap of misfortunes. The intention is clearly to soften the middle- or upper-class readers to the misfortunes of the poor, and to evoke the sentimental broodings in lower-class readers. The fact that most of the rebels are sympathetic in a way that reflects their investment in the roots of the rebellion further points to the fact that the rebellion authors were sympathetic to the causes that the rebels stood for. Another commonly recurring character type is the strong female "Amazon" rebel: Sybil in Disraeli, Die Vernon in *Waverley*, Helen MacGregor in *Rob Roy*, and Catriona in *David Balfour*.

The binary character types of rebels and rulers in rebellion novels are not accidental, but are done with the intention of conveying symbolic tensions between classes. Eagleton wrote: "With Scott..., the idea of characters as representing social forces enters the major novel for the first time"; the characters are "representing abstractions like nation and culture, church and state, sovereignty and rebellion."[16] At the same time, the characters are not only symbols for larger social tensions, they are also drawn with close realistic detail to make them more sympathetic when they frequently end in tragic deaths. On Dickens, Eagleton writes that his characters are a "bunch of grotesques, perverts, amiable idiots and moral monstrosities," because "they are realistic," and "true to a new kind of social experience. Dickens's grotesque realism is a stylistic distortion in the service of truth, a kind of astigmatism which allows us to see more accurately."[17] If Dickens is sincere in his depiction of characters, readers are more likely to believe in their reality, and in turn to sympathize with the poor characters' sentimental plights.[18]

Linguistic Features

To understand how formulaic the linguistics of Scott, Dickens and Stevenson are, one should compare examples of broken English in their works with the English in the following 1812 letter to Coroner Salford, who returned an anti-radical decision on a murder case, saying that a man being shot at Burton's mill was a case of "justifiable homicide":

> I Ham going to inform you that there is Six Thousand men coming to you in Apral and then We Will go and Blow Parlement house up and Blow up all afour hus/labring Peple Cant Stand it No longer/ dam all Such Roges as England governes but Never mind Ned lud when general nody and is harmey Comes We Will soon bring about the greate Revelution then all these greate mens heads gose of.[19]

Random broken or dialect speech is different from "standard" English in nearly every word an uneducated or a provincial character utters. But novelists in the 19th century developed a few specific tricks to enrich their dialogues with linguistic diversity, without overwhelming the reader with an avalanche of misspellings.

There are several microlinguistic rules that rebellion novelists follow, but there is one general linguistic formula used in all rebellion novels. It can be simplified as:

> Linguistic Formula of All Rebellion Novels = Regional, National or Class Dialects + Complex Sentence Structure and Vocabulary (Including Many Allusions) + Social/Rebellious Slogans/Rhetoric.

Some rebellion novels include other elements, such as epic characteristics, or focus on either regional or class dialects, but all rebellion novels use some dialogue in nonstandard dialects, some highly complex sentence and word structures, and make some arguments on behalf of the rebels or the poor. Combining high English prose and poetry with sympathetic regional and impoverished speech, and adding to these detailed and sympathy-provoking speeches and narration on behalf of the rebels and other oppressed people in England and abroad, all work to subversively make radical and socialist political statements, which would have otherwise been outlawed by English treason, sedition and censorship laws and publishing limitations.

Eagleton notes: "Almost everyone in Dickens ... has his or her inimitable quick-fire delivery, churlish mumble, wheedling whine, verbose ramblings, pious cant or portentous rhetoric."[20] The linguistic quirks in Dickens at first appear like the same foolery that populated the language of Shakespeare's fools and jokers. But they are not accidental; they exist to carry social messages for literacy, against poverty, and for other social causes. On the surface, Dickens' linguistic dialects and slips appear accidental or comedic, but they reveal a hidden political message. This fact means that Dickens is using subversive linguistics to hide a radical message from all but those who know where to look for it. One example of Dickens' use of the poor class dialect to depict a subversive rebellious message is when a housekeeper, Miggs, joins a mob of rioters by pouring a barrel of "table-beer" on her boss, the old locksmith, who was trying to prevent the attack. "My sentiments is of little consequences, I know ... for my positions is but a servant, and as sich, of humilities; still I gives expressions to my feelings, and places my reliances on them which entertains my own opinions!"[21] By using substandard grammar and misspellings like "sich," Dickens makes her violent action seem more innocent, as if it is coming from an ignorant babe, rather than from a grown and hostile woman. Poussa writes: "Sir Walter Scott's *Heart of Mid-Lothian* (1818) was a pioneer in the serious use of literary dialect, 'for purposes no longer exclusively comic and eccentric, but heroic and even tragic.'"[22] *Mid-Lothian* was Scott's last rebellion novel, so it is more likely that the real pioneering work was made in the earlier rebellion novels, like *Waverley* and *Rob Roy*, with *Mid-Lothian* simply furthering and developing earlier linguistic techniques. Scott, Dickens and Stevenson share this technique in common — they all used linguistic quirks to make their characters more tragic and sympathetic. For example, when Dickens enriches even his raven in *Barnaby Rudge* with quirky language, readers are far more affected by the tragedy of the raven's potential death with Barnaby in prison, or of starvation by himself. This elicits sympathy, not only for the raven, but for the rest of the rebels as well. Poussa calls Dickens a "dialect reporter," for his close representation of the Preston, Lancashire working-class dialect. He took notes on it while he visited the area, and he studied Mrs. Gaskell's husband's "lectures" on this lexicon. Poussa goes on to study the details of the linguistics in Dickens' *David Copperfield* and finds that they confirm what some of the best sociolinguists have had to say about dialects. For example, the upper-working-class women in the novel have a more standardized East Anglian dialect of Yarmouth because women typically had more interaction (as domestic servants, etc.) with middle- and upper-class visitors, who spoke the standard dialect. Poussa studies Dickens as if he were a sociolinguist reporter, rather than a novelist making up fictional dialects. Many other linguists have used the linguistics in Scott, Dickens and Stevenson to make sociolinguistic points about various regional and national dialects, as I will show in the main chapters. Why this type of sociolinguistic studies by these great novelists was subversive can perhaps be best understood with the following example from an introductory book on sociolinguistics.

> Following the military coup in Spain in 1936, Anibal Otero (1911–1974) was arrested while undertaking fieldwork in northern Portugal. He had sent a letter back to his family in Galicia commenting on the legitimacy of the Republican government. On the basis of "evidence" that he was a spy — which included, especially, his suspicious notebooks full of incomprehensible notes in "code"— Otero was convicted of treason and sentenced to death by firing squad. The testimony of scholars that Otero's notebooks were not in fact a spy's code, but rather linguistic transcriptions, enabled him to have his sentence commuted to life imprisonment.[23]

Even in the twentieth century, sociolinguistics was a field that could rouse nationalist or seditious suspicions, which, is shown above, could lead to an execution. As I discussed earlier, at least one author was refused publication because of his use of a Scottish dialect in his novel. This was not an isolated case, and writers knew that they could be censored even for using a nonstandard poor, regional or national dialect because these dialects became synonymous with the struggles for national, regional or class rights of these various oppressed groups. Subversive linguistics was a form of "code" that could be understood by those who shared the dialect, but was difficult to grasp or incomprehensible to "outsiders"— for once, the outsiders were members of the upper and middle classes rather than the poor, and residents of the core instead of the periphery.

Subversive linguistics in the parameters of rebellion novels meant that the author had to use language to simultaneously appeal to the rich and poor. Both realistic and rebellion novels try to home in on authentic dialects to make them more realistic. Rebellion novelists simply also use these authentic dialects to win working-class readers' sympathy for rebellious characters. Thus, the writer criticized the union, capitalists or the empire, but without inspiring a ban on the book by English censors. Scott used the Scottish tongue to make insulting, anti-empiric or anti-union with England statements in his rebellion novels because the English public did not understand Scottish words and expressions and therefore could not take offense at their use.

D'Arcy's book-length study of subversive linguistics is the best source for understanding how the use of Scots and other Scottish dialects in both Scott and Stevenson helped them to bypass some censorship, as their sly anti–English remarks were not understood, but simultaneously the same use of Scots led these authors to be censored by critics and publishers for the use of this "nationalist" language. D'Arcy quotes from Murray G. H. Pittock that "in the years after 1707, the defense of Scottish culture and the Scottish language were in themselves nationalist acts."[24] "Bearing in mind the English and American critics' complaints about the Scots language..., it is quite clear that early nineteenth-century critics, both north and south of the border, immediately discerned at least two sets of readers, one essentially English, the other Scottish." This meant that there was a reading of Scott's novels that was "only accessible to Scots."[25] And this latter Scots language included subversive criticisms of the English people and of England that non–Scots readers could not discern, and therefore did not censor these rebellious words out. D'Arcy brings up "a whole scene" in *Waverley* that is "clearly a droll joke for the benefit of this Scottish/Highland reader at the expense of the ignorant English one."[26]

Stevenson followed Scott's linguistic tricks closely, also utilizing heavy Scottish dialects. Fleishman writes that the prehistorical genre, typified by the 18th-century *The Castle of Otranto*, by Horace Walpole,[27] "romanticizes the past," using "psychological realism" instead of historical facts. Fleishman concludes that the "final stage in the pre-history of the historical novel" is "circumstantial realism," or the use of "regionalist antiquarianism and historical chronicle," as in "the local-color history, dialect and manners in Maria Edgeworth's *Castle Rackrent*."[28] Scott borrowed this use of local color and especially dialect to recreate historical events for readers with historical facts, dialects, manners and enough other details to allow readers to feel as if they are actually stepping into a different historical period.

Some linguistic subversion is so complex that it is intended for a highly intelligent radical readership, as opposed to a section of the Scottish population like poor Scots. Scott and Stevenson occasionally made up Scottish words and phrases by using derivatives of or the original Old English archaisms, as they both spent a lot of time in England, or in the south, and read more books in English, even if in Middle English, than in Scottish.

More frequently, Standard English is only slightly altered. Insults against a country or royalty sound less harsh when they come from the homeless, servants, or squires with unusual accents. But it is a mistake to ignore the content of the criticism, dismissing it as a satire or parody, when these insults carry a heavy political purpose. Dickens, as well as many other rebellion novelists, employed regional or ungrammatical poverty-implying dialects, accents or slang that allowed him to insult, deride, and otherwise criticize wealthy characters by putting this anti–English bellowing in the mouths of those who might have been excused for it due to their "ignorance" of "proper" English etiquette. The Irish Joseph Sheridan Le Fanu writes in *Colonel Torlogh* that he will "borrow the language of knight errantry," before putting into the dialogue of two "squires" misspellings, abbreviations, and regional pronunciations such as: *id* for *is*, *iv* for *if*, *differ* for *difference*, and *murdher* for *murder*. One of the squires, Tim, reflects, "ignorance is a poor thing." To which his companion squire echoes that the country of Ireland is "a low, dirty, vulgar, 'owling desert."[29] Similarly, the old witch Ursula, in *White Hoods*, "publicly insulted" and threatened the prince, but her poverty and apparent frailty shielded her from immediate retaliation.[30] George Eliot also uses ungrammatical dialect to portray poverty or a lack of a proper education. The landlord, Spilkins, uses abbreviations like *o'* and *'em*, and Tommy argues in defense of his right to poach on the land where, he says, "every hare and pheasant ... is mine," despite the rights of its legal owner, with unusual abbreviations like *y'aren't* and *kep'*.[31] Similar examples can be found in all rebellion novels as they all involve situations where the writer has to distinguish "us" from "them" or the rebels from the aristocracy. This separation of character types can best be achieved through varying their linguistic characteristics. When the linguistics became so convoluted that an average English reader was unable to understand the slang or the regional dialect, the author was using subversive linguistics to carry a message to a small portion of the population that would not be understood by the censoring establishment. At the same time, lightly complex linguistic tricks, such as the slight abbreviations used by Eliot as mentioned above, created denser and more sympathetic poor characters.

Another technique employed to criticize the aristocracy and capitalists is framing the criticisms as a question, as Thackeray does: "Suppose no coppers ever were known to come out of the royal coach window?"[32] This, and a string of other similar questions and semi-conclusions, Thackeray introduces by saying that in an ideal country village, the lord's neighbors would adore him and he would live in perfect harmony with them and himself if he were charitable and kind. You can see that even with this satiric trick, criticizing the rich in the language of an affluent bourgeois author, sounds preachy and does not have the same impact as similar criticisms coming from the mouths of the poor.

Genre is commonly studied either with structuralism or with linguistics, but it is illogical to separate linguistics from structure in a discussion of a literary category. In order to create a unified, single argument, I am focusing on the radical purpose rebellion novelists had in mind when they wrote rebellion novels, and I am extending the discussion of purpose into the linguistic and structural sections for each author, to explain subversive and radical politics at work even in the structural and linguistic elements. As some of the most popularly read novelists of the nineteenth century, Scott, Dickens and Stevenson knew how to manipulate the censors and the public to sympathize with the justice of the arguments they presented in their rebellion novels. While there is some proof that Stevenson was a radical revolutionary, that Scott was a pro–Scottish nationalist, and that Dickens held deep-rooted socialist beliefs, I am not arguing that these writers created rebellion novels with the sole purpose of inciting rebellions. If I occasionally slip and call them "revolutionaries," I am referring to the radical and socialist nature of their beliefs, rather than to any overwhelming desire on their parts to see a total violent overthrow of the English empire. After all, they were not revolutionaries but writers. They were not violent but spent their lives in study and focused their energies on making arguments with legal motions and literary battles. Scott, Dickens and Stevenson used the tools of political literary propaganda to assist the poor, disenfranchised and peripheral people with whom they identified and hoped to see free from oppression and poverty.

PART II. SIR WALTER SCOTT AND THE INVENTION OF THE REBELLION GENRE

7
Scott's Scottish Nationalism

Sir Walter Scott was the founder of the historical novel genre, of which the rebellion novel genre is a subgenre. Several critics have claimed that Stevenson, if not Dickens, mimicked many of the elements that Scott used. In order to examine how later rebellion novels developed, it is essential to look at Scott's work and to study its elements and origins. As Scott wrote, "Notwithstanding the name of *novel* they are in a great measure copied from each other."[1] Scott is playing on the two definitions of the word "novel," one that refers to the novel genre, and the other that means "new" or "original." Scott frequently explained whom he was mimicking in his works, and complained that he noticed that even during his lifetime numerous authors started copying the techniques he used in his "novels." A new genre can only be built through mimicry of some of the elements of prior genres, and to survive, the genre's elements need to be mimicked by future writers. If Dickens, Stevenson and other writers did not mimic Scott's historical and rebellion genres, his works would have been isolated oddities. Because their elements were "copied," we have proof of a new generic form.

The main plot in a rebellion novel is a rebellion; the characters are rebels; and the characters and narrator use linguistic tricks to inspire sympathy in the reader for the rebels. A study of the rebellion novel genre has to coincide with a study of the rebellious biographies or actions and statements of the writers who wrote these works. The author's purpose is an ingredient in the structural dimensions of a genre, and in the rebellion genre it carries more significance. But, because the purpose is infrequently given by rebellion writers directly, for fear of sedition charges, it needs to be uncovered by studying the details of the other rebellion genre ingredients.

> Seriously I am very glad I did not live in 1745 for though as a lawyer I could not have pleaded Charles's right and as a clergyman I could not have prayed for him yet as a soldier I would I am sure against the convictions of my better reason have fought for him even to the bottom of the gallows.[2]

Figure 9. "Abbotsford, the Residence of Sir Walter Scott, Scotland: Library, with portrait of Lieut. Scott, son of the poet," 1903 (Library of Congress Prints and Photographs Division).

The quote above, from an 1813 letter of Scott, when he was writing his first rebellion novel, explains why the subversive or wavering, on the surface, elements of Scott's rebellion novels were essential to the genre's acceptance by the monarchy. If, instead of writing rebellion novels, Scott tried making a legal case for Charles and his successors' rights to the throne, in opposition to the ruling monarchs, he would have been taken to the gallows, even if he did not fight with a weapon for the cause. Therefore, Scott had to make a fictional appeal, and inserted a counter-argument to the Jacobites' cause to make an apparently impartial and detached appeal for the rights of the Jacobites. The above quotation points to a definite bias towards supporting the Jacobites, to the point of wanting to pick up arms in their cause. Scott was being prescriptive rather than descriptive. Scott could have potentially gone to the gallows for *fighting*, rather than for *writing*, for the Jacobite cause. If writing about the Jacobites or about other rebellions was a punishable offense, Scott, Dickens and Stevenson would have all been hanged for it. Writing about rebellions was a legal practice in the British Isles in the 19th century. On the other hand, fighting with weapons on the side of the Jacobites was a treasonous act punishable by death. Some examples of nineteenth-century hangings for rebellious, violent treason are the executions of Edward Despard (1803), Jeremiah Brandreth for the Pentrich Rising (1817), and five men involved in the Cato Street Conspiracy (1820). In fact, the death penalty for treason in England was abolished only in 1998, and remained a potential threat until the end of the twentieth century. Thus, Scott, in theory, could have been accused of treason and could have been sentenced to death if it was proven that he participated in the Scottish Insurrection. He could not be executed for treason by writing about past rebellions.

The above quotation, where Scott openly confesses his sympathy with the Jacobites, is not frequently cited. Scott and his fellow Scottish lawyer and politician Tories did not typically practice what Daniel O'Connell, an Irish lawyer, did to incite the 1820s Irish Catholic emancipation debate and insurrection, which went partially hand in hand with an argument for Ireland's separation from England. In contrast to the common descriptions of Scott as a "waverer," in a critical study on the Irish national tale, Ferris describes O'Connell's discourse thus: "When language moves into the temporality of demand, it loses its distance and its moderation; harnessed for purposes of agitation, it casts off the protocols of rational and gentlemanly discourse. O'Connell ... was routinely charged with 'demagoguery,' shorthand for a language outside that of a liberal politics of consensus, balance, and decorum."[3] Instead of taking this imbalanced route, Scott chose to dance around his beliefs in the Jacobites and the Scottish nationalists' cause that he felt passionately about when he spoke publicly in order to avoid this injurious title of "demagogue." Of course, Scott was a novelist and not an orator. The novel is a genre that is more subtle about its political declarations than partisan pamphlets and oratorical deliveries. Therefore, a novelist like Scott could avoid accusations of "demagoguery" by making indirect criticisms of past political crimes by the government, instead of making propagandistic orations about the current political events of his own time.

The rebellion novelists who followed Scott's lead learned from his novels and actions. In fact, O'Connell made his public nationalist outcries in the decade after Scott published his fifth rebellion novel in 1818. To understand how a Scottish sheriff, a clerk of the court, and later a knight and a baron came to write the first five rebellion novels, and yet avoided prosecution for treason, we have to look at the sequence of the major events in Scott's life.

Scott had a power that few authors claim, as from 1805 onwards, he owned half the shares of his publisher, Ballantyne and Co. He published his first work with them (a translation from German) in 1799. This power allowed Scott to publish whatever he wanted, as he was the author or copyright holder and the publisher. In 1813, due to the first banking crises, Ballantyne and Scott sold most of their shares to Archibald Constable, to avoid acknowledging Scott's ownership of the company, which would have meant that he would have been "forced to resign as Clerk to the Court of Session and thus lose his regular income."[4] To restate, it was illegal for Scott to act as both the clerk to the court and to also own a major share of a publishing house in the same jurisdiction. Scott neither gave up ownership of Ballantyne, nor did he resign from his clerkship.

He kept both posts because he won the clerkship through patronage from the duke who owned the district, and Ballantyne was a childhood friend of his. Sutherland explained, "Through the influence of his," Scott's, "'kinsman' the Duke of Buccleuch and the goodwill of Henry Dundas, he was appointed Sheriff-Deputy of Selkirkshire, at a salary of £250 (later raised to £300).... The duties of the office, Lockhart adds, 'were far from heavy; the district small, peaceful, and pastoral, was in great part the property of the Duke of Buccleuch.'"[5] Scott was appointed through patronage to a position by the same duke who owned the jurisdiction. He served as a sheriff until 1806, when he was appointed as the clerk of session. This was not an easy appointment, as it happened during a time of turmoil, when Scott suspected that the government that first hired him as a sheriff in 1799 was about to fall, and so he settled for what he later described as a "mere Clerkship" as payment for his support of the Tory government.

Similarly, in *Waverley*, Sir Everard, the brother of Richard Waverley, Edward Waverley's father, "inherited" from "his sires the whole train of Tory ... predilections and prejudices, which had distinguished the house of Waverley since the Great Civil War."[6] As a result of this Tory heritage, Edward's uncle is a highly respected baronet, and can assist Edward in his ambition to succeed, while his father, a new Whig, cannot be of equal assistance.

When Scott first took the post, his job was more similar to that of a sheriff substitute, because he did the active duties for the deaf George Home, the prior clerk, until Home died.[7] One of the reasons Scott was not promoted above the post of clerk of sessions is that the Tory government did fall shortly after the appointment, and this made it nearly impossible for him to find the needed patronage to advance, as most of his "friends" were Tories. Tories were the radicals of the period, and had supported the Jacobite cause in the prior century, so writing Jacobite rebellion novels might have been a vent for Scott's frustration over the fall of the radical party's rule in Scotland.

Because Scott's job was primarily researching the legal system and mailing back his rulings on the more difficult, disputed cases, he was adept at legal research. The frustration about being stuck in a monotonous, dead-end job was a possible motivation for Scott's dissatisfaction with the monarchy and especially with the Whig government. Partially because of these frustrations, Scott used his knowledge of the legal system to create the rebellion novel genre, which bypassed the Seditious Act with subversive structural and linguistic techniques. Rebellion is a form of political crime, and a lawyer was more likely to be familiar with the details of the actions and motivations of past rebels, and with the judicial challenges that the rebels would face if they were discovered. While Scott lived in and ran a publishing house in a slightly different jurisdiction than where he presided as clerk of sessions, if somebody brought a complaint that his rebellion novels were seditious while he was in session and at the location of his job, he would have heard the complaint as the judge on the case, before it was transferred elsewhere due to a conflict of interest. There is no evidence to support that any such charges were brought against Scott in his own court, but it is important to think through this possibility to understand one of the reasons such charges did not take shape. Of course, regardless of whether he was the superior judge in charge of sedition complaints in his region, as a superior judge, the person who brought a complaint against him had to have an extremely strong case and would have been making a political attack on a representative of the Scottish legal system. To continue this line of hypothetical conjectures, if King George IV, instead of rewarding Scott, had charged him with a violation of the Seditious Act, he would have been making a political attack on Scotland, in a time when his own reign was new and vulnerable to attacks.

Eight years into his term as the clerk of sessions, the highest legal post that he would attain, he began writing rebellion novels with *Waverley*, and stopped writing rebellion novels around the time King George IV titled him "Sir Walter Scott, Bart" in 1820. Scott never lost his clerkship, despite a close call when the bankruptcy of Ballantyne revealed his identity, and he was forced to confess that he simultaneously owned a share in a publishing house and served as the clerk, which was an illegal dual income.

To further understand the relationship between Scott's legal and literary careers, one has to look at the timeline of Scott's five historically accurate rebellion novels, ordered by their publication date: *Waverley* (1814), *Black*

Figure 10. "Sir Walter Scott, Bart. in his study at Abbotsford," painted by W. Allan, R.A.; engraved by H. S. Sadd. New York: J. Neale at the Albion Office, 1846 (Library of Congress Prints and Photographs Division).

Dwarf (1816), *Tale of Old Mortality* (1816), *Rob Roy* (1817), and *Heart of Mid-Lothian* (1818). All five of these rebellion novels consistently center on Jacobite rebellions. In *The Historical Novel and Popular Politics in Nineteenth-Century England*, Nicholas Rance calls Scott's *Waverley* "the first genuine historical novel"[8]; the same sentiment is echoed in most studies of the historical novel genre. So, in 1814 Scott created the historical novel genre, but he also created the first major rebellion novel, and sailed forward with publications of four very similarly plotted and themed rebellion novels. These dates gain a still greater significance when we consider that the biggest and most violent Scottish uprising of the century occurred in 1820: the Scottish Insurrection. D'Arcy wrote: "Between 1815 and 1820 the so-called 'Peterloo Massacre,' the march of the Blanketeers, the Spa Fields riot, the Cato Street conspiracy to murder the Cabinet, the Six Acts, and in Scotland itself, the 'Radical War' requiring troops to quell a rising, all revealed how Great England came nearer to a bloody revolution than at any time since the seventeenth century Civil War."[9] While it is too much of a stretch to insist that Scott hoped to tip the scale by inspiring rebellion or Scottish separatism and independence with his fiction, it is fair to conclude that Scott was aware of this vulnerability.

When the Scottish Insurrection failed, Scott bounced directly in the other direction, publishing anti-radical short essays, under the name "The Visionary," against the insurrection in the *Weekly Journal*. Although this might suggest that Scott became anti-radical after the Scottish Insurrection, I would suggest that he simply retracted his rebellious beliefs and refrained from publishing rebellion novels. As I demonstrated in the introduction, he had at least one other Jacobite-themed story, "Aunt Margaret," which his publisher censored from publication. Declaring open support for the Scottish Insurrection would have led to his execution, as several affiliated rebels were executed. Fear of a potential execution is the reason Scott wrote against the insurrection, until this fear somewhat dissipated with the years and he felt comfortable enough to publish "Aunt Margaret" at the end of his life. As a judge and publisher, Scott had a sense for when it was no longer legally prudent to continue publishing Jacobite rebellion novels. Scott never really gave up the rebellion or the Jacobite cause, but his publisher insisted that such publications were no longer safe.

As described by John Prebble in *The King's Jaunt* (1988), Scott and King George IV first met in London in 1815, when the king was still a Prince and met Scott as the "author of Waverley."[10] During this initial chat, Scott convinced George IV that as a Stuart prince, he was a Jacobite Highland chieftain. Scott advised the new monarch, King George IV, that as a chieftain himself and in order to quash the need for rebellion among the poor in Scotland, the king should show his care for the country with a visit in 1822, and Scott encouraged the king to wear the tartan as a symbol of his support of Scottish nationhood. The dress as well as the other elements of this "extravaganza of Highland culture ... helped to re-establish [the] tartan as the national dress of Scotland," because the English king wore it.[11]

Because Scott's publishers, Constable and Ballantyne, kept lowering the prices of Scott's novels, Scott's sales records, Sutherland wrote, "inaugurated the new era of huge readership." (Due to the fact that Scott's epic, historical rebellion novels were read by an incredibly high percentage of Scots, it is very likely that they had some influence on the leaders of the 1820 Scottish Insurrection. Because a "revolution" in readership also suggests that before 1814 a significantly smaller quantity of books were available and purchased, one of Scott's rebellion novels might have been the only book a poor Scottish countryman might have owned.

The event that Scott was dreading for a decade finally happened in 1825. Scott's new publisher, Constable, went bankrupt in the middle of a great banking crisis, leaving Scott £120,000 in debt. Scott became politically active during the banking crisis, publishing a sensational, humorous political tract in the *Weekly Journal* under the name Malachi Malagrowther, and otherwise lobbying on the part of Scottish banking. Because Constable's books were examined during the bankruptcy settlement, Scott "stood fully detected as the author of Waverley" after 1827.[12] He was then called out as the author in the same year, during the meeting of the Edinburgh Theatrical Fund Association, and replied that he was then "understood to be on his trial before Lord Meadowbank as an offender; yet he was sure that every impartial jury would bring in a verdict of *Not Proven.*"[13] Scott was directly referring to being revealed as the author of the Waverley novels, when he said that the verdict would be "*Not proven.*" Indirectly, he must have been conscious that this revelation was also exposing his ownership of the publishing house and could have jeopardized his clerkship at a time when he was financially vulnerable. He was probably also sensible to the fact that having a judge acknowledging publishing rebellion novels openly might have been potentially seen as a seditious act, while publishing the same works anonymously was a bit less outrageous. No trial for treason, or of publishing rebellious novels, followed. Scott waited two years and then retired from his post as principal clerk of the Court of Session in 1830. Though he retired in the workload, he continued as an honorary absentee judge until his death. Two years after this, at age 61, in September 1832, Scott died in bed after a long illness in Abbotsford, Scotland.

The debate over Scott's authorial intent was revived over a hundred years after Scott's death, when Edwin Muir's essay proclaimed that Scotland lacked a unified national language and that, therefore, both Scott and Scotland were

Figure 11. "Abbotsford, the Residence of Sir Walter Scott," 1933 (Library of Congress Prints and Photographs Division).

incomplete.[14] In 1956, David Daiches wrote a rebuttal, "Scott's Achievement as a Novelist," where Scott was put on a pedestal as a great historical novelist.[15] Scott was simultaneously proclaimed as a waverer, or an "ambivalent" man with a "double attitude," one who supported Scottish nationalism and the Jacobites, but who, on the other hand, wanted to show his allegiance and loyalty to King George IV and the English empire. Since this publication, calling Scott a waverer has been fashionable, and critics like McLaren have pointed out biographical facts, such as that by the time *Waverley* was published, "Jacobitism was completely dead (in that there were no Royal Stuarts left alive)," as "the very last of the male Stuart line in succession" died in 1807.[16] However, the last Stuart was still alive in 1805, when, Scott says, he first conceived *Waverley*. Scott could have been inspired with the idea of writing a Jacobite rebellion novel to directly support the cause of the then-living, last Jacobite heir to the throne. The perspective and political bias of the critic plays a significant part in identifying Scott as a waverer, as opposed to a radical rebel. Further still, subversion, or "true Scottish indirectness," as Scott calls it in *Mid-Lothian*,[17] must include opposing statements, or it would not be an effective form of veiling the author's true radical intent. The "wavering" argument is, in part, convincing because the title of Scott's series includes the word "waver," and the main characters frequently appear to be wavering between camps. In fact, if we look back at Scott's biography, Scott wavered between supporting and opposing reform in his public statements. But if we return to the idea that it would have been unheard of for a superior judge to exclaim publicly that he supported rebellion against the English monarchy, his tame public statements and contradictory political arguments in the rebellion novels can be viewed with the suspicion that they deserve.

An abrupt turn in the critical perception of the rebellious nature of Sir Walter Scott's work came with Julian Meldon D'Arcy's 2005 *Subversive Scott: The Waverley Novels and Scottish Nationalism*. D'Arcy made the unique claim that Scott was *not* a "waverer" between the nationalist Jacobite and pro-union English camps but instead was a firm believer in the nationalist (as opposed to the Jacobite) cause, hiding these views subversively in the subtext of his novels to avoid censorship. D'Arcy lists hundreds of examples for how this view has been neglected or intentionally avoided by earlier critics. According to D'Arcy, Scott is subversive because his Lowland Scottish vocabulary and grammar, onomastics and topography are only comprehensible to a Scottish reader, who understands Scott's biting critiques of the empire; "his narrative denouements and endings can deflate more superficial interpretations of his plots"; "his imagery and metaphor can frequently subvert more politically correct readings"[18]; and Scott frequently uses unreliable, or "'deliberately misleading' narrators, who stand in the way of our acceptance of the joyful union between Empire and Scotland," which is the common theme of nationalist tales, "that is presented by the biased narrators."[19] Carlyle wrote, "No Scotchman of his time was more entirely Scotch than Walter Scott."[20] D'Arcy further explains that not all Scots knew the dialect Scott's characters spoke even in 1814 (Highland versus Lowland dialects), and still fewer Scots spoke Scott's Scottish a decade after the book was first published, so Scott was even subversive towards some Scots, speaking primarily to his own clan or to those who shared his dialect.

What motivated Sir Walter Scott to write about the Jacobite rebellions? It seems that Scottish clan and family loyalty motivated Scott's actions. In his memoirs, Scott talks about his great-grandfather Beardie, an "ancient chieftain, whose name I have made to ring in many a ditty," who wore a "beard ... in token of his regret for the banished dynasty of Stewart. It would have been well that his zeal had stopped there. But he took arms, and intrigued in their cause, until he lost all he had in the world, and, as I have heard, run a narrow risk of being hanged." Later in life, Beardie joined "a Tory or Jacobite club in Edinburgh."[21] Jacobite and Tory sentiments are Scott's inheritance and inevitably saturate his work. You might have noticed that Scott expresses apprehension about Beardie's "zeal," but the reality that Scott wrote five novels about such rebellious ditties overrides any potentially genial meaning in these clearly satiric statements. Carlyle called Beardie "the old fighting Borderer of prior centuries," and expressed a yearning for what Scott could have become if he had followed Beardie's rebellious path.[22] Yes, Scott knew that Beardie's open rebellion did not pay, and this is why Scott instead subversively expressed his support for radicalism, Scottish nationalism and the Jacobites' cause. While Beardie suffered, Scott won praise for his sympathetic rebellion fiction. Scott watched the Scottish people taking arms in the Scottish Insurrection, partially inspired by Scott's nationalist call, an event on a scale that did not result from any direct actions that Beardie took. A writer contributes by inspiring others to action, instead of risking his neck by picking up a weapon (as Beardie or Fergus did) in any radical cause.

Scott's family allegiance was with the impoverished but also with wealthy Highlanders and Lowlanders whom he portrays in his rebellion novels. Similarly to Rob Roy, a member of Scott's family was among the "first ... in the cattle trade," but unlike Rob, he was financially successful at his legal cattle enterprise.[23] Due to the herding members of his family, Scott sympathized not only with Jacobites, but also with Highlanders, including Rob Roy. During the writing of *Rob Roy*, Scott had Rob Roy's gun and "ammunition pouch" hanging "over his writing desk."[24] Figure 9 and 14 include characters in kilts and other traditional Scottish garments through which Scott and his publisher created an epic mythology around the historical figure of Rob Roy and the Highlanders.

Scott might have also opposed the colonial triumphs of the English empire because one of his brothers, Robert, joined the East India Company, and died after only two voyages due to the "climate."[25] Scott knew that colonialism could be deadly. Scott's family suffered from harsh English laws and work conditions. Scott inherited money and an estate from his family, so following his family's radical leanings was a financial, as well as a familial, obligation.

Scott's family, friends and instructors influenced his liberal and nationalist views. Scott's friends were also his close allies; for example, Ballantyne began

Figure 12. "The armory [at Walter Scott's Abbotsford]," drawn by Frank Vincent DuMond, 1888 (Library of Congress Prints and Photographs Division Washington).

as Scott's childhood friend and then served as his publisher for many decades. The fact that his early friends and relations were from radical or revolutionary families points to a clear pro-rebellion bias in Scott. Scott was born on August 15, 1771. He was over twenty by the time of the French Revolution and was surrounded by pro-revolutionaries. Scott's wife was French. Sutherland wrote: "Mr. and Mrs. Scott maintained excellent relations with French officers, prisoners of war, held around Edinburgh during the hostilities," at the end of the Napoleonic War in 1814, the year when *Waverley* was published.[26] Mrs. Scott's French upbringing is significant because of the relationship the two countries had during the period when Scott started writing rebellion novels. Because of the lengthy and violent Napoleonic wars, and because France sided with America in the American Revolution, English monarchs and the upper class sponsored and gave social support to fictional characters that made French rebels and revolutionaries appear as heroic "guerrillas" fighting against unjust invaders.

One example of the support the English monarchy gave to English writers

7. *Scott's Scottish Nationalism* 75

Figure 13. "Sir Walter Scott and his literary friends at Abbotsford: Scott, Mackenzie, Wilson, Crabbe, Lockhart, Wordsworth, Jeffrey, Ferguson, Moore, Allen, Campbell, Wilkie, and Constable seated at table," painted by Thos. Faed; engd. by J. Sartain [1830–1890] (Library of Congress Prints and Photographs Division).

depicting the French Revolution and France in general in a negative light is William Wordsworth's 1793 publication of *Salisbury Plain*, a long poem which was later published as *Guilt and Sorrow: Or Incidents upon Salisbury Plain* in 1848, and his later publication *The Prelude* and the related *Recluse*. Coleridge encouraged Wordsworth to pen the epic *Recluse*, writing, "I wish you would write a poem in blank verse, addressed to those who, in consequence of the complete failure of the French Revolution, have thrown up all hopes of the amelioration of mankind, and are sinking into an almost epicurean selfishness, disguising the same under the soft titles of domestic attachment and contempt for visionary philosophes."[27] In the initial version of *Salisbury Plain*, a female vagrant loses her family to the Napoleonic wars. The revolution is justifiable from the perspective of the poor in Wordsworth's poetry.

This split in sentiment away from the previous view that all rebellion against monarchies had to be suppressed led to the "discourse of primitive liberty" and the championing of the "pre-modern."[28] Thus, by the time Scott wrote *Waverley* and *Rob Roy*, describing a rebellion's leaders in glowing and heroic terms was legally and politically acceptable. The rebellion novel started with Scott because before the Napoleonic War and the French Revolution, England did not have a political reason to support rebellions or revolutions anywhere; but, after the revolution, rebellion started to look like a successful strategy for ridding the empire of competitors. This is one of the reasons Scott

occasionally makes open radical statements in his novels, direct statements of support for the Jacobites in the English language, as opposed to in Scots or Gaelic. Some of the rebellious or radical statements are hidden with subversive techniques, while others are flaunted. This apparent wavering is present because of the two contradictory realities:
1. English monarchs supported depictions of rebellions against France and other foreign foes
2. English monarchs still wanted to keep their throne, and did not want to see a revolution in England.

These two opposing objectives led to the split between open and subversive criticism of England and the English monarchy in Scott's rebellion novels.

Critics before D'Arcy have called Scott a waverer because he frequently calls himself indecisive and wavering. This indecision was a self-defense mechanism of a strategic politician who is running in two directions, one towards his poor reading public, and the other towards his wealthy patrons, regardless of his deep-seated rebellious beliefs. When stating a party allegiance, Scott is careful to note that "there was no real conviction on my part" towards any one party.[29] In what appears at first to be a jovial wavering, Scott further writes across different sections of the memoirs that he is politically independent, even after stating a firm political identification as a Tory. In Chapter XIV of Scott's memoirs, Lockhart quotes him as writing in a letter in 1805 that he felt split, "half-lawyer ... half-crazy ... half every thing."[30] Clearly, Scott was once again using satire to express subversively, instead of openly, an unpopular or rather an anti-empiric pro-rebellion view.

As a superior court judge or as the clerk of sessions, Scott was a politician (in other words, his potential promotion up the ranks depended on who was in power), which influenced his first rebellion novel, *Waverley*. It was brewed during a Whig administration, when he felt an urge to support his deteriorated more radical Tory Party. He actually published all of his rebellion novels during a period of resurgence of the Tory Party, when rebellious feelings were more acceptable and he felt more secure in his clerkship job. In the period when Scott's rebellion novels were published, there was a Tory prime minister in England, Robert Banks Jenkinson, second Earl of Liverpool, who served between June 8, 1812, and April 9, 1827. The Tory Party was initially founded in 1678 as an opposition party to the Whigs, and in support of the Jacobites. It is clear that having a Jacobite prime minister in office allowed Scott the freedom to publish novels about Jacobite uprisings. The fact that the king was convinced of his Scottish heritage also made the climate ripe for such publications. The Tory Party died in the 1760s, when the last Jacobite uprisings failed, and reemerged as a new kind of party in 1783 and remained basically stable in this form through Scott's lifetime, before eventually translating itself into the Conservative Party that Benjamin Disraeli subscribed to, and which is still a strong party in England today. Oddly, a Tory, Viscount Bolingbroke, was the chief minister in 1714, just before the first major Jacobite rising, but he did not proclaim the son of James II, the "pretender," as the new king when Queen Anne died, allowing Elector George to succeed to the throne "peacefully," at least until the uprisings started a year later. Viscount Bolingbroke acted oddly because he assumed that King George would accept his assistance and would keep him on as the chief minister, but instead King George fired him and hired an entirely Whig staff. Fearing further retribution, Bolingbroke fled to France, where he found the "pretender" and assisted in the 1715 Jacobite rising. The term "Tory" went through numerous changes across different administrations, and encompassed both supporters of an autocratic monarchy and prolower class reforms, the latter exemplified by Disraeli, who initially ran on a radical ticket but failed to win until he adopted a Tory or a Conservative tag. Dickens and Stevenson also subscribed to similar radical or oppositional political parties.

The motive for writing about rebellion was the political climate in England and Scotland in the years surrounding 1814. For some, the problem, but for others, the solution, began in 1707, when Scotland and England united. This union was a major historic shift because, since the Roman invasion of England, Scotland's history was characterized by its resistance to foreign domination. The Romans never conquered the area, and when the Scots extended their kingdom to its present boundary in 1018, a long era of conflict began with England. After many wars, the Scots finally accepted union with the "auld enemy": first with the Union of Crowns, and then with the Union of Parliament in 1707.[31]

The union was shaken by repeated Jacobite and other uprisings until 1778, when the Highland Society of London was born to improve Scotland's agricultural and economic competitiveness and to preserve the Scottish heritage, including dress, language, and literature. This move was a response to the continued cultural resistance in Scotland to English cultural and economic domination. Scots had a desire to promote their heritage and to their roots survive, in parallel with the anthropological school of thought that developed at this time, which promoted preserving "ancient" or dying-out cultures, languages and traditions. In part, Sir Walter Scott's purpose in writing the Waverley novels (most of which take place in Scotland) was to showcase the Scottish dialects and history to the English empire and to the world. This desire to preserve the Scottish nation's culture, despite the union, was similar to the motives of writers of Irish national tales. Scott made "raids" to Liddesdale, "for the purpose of collecting the ballad poetry of that romantic district. He not only visited many of the scenes alluded to in the metrical narratives, but

Figure 14. "The Highland visitors," Van Guzzel delin.; Van Duivel Kind, engraver. "An open space in a country town where 'The Post House' is at the sign of 'The Old Crown, kept by George King with ye best of Usage.' Highlanders are plundering and abusing the inhabitants in all directions. A distant road is filled with the approaching rebel army." London: Publish'd according to Act of Parliament by I. Dubois, 1745 (Library of Congress Prints and Photographs Division Washington).

gathered all the local anecdotes and legends preserved by tradition among the peasantry."[32] As the above quotation shows, Scott was a close student of the Scottish heritage. He was helped in his research, not only by the Highlanders that he met on his travels, but also by Scottish highsociety, such as Captain James Denniston, who at one point "accumulated a large amount of information relative to the history, antiquities, manners and customs of the former inhabitants of the district," and donated it to Scott, "to be used" in "various publications." Later on, Mr. Train gave Scott a "*spleuchan*, at one time the property of Rob Roy, which he had obtained indirectly from a descendant of 'the bold outlaw.'"[33] Thus, through the accumulation of scraps of information, Scott gathered enough research to create the type of historical novel that was based on the "truth,"— facts, as opposed to the mostly "imaginary" histories that were written by earlier novelists.

A few examples of how Scott utilizes "truth," or accurate history, in *Waverley* and *Rob Roy* should help to explain this point. *Rob Roy* and *Waverley* appear to have two of the longest combined introductory and closing remarks and notes of most nineteenth-century English novels. In the Signet Classics edition of *Rob Roy*, pages 400 through 490 are the: "Author's Introduction,"

"Appendix to Introduction" (with evidentiary documents from the historic period), "Postscript," and then a relatively brief "Glossary" of Scottish terms (471–483) and an even briefer "Afterword" by the editor of the volume, A. N. Wilson (485–490). Thus, a fifth of *Rob Roy* is introductory and closing notes. In the Penguin edition of *Waverley*, the text is surrounded with supplementary materials. The book begins with an "Advertisement," continues with the "General Preface," then three "Appendixes to the Preface" (works previously published by Scott), an "Introduction to Waverley," a "Preface to the Third Edition of Waverley," and finally "Chapter 1: Introductory," in total 56 pages. The book bravely concludes with "Chapter LXXII: A Postscript, which should have been a Preface," and "Notes to Waverley," another 20 pages; all totaling once again a fifth of the book in explanatory notes. Most of these notes were written by Scott and contain various types of proof in the validity or the truth of the historical accounts portrayed in Scott's rebellion novels. The best example from the above of Scott working to show that the events in these rebellion novels are true is in the "Notes to Waverley," where Scott explains the textual origins behind his story. Scott explains that one of his allusions, Nicholas Amhurst, was a real political writer, and cites, "*Lord Chesterfield's Characters Reviewed*, p. 42." Other sources for historical facts directly cited by Scott in these notes are: *Hibbert's Philosophy of Apparitions, Travels, Some Remarkable Passages in the Life of Colonel James Gardiner*, and *Account of Somerset's Expedition*.

Scott needed to prove the "truth" behind the rebellions for them to be indisputable historical and legal facts. If Scott was depicting history, it could not be treasonous libel against the English monarchy. England had laws against libel and against published threats against the monarchy, but it did not have laws against truthful historical accounts of previously committed treason, rebellion, revolution or any criminal misdeeds. As a lawyer, Scott knew the distinction between libel, treason and nationalistic historical portrayals. Scott took the fine print of the law to his political advantage. Scott did not want to turn out like Beardie, nearly hanged for expressing nationalist sentiments, but he did want to express his nationalist pride, and this is the balance that he achieved in his rebellion novels. Perhaps, without intending the latter, Scott also created the historical novel genre, a field that works to describe only the "truth" about historical events, an odd challenge when we consider that truth is in direct contradiction to fiction, which by its nature is supposed to be fabricated. Either way, it was clearly Scott's intent to portray epic and heroic rebellions of oppressed Scottish people against an oppressive and corrupt English Empire in his rebellion novels.

8

Scott's Structural Features

Genre Categorization, Mixture and Influences

Scott easily created a formula for the unique, upon its creation, rebellion novel because as a literary critic Scott studied and dissected the rules of genre formulation. Scott wrote several essays that dissected the structure and form of novels. One frequently cited essay is titled, "Essay on Romance." It originally appeared in the *Encyclopædia Britannica* in 1824, six years after the publication of *Rob Roy*. Scott makes a "generic/typological" distinction between romance and the novel which has contributed to our modern-day definitions of these terms. Thus, today literary critics call *Don Quixote*[1] the first modern novel, as opposed to a romance, because it describes many grotesque details, the reality of the existence of an aging and sickly man, as opposed to the beautiful damsels in distress and heroic knights that dominated "romantic" fiction ever since the chivalry tales of the Middle Ages, including works like *Amadis of Gaul*.[2] Scott explained that romance disregards "the dictates of plausibility" by using "marvelous and uncommon incidents," while the novel follows the "ordinary train of human events."[3] In this quotation Scott shows his expertise as a literary critic and as an author who is vividly conscious of his craft.

Scott utilized generic mixtures when he concocted the rebellion genre. Scott's rebellion novels are an example of "pathbreaking generic prototypes," as opposed to the work of a "herd of imitators" because Scott was first in the fields of the rebellion and the historical novels and established the generic norms that later novelists imitated. Trumpener writes that new genres are formed when "new social, historical or national" characteristics arise and "literary" representations no longer match "lived reality." The need to reclaim and promote Scottish national identity and rights prompted Scott to begin the rebellion genre. Trumpener distinguishes between "original, pathbreaking generic prototypes and increasingly convention-bound copies."[4] In a way, it was only Scott's *Waverley* that was truly a prototype for the rebellion and historical genres. The four rebellion novels that Scott wrote after *Waverley* technically are reproductions of the same generic formula. Trumpener's elements of genre are: narrative voice, perspective, tone, characterization, sociopolitical narrative, a "range of social and literary concerns" addressed, "conscious recycling of a preexisting range of plot patterns and moves," borrowings of "tropes, themes, characters from earlier works," and other forms of announcing the genre one has chosen.[5] When several elements of genre are unique among a group of novels, they can be placed into a separate genre, such as the rebellion novel.

Deriving a new generic formula is work only a literary giant can achieve with great success. In fact, we can think of Scott as the man who established genre fiction in general, when *Waverley* outsold all previous book sales records. Carlyle writes gloatingly about the "literary statistics" that show that Sir Walter Scott outsold all other authors of his time, and that he caused "universal reading" among "Princes" and "Peasants" alike. Carlyle even sees something "distracted" or delirious about, "Walter Scott writing daily with the ardor of a steam-engine, that he might make 15,000£ a-year, and buy upholstery with it." Still, Carlyle realizes that at the end Scott's books "were faster written and better paid for than any other books in the world." Carlyle objects that the speedy or the "extempore method" that Scott was forced to employ detracted from the quality of the works, in comparison to Shakespeare and other great classical writers. Still, in jest or in earnest, Carlyle does conclude that there is "indispensablest beauty in knowing how to get done" and leaving literature "right enough."[6] If novel-writing was not profitable before *Waverley*, there was no motivation to mimic the plot formula that previous writers used. When Scott saw the sales figures for *Waverley*, he knew that he had to write novels using a similar formula if he wanted to match the first work's success. Scott was the first in a "herd of imitators" who mimicked generic elements of *Waverley*. In an essay on Lord Byron in the *Quarterly Review* in 1818, Scott wrote in part about himself, or perhaps *against* himself,

> Originality, as it is the highest and rarest property of genius, is also that which has most charms for the public.... The vulgar author is usually distinguished by his treading or attempting to tread, in the steps of the reigning favourite of the day. He is didactic, sentimental, romantic, epic, pastoral, according to the tastes of the moment.... The consequence is, not that the herd of imitators gain their object, but that the melody which they have profaned becomes degraded in the sated ears of the public — its original richness, wildness, and novelty are forgotten when it is made manifest how easily the leading notes can be caught and parodied, and whatever its intrinsic merit may have been, it becomes, for the time, stale and ful-

some.... The true poet attempts the very reverse of the imitator. He plunges into the stream of public opinion even when its tide is running strongest.[7]

Scott was aware that great generic innovation comes from mixing other previously established genres, such as the "didactic, sentimental, romantic, epic, pastoral" that Scott discusses in the quote above. In his memoirs, Scott also closely dissects the use of "adoptions" or "plagiarism" by classic authors. He writes that Macpherson "very cunningly adopted the beginning, the names, and the leading incidents, etc. of an old tale, and dressed it up with all those ornaments of sentiment and sentimental manners, which first excite our surprise, and afterwards our doubt of its authenticity." In addition to considering the repercussions of mimicking Homer and Ossian poetry, Scott was also questioning the wisdom of mimicking true historical tales by sticking as closely as possible to the truth. This would later become known as Scott's unique form of historical fiction. Scott writes:

> Suppose I was to write a fictitious book of travels, I should certainly do ill to copy exactly the incidents which befell Mungo Park or Bruce of Kinnaird. What was true of them would incontestably prove at once the falsehood and plagiarism of my supposed journal. It is not but what the incidents are natural — but it is their having already happened which strikes us when they are transferred to imaginary persons. Could any one bear the story of a second city being taken by a wooden horse?[8]

Scott was aware that copying history had in the past been viewed as plagiarism. Because using primary sources meant plagiarizing past historians, writers before Scott did not create the historical novel genre. Scott walked a fine line between history and fiction, between originality and plagiarism, solving this duality by leaning more on fiction and heavily editing the "true" story of rebellious historical events.

Regardless of Scott's desire to avoid mimicry, the rebellion genre would not have materialized without several inspirational sources, the remnants and influences on this genre from other genres. Rebellion novels have so far been misplaced into a myriad of other genres. After the historical novel, the genre that rebellion novels are most frequently classified under is tragedy. This is a reasonable conclusion, as most rebellion novels end with the execution of the leading heroic rebels. The leading study in this pack is *Revolution as Tragedy: The Dilemma of the Moderate from Scott to Arnold* (1980) by John Farrell.[9] The title is very telling as it calls Scott a moderate because he portrayed revolution in a tragic light. In contrast, I believe that portraying a rebellion or a revolution in a tragic light implies a desire to elicit sympathy for the executed rebels. For example, when in a realistic novel, a poor, starving girl dies of disease and hunger, readers sympathize with the poor and want to help their cause. Similarly, depicting a revolution as a tragedy is not the work of a moderate, but of a staunch radical who wants to encourage revolution against an empire. Some of the tragic revolutionary works on Farrell's list are also examples of the rebellion novel genre. Farrell looks at two rebellion novels by Scott that I consider: *Old Mortality* and *The Heart of Mid-Lothian*. Farrell ignores three other rebellion novels by Scott: *Rob Roy*, *Waverley* and *Black Dwarf*. This selection is too random, as all five novels end tragically for some of the rebellious characters, and all center on a rebellious or revolutionary theme. Most of the other works Farrell covers did not make my study because they were in mediums other than the novel. For example, Farrell spends a lot time on Lord Byron's plays and poems.

Some of the most obvious generic inspirations and origins for the rebellion novel are Irish and Scottish national tales. The publication of Joanna Baillie's *Family Legend* about the Highland clans, Jane Porter's *Scottish Chiefs*, Peter Middleton Darling's *Romance of the Highlands* and Honoria Scott's *Vale of Clyde*, all in 1810, four years before the publication of *Waverley*, also meant a newfound interest in Scottish tales that Scott might have wanted to exploit for commercial reasons. Scott's close relations with these national tale writers can be proven with details like the fact that the play *Family Legend* was dedicated to "Walter Scott, Esq." for his "encouragement." Scott also wrote a rhyming prologue to Baillie's *Family Legend*, honoring the nationalistic treatment of a 15th-century Highland legend and tradition. The work is about a clan conflict over a murderous disagreement between a father, a daughter and a husband, between the Maclean and the Campbell clans, both of which tribes also appear in *Rob Roy*.[10] Not surprisingly, the *Romance of the Highlands* also opens with a Campbell, Malcolm, who is seized in his own home by three "ferocious ... ruffians," and taken to a wood to be given a child, Kenneth, whom he would later raise as his own.[11] In a somewhat parallel scene in *Rob Roy*, a different Campbell is on the other side of the scene, as the ruffian outlaw that guides Frank through the Highland wilderness. (As a side note, in Stevenson's *Kidnapped*, yet another Campbell is assassinated in a wood.) It so happens that Scott traced his heritage to the Campbells. There are also parallels, similarities and connections between Scott and the *Vale of Clyde*, which "included dialogue in Scots and a heroine called Flora, who visits the Highlands."[12] Clearly, when in *Waverley* and *Rob Roy* Scott uses the name "Flora" as a leading heroine, he echoes some of the revivalist and romantic ideas that these early national tales utilized.

Waverley and *Rob Roy* were initially designed to join, despite several divergent characteristics, the "national tale" genre, which flourished in the first two decades of the nineteenth century,[13] primarily in Ireland. Robert Colby and Peter Garside have cited one national tale, *The Wild Irish Girl; A National Tale*, as the origins of *Waverley's* Flora Mac-Ivor's "gardening and harping in the Highlands."¹⁴ The national tales frequently focused on rebellions and revolutions because these accounts typically supported nationhood and separation of the periphery, usually Ireland or Scotland, which they covered. More frequently, national tales argued for unification by describing unrest and other negative elements of personal, clan and political rebellions. National tales don't fall under the rebellion novel umbrella because of predominance in them of personal or clan rebellions by individuals, unlike the rebellions against the empire or the English establishment that Scott used in his rebellion novels. Of course, some national tales are in the very gray area between personal and national rebellions; for example, *The Milesian Chief* (1812) describes the failure of a national revolution put down by the brute force of the English. Scott inherited the national tales' mixture of both peaceful celebration of the history and nationhood of peripheries, like Scotland and Ireland, and a celebration of a more violent, "fierce patriotism,"¹⁵ which is a patriotism utilized by peripheries that claimed individual nationhood.

The flood of nationalistic tales began as early as 1783, with the publication of Sophia Lee's *The Recess: or A Tale of Other Times*. By 1806, a national novel was published at least once per year, with the exception only of five years, 1826 through 1831. After 1832, other genres started to dominate the Scottish and Irish peripheries, as well as the rest of Europe. A few national tales with rebellion themes include: Jane West's 1812 *The Loyalists: An Historical Novel* (shows the outcome of a civil war, and expresses hope for the restoration of a king who unjustly lost his throne), and Sydney Owenson's 1809 *Patriotic Sketches of Ireland* (which includes a quote from Burke's *Reflections on the Revolution in France* on the concluding pages of the second volume). One of the earliest national novels by Charlotte Smith, *Desmond* (1792), even debates the "Social questions raised by the Revolution itself," as "Lionel Desmond is enlisted to accompany a flighty youth on a pleasure trip into revolutionary France," where the narrator develops "Jacobite sympathies," while he "wavers" between the pro- and anti-revolutionary sides of the debate.¹⁶

The nationalist tale inspired Scott to write about a previously censured topic of rebellion against the empire, and to express pro-periphery or pro–Scottish nationalism. Law is based on precedents. If something was legal in the past, it is likely to be legal if repeated. Scott needed a precedent to make an aggressive move against the empire in writing five rebellion novels, and he found this legal support in national tales with rebellion themes. If England could not censor or imprison the writers of national tales, Scott assumed that he was also going to be spared. However, Scott made several changes which meant that his rebellion novels had far more impact than national tales. Scott made the claim that his tales were "true" and based on history. National tales also utilized occasional historical backgrounds, but they did not provide the full panorama and historically accurate details that Scott brought to his historical novels. Scott sold an enormous quantity of books, a number that broke all past sales records, and certainly beat, in popularity, all national tales. Scott also wrote five novels with the same rebellion theme, instead of single national works as had earlier nationalist novelists.

One of the key differences between the nationalist tale and Scott's historic rebellion novels is his use of "scandal." In Ireland, "scandal fiction" bloomed between 1806 and 1810, with works such as *A Winter in London; or Sketches of Fashion* (1806) by T. S. Surr, which, Garside writes, Scott read closely, shortly before writing *Waverley*. *Winter*'s Chapter 1 begins with the narration of Sir Alfred Beauchamp being "attacked by banditti," or rather "five ... assassins," who aimed at "murder, and not plunder" of Sir Alfred, in an Italian wood, far from his London home.[17] The scandal lies in the fact that the hero's own brother planned the attack, and "rioted in his bloody spoils with the harlot that had excited him to murder."[18] These scandalous works were more fun to read than the happy-ending, pro-union nationalist tales. While the national tale and other influences are far more prevalent in Scott's works, it is apparent that Scott also used some elements from scandal fiction. The repeated use of terms such as "assassin" and "riot" in *Winter* gives the events a political shade, as opposed to a family tragedy. A technique that Scott borrowed from scandal fiction is to contrast dramatic violence with the "tranquility of the scene" of, say, Switzerland's mountains,[19] which is similar to the use of Highland mountains as soothing elements between violent rebellious action scenes in Scott's *Waverley* and *Rob Roy*. The scandal novel was probably in the back of Scott's mind when he wrote his scandalous spectacle of rebellious violence, with its rapid plot movement, brisk character interactions, adventure, and rebellious military action.

Scott frequently mixed in mimicries of national tales, scandal, epics, tragedies, romances, realistic stories, satires, and histories into his rebellion novels, among them *Rob Roy* and *Waverley*.

Scott's Rebellion Novel Formula

As a pioneer in mass-production fiction, Scott wrote highly formulaic novels, and therefore it is fairly easy to detect a formula he used in his rebellion novels. What were the components of Scott's rebellion genre formula? How does this formula differ from prior formulas for the structure of Scott's novels, which were deduced by other researchers? The term "formulaic" fiction means literature written according to a logical or mathematical formula. It is designed with two purposes in Scott's rebellion novels: S = Creating an exciting story that sells copies of the book, and **P** = Creating a convincing work of political nationalist propaganda. What are the repeating ingredients in all five of Sir Walter Scott's rebellion novels that lead to these two outcomes, or S + P? These repeating elements are:

> **J** = Violent Jacobite uprisings and revolts
> **T** = Travel between periphery and core, or Scotland and England
> **L** = Love partially motivates the rebellious actions of the protagonist
> **S** = Protagonist or narrator of the novel always escapes retribution or succeeds in his primary goals

Thus, the formula for Scott's rebellion novels is:

> **S** (Sales) + **P** (Scottish Nationalist Propaganda) = **J** (Violent Jacobite Uprising) + **T** (Travel) + **L** (Love) + **S** (Success of Protagonist)

The table (Figure 15) gives examples of these four ingredients of Scott's structural rebellion novel formula from Scott's five rebellion novels.

This formula has several structural elements that differ from the formulas of other rebellion novels and the national tale. Some of the features of the rebellion novels that Scott, Dickens and Stevenson wrote are unique to each of the writers, while other features are shared by all who wrote in this genre. Scott in part adopted, and in part altered the national tale formula. Scott followed the guidelines set in national tales in his rebellion novels. The central

	Waverley	*Black Dwarf*	*Old Mortality*	*Rob Roy*	*Mid-Lothian*
J (Rebellion)	1745 Rising Jacobite Battle of Prestonpans	Jacobites kidnapping of Isabel Vere	Assassination of Archbishop James Sharp; Battles of Bothwell & Drumclog	1715 Rising Jacobite battles	Porteous is killed by a lynch mob
T (Travel)	Scotland & England	Scotland & England	Scotland & England	Scotland & England	Scotland & England
L (Love Interests)	Rose & Flora	Isabel Vere	Edith Bellenden	Diana Vernon	Jeanie Deans & sister
S (Success)	Edward Waverley escapes retribution & marries	Earnscliff marries Isabel	Henry Morton escapes retribution for rebellious actions	Frank Osbaldistone inherits property & marries Diana Vernon	Jeanie Deans gains her sister's pardon

Figure 15. Scott's Rebellion Novel Formula

plot device that was borrowed from the national tale was "specialization of political choices, presented as a journey of discovery through the English peripheries."[20] After the genre-setting publication of *The Wild Irish Girl: A National Tale* in 1806 by Sydney Owenson, the national tale frequently relied on:

> stylized repetitions of this basic plot, with its allegorical presentation of the contrast, attraction, and union between disparate cultural worlds. In each subsequent version, an English character will again travel to the English periphery, which he or she expects will be devoid of any culture at all. Instead, under the tutelage of an aristocratic native friend, he or she will come to appreciate its cultural plenitude and self-sufficiency to such a degree that he or she will decide to settle there permanently. Each book ends with the traveler's marriage to his or her native guide, in a wedding, which allegorically unites English and Celtic "national characters."[21]

Here is a summary of the national tale formula above:

> National Tale Formula = Travel to Periphery + Cultural Appreciation of Periphery + Marriage and Settlement in Periphery

Trumpener's summary of the national tale ignores the violent uprisings that national tales sometimes include in their centers. Thus, while the national tales' protagonists typically end up settling in the periphery, sometimes there is turmoil and violence before this "happy" union between the core and periphery can take place. Logically, the national tale and rebellion novel still fall into separate categories, as a few national tales did not include tales of violent rebellions, but all of Scott's rebellion novels were about Jacobite uprisings. The table (Figure 16) gives a brief summary of how the rebellion plot elements of both *Rob Roy* and *Waverley* can also be simplified to match the basic ingredients in national tales.

Since travel to the periphery is an important plot element in these rebellion novels, the setting of the plot is essential. It is not a coincidence that all

Plot Element	*Rob Roy*	*Waverley*
Travel to Periphery	Frank travels to Scotland's Lowlands & Highlands	Waverley travels to Scotland's Lowlands & Highlands
Assistance by a "native friend"	Frank is assisted by Baillie Jarvie & Rob Roy	Waverley assisted by Fergus Mac-Ivor
Settlement & marriage in the periphery	Frank marries the Lowland, Jacobite Di Vernon	Waverley marries the Lowland Rose

Figure 16. Scott's Plot Elements

of Scott's rebellion novels take place in Scotland, about whose national future he was most concerned, politically as well as financially. Scott frequently mentions the environs of his childhood Scottish homes in his memoirs, writing about Kelso, "the most romantic village in Scotland," describing its rivers, songs, ancient abbey, Roxburgh Castle and other wondrous sights and monuments. Scott then writes that later in life his "principal object in these excursions was the pleasure of seeing romantic scenery, or what afforded me at least equal pleasure, the places which had been distinguished by remarkable historical events."[22] These and many other passages betray Scott's passionate nationalism for Scotland.

Besides the central rebellion theme, there are several crucial points of divergence between the national tale and the rebellion novel. In Scott's rebellion novels, the travel and potential marriage in the periphery merely assist the primary rebellion plotline. In addition, some of Scott's main characters are Scottish and they appreciate Scottish culture at the beginning of the novel, instead of at first seeing it as simplistic and backwards and then slowly coming to appreciate it, as frequently happens in national tales. In addition, two out of five of Scott's rebellion novels do not end with a happy marriage between a Scottish woman and a border dweller or an English man. For example, *Mid-Lothian* ends with a woman rescuing her sister from execution, without a major character becoming engaged or marrying. While national tales and Scott's rebellion novels share the purpose of promoting Scottish or Irish national identities, Scott presents a violent, contentious union between Scotland and England, which is ripped by constant rebellions. Meanwhile, national tales typically focus on the hope for acceptance and peace within the union. The death toll is much higher in Scott's novels. The main characters are typically in the midst of violent rebellions, and only marry accidentally or in an afterthought, at the end, being busy through most of the plot with escaping retribution for their rebellious actions. Lastly, Scott created the historical novel genre simultaneously with his creation of the rebellion novel genre, so the historical details of past rebellions charge these stories with the radical sting of "truth." Reading about wrongs perpetrated by England against Scotland in a "real" past conflict made a stronger political or propagandistic impact on the readers than reading about purely fanciful or fictional ladies in distress or gentlemen searching for adventure in the Irish periphery.

The rebellion genre formula between the three main authors is highly repetitive. For proof of the degree of the formulaic nature of Scott's rebellion novels, one need only look at D'Arcy's interesting comparison of the surprisingly similar fates of Henry Morton in *The Tale of Old Mortality* and Edward Waverley in *Waverley* in a table in the "Mortality" chapter of D'Arcy's book. D'Arcy writes almost identical sentences into both columns. Figure 17 shows

Edward Waverley (D'Arcy, pages 117–8)	Frank Osbaldistone (Rob Roy)
Visit to pre-rebellion place	Visit to pre-rebellion place
Involvement in love triangles: Flora & Rose, then Rose & Mac-Ivor	Involvement in a love triangle: Diana Vernon & Rashleigh
Plans to leave Scotland and clear name from treachery allegations	Travels to Highlands to clear his & father's name from financial crimes allegations & ruin
Not present when rebellion begins, but hunting with lead conspirator (Mac-Ivor), which leads to his arrest	Present when Helen MacGregor has Morris thrown off a cliff for raping her & arresting her husband; Frank protests against it
Interviewed by Cpt. Melville & Rev. Morton on capital offense charges; saved by intervention of one of the "love triangle" (Rose)	Accused of a robbery & prosecuted by the local magistrate; saved by intervention of one of the "love triangle" (Di)
In battle, sees officer cut down & slain (Gardener)	In battle, sees many officers cut down and slain
Bravely saves fellow countryman, fighting for government, from death (Colonel Talbot)	Bravely saves his family from financial ruin & bails out his father's clerk, Owen
Prince needs him in the top echelons to help influence English Jacobites	Prince needs him in the top echelons to help influence English Jacobites
Later military exploit (Clifton) ends in defeat & flight	Later military exploit ends in defeat & flight of the Jacobites
Life saved by powerful friend (Talbot); can't prevent torture & death of friend & ally (Fergus)	Life saved by a powerful friend (Rob Roy); can't prevent torture & death of friends & enemies (Sir Hildebrand, his sons, and other Jacobites)
Lives under assumed names, awaiting pardon	Hides identity, traveling through Highlands & Glasgow to clear father's financial crisis
Lands of beloved (Tully-Veolan) lost to unscrupulous relative (Inchgrabbit)	Lands of beloved (Di Vernon) lost to unscrupulous relative (Frank)
Edward & Rose marry	Frank & Di marry

Figure 17. Scott's Rebellion Plots: *Waverley* vs. *Rob Roy*

the degree of the plot-element repetitions across various rebellion novels. It shows D'Arcy's summary for *Waverley* and my own miniature plot summary for *Rob Roy*.

Most of the rows can be repeated with almost identical summaries. Many of the repeating elements in these plots stem from the basic J + T + L + S formula of the sequence and direction the events in Scott's rebellion novels always take. For example, the protagonist typically begins by journeying to a non-native for him or her territory — usually from England to Scotland, but occasionally, as in *Mid-Lothian*, in the opposite direction, from Scotland to England. Because love would be dull without a struggle, the protagonist typically has to battle for the heart of his beloved with a rival. While the plots are strictly formulaic, the details in these novels are realistic, historically accurate, and include many individual twists in the characters' fortunes, so they do not read like formulaic fiction. The reader is frequently surprised by the endings and the characters' actions. For example, Jeanie Deans is (oddly for Scott) a female protagonist, and she travels in the wrong direction, to London from Scotland. Scott's generic variations, within his formulaic rules, are the reason he is still respected as one of the best nineteenth-century novelists.

The fact that Scott wrote about places that he had seen and studied made his histories superior, so that a new genre of realistic, thoroughly researched historical fiction was born. The use of strict formulas also helps to tie Scott's five rebellion novels into a compact and clearly defined genre. The formula can be broken down into several structural elements: characters, plots and narrators. These elements betray Scott's pro-rebellion authorial bias in his repeating Scottish nationalist or Jacobite rebellion theme.

Rebellious Plots

The four ingredients of Scott's rebellion plot are: travel, love, rebellion, and eventual success of the main character. The tragic ending of failed rebellions inspires sympathy for the fallen, brave rebels in readers. In general, if Scott intended to repel readers from rebellious plots, he would not have made them as exciting and adventurous as they are. The rebellious plots are typically rapid and jump between varied exciting actions. In the introduction to *The Black Dwarf*, Scott writes that he followed the advice of his Edinburgh publisher, Blackwood, "an excellent judge of public opinion," upon whose prompting Scott "got off" his "subject by hastening the story to an end, as fast as it was possible," thereby producing "a narrative as much disproportioned and distorted, as the Black Dwarf, who is its subject."[23] The rapid gallop at which the action begins on the first pages continues until the end, and pulls readers into the stories of these rebellions.

Rebellious Characters

Readers also admire the vigorous characters who are revealed in rapid succession. The objection readers are likely to raise when they encounter the idea that Scott's rebellion novels are subversive or radical is that the rebels typically lose at the end. If the rebels lose, how can Scott be encouraging others to rebel or applauding the actions of prior rebels? It is not exactly true that the rebels always lose in Scott's novels. In fact, it is a constant fact that the main characters always win. But they win only after at least some of the rebels are executed or forced into exile. Thus, a reader feels sympathy for the executed rebels and rejoices and feels empowered by the fact that the main semi-rebellious character escaped without significant punishment, and typically with a reward, such as marriage.

Another objection that critics have raised is that Scott's characters "waver." On this point, I agree with D'Arcy in that while some of Scott's characters might switch camps at convenient times to avoid hanging, Scott does not waver—he remains a nationalist and a radical believer in the rights of the Scottish people. It is easy to stop the analysis on the obvious waverers in Scott's rebellion novels, and primarily Edward Waverley himself, whose name includes the term, "waver." Waverley is also the name of the first rebellion novel, which leads its name to the series. But, as D'Arcy shows, the wavering characters are depicted as cowardly, morally unjustifiable or insane. Scott uses "wavering" as a synonym "unsettled habit of mind," and calls Waverley disturbed or crazy due to his inability to commit to a single side of a conflict or cause.[24] Scott clearly ridicules characters who waver, and does not support the wavering political position.

Scott portrays anti-heroic or anti-epic waverers who spend most of the tales running away from fights and only accidentally find more trouble. Scott even refers to the concept of "Wavering Honor" in *Rob Roy*, mocking his wavering "hero." According to Scott's code of honor, the hero knows which side is good and which is evil, and does not switch alliances in the middle of a conflict. The wavering in the characters in the narrative, as opposed to Scott's own position, from one side of a rebellion to the other, repeats in *Rob Roy* as Frank and Jarvie "scramble sensibly away when the fight starts, because they are on no one's side but their own." Frank is "fully free of political entanglements." Critics have noted how he whistles calmly due to his freedom from dedications "to extreme causes."[25]

Cadbury writes that the "best" of worlds for Scott is to be "decently Whiggish but sympathetically Tory, tolerantly Protestant and guardedly Catholic, appropriately commercial and validly bucolic."[26] Cadbury's summary of Scott as a waverer is erroneous, when one studies the implications that the wavering characters are making. Wavering characters are unsympathetic and unheroic, especially when they are put in contrast with hyper-heroic, epic rebels. To call Fergus a fool might be accurate, but without such foolish heroism Karl Marx's *Communist Manifesto* and Scott's pro-rebellious fiction and political treatises would have been far less impactful. If the violent 1848 revolutions or the Scottish Insurrection did not occur, the theoretical and fictional rhetoric of a subversive political novelist or of the far more direct pro-revolutionary theorist would not have led to the social impact that the neighboring violent rebellions brought about. Scott and Marx survived and were not executed, similarly to Waverley and Frank, but it is a political judgment to call the rebels, who were hanged for treason and sedition for participating in the 1848 revolutions or in the Scottish Insurrection, fools. Depicting the heroic death of the rebels for their just cause and arguing that violent revolutions are just were the roles in the "literary battle" that Scott and Marx waged to contribute to the struggle, without losing their heads. Neither Scott nor Marx wavered; they were simply lawyers and navigated legal, political and literary venues with focused single-mindedness, just as the rebels who were executed fought for a single cause that they believed in. Thus, logically, Scott's readers are led to conclude that rebellion is heroic, but wavering is unheroic and cowardly. Scott is subversive in the depictions of his characters' wavering and anti-heroic elements, and does not waver himself. Scott's puppets, Waverley and Frank, waver wildly between extremes (partially due to their romantic attachments to Flora or Di). Scott remains firm in his belief in the virtues of the rebellious causes. In contrast to some of his contradictory statements, Cadbury himself claims that Scott believed that "the virtues that gave rise to" the Jacobite rebellions "need not be lost, and must be saved."[27]

Some of Scott's rebellious characters survive, despite temporarily refusing to waver, as happens with Dalgetty in *Black Dwarf*. Dalgetty fought with the Jacobites, and after the rebellion failed, "his principles would not permit any shadow of changing,"—joining the English troops to save himself from being a "martyr" in the Jacobite cause. He initially refused to switch sides simply because he felt it was honorable to follow "strict ideas of a military enlistment," and to stay loyal to his commission. This matter was resolved when his friends waited for Dalgetty's contract with the rebels' troops to expire, and then he obliged by switching sides.[28] Scott explains that there are some military situations in which switching sides once your side has already lost is not an act of wavering, but rather a form of logical self-preservation. The fact that there was no viable Jacobite or nationalist party for Scott to join is one of the reasons he joined the establishment as a judge, and did not pick up arms in any cause, instead choosing to argue with his novels.

Some of Scott's rebellious characters do not waver in their beliefs and then end tragically. One of the best examples of this is Fergus in *Waverley*, who dies tragically. Sympathy for Fergus, one of the leaders of the 1745 Rising, is inspired not only by the narrator or by his death, but also by the plea from his comrade, Maccombich, who pleads with the court to first take his own life and the lives of several other Highlanders in place of Fergus', and when this is refused, asks to "die with his Chieftain" during their trial.[29] This self-sacrificing gesture suggests not only the love and respect that the Highlanders have for Fergus but also inspires sympathy for the rebels as a group in the readers, who cannot fail to appreciate the sentimental value of these gestures. Another example of a character who retains rebellious beliefs and ends happily is Die Vernon, whom Andrew calls "the bitterest Jacobite in the haill shire"[30] at the beginning of the novel, and who marries Frank, the narrator, at the end, after the end of the 1715 Rising. The rebels are raised to epic heroic status with their tragic ends. The tragic endings also betray Scott's radical, pro-rebellion bias.

On the other hand, there are several rebellious characters who never waver in their beliefs, and end happily. For example, the preacher, Morton, is asked by Claverhouse, a general, to waver and switch sides, to "instantly come over to our army and surrender yourself," at the beginning of the rebellious actions in the book, but Morton squarely refuses, insisting that instead he will return to the rebel side and will face Claverhouse shortly, "with my sword in my hand."[31] Surrendering and wavering are seen as immoral when a preacher insists that despite the fact that the odds are against the rebels, he is willing to return to their side and potentially to suffer as a martyr to the rebellious cause. In the end, Morton keeps a "high ... reputation," and marries Lady Margaret, his ideal wife.[32] Thus, some rebels succeed in keeping their political beliefs and also their necks. Readers who read about Morton's success might have wondered if joining a rebellion might not necessarily mean death at the gallows. The fact that some rebels survive goes against the hypothesis that Scott was teaching his readers not to rebel by showing that rebels are typically executed.

The most blatant proof that Scott was on the side of the rebels is in the passionate pro-rebellion statements that many of his rebellious characters utter. Even when they are contemplating surrender, they cry out, "bear terms of peace to the tyrant," calling the opposition "tyrants," rather than seeing justice in the opposing position.[33] In fact, the rebels do not view themselves as supplicants, or rebels, but as honest people who feel there is "general justice" in their demand for Scottish independence or for the rights of the Scottish people and monarchs. As the preacher, Mr. Morton, exclaims in *Mortality*, "Our swords are drawn for recovery of a birth-right wrested from us."[34] The Scottish people are shown as being forced into armed combat by unjust English laws, tyrants and other misuses of English power. An interesting case, in which Scott semisubversively inserts a very strong insult against the English monarchy, is when, in the middle of an avalanche of a dozen Highlander toasts in *Waverley*, one character exclaims, "Hospitality to the exile, and broken bones to the tyrant."[35] This toast clearly implies giving shelter to the exiled king, and breaking the "bones" of the reigning king of England. Clearly, if Scott sided with the king of England, it would not have been prudent to insert a threat of physical violence in a side comment, a toast by a minor character, where it is also nonessential to the unraveling events.

Characters frequently make many other political statements that side with Tories, rebels, Jacobites, Scots or other radical, national or liberal factions that Scott supported. For example, upon his departure, Edward Waverley's uncle advises him to "keep no company with rakes, gamblers, and Whigs,"[36] equating Whiggery with gambling and criminality. Frequently, thieves like Rob Roy and Donald Bean Lean defend stealing from the English and from the aristocracy as their right, rather than a crime. Donald argues, "He that lifts a drove from a Sassenach laird, is a gentleman-drover. And, besides, to take a tree from the forest, a salmon from the river, a deer from the hill, or a cow from a Lowland strath, is what no Highlander need ever think shame upon."[37] Scott shows that the Highlanders are justified not only in the Jacobite rebellions that they lead but also in the thefts that they perpetrate during peacetime due to their impoverished state.

Scott frequently depicted the deaths of rebels in order to bring them to an epic, heroic status, and to make their deaths tragic. Scott's characters fall into common epic character types: the bard, the traveler, and the man who seeks his inheritance. Fiske writes that Scott uses "typical Homeric" or epic "personages — the bard, the seer, the returned heir, the ancient nurse, the captive maiden of noble birth."[38] Both *Rob Roy* and *Waverley* have these and other Homeric character types: Frank and Waverley both seek their inheritance; Flora Mac-Ivor, in *Waverley*, sings Scottish ballads; Nicol Jarvie, the bailiff, tells stories about his ancestors and about the Highlanders; and most clearly both Frank and Waverley are Odysseus-like figures, who make a journey to distant lands in search for adventure. Most of the characters in Scott's rebellion novels carry epic symbolic weight, so those who die heroically in a rebellious cause affect the readers' sympathy.

Rebellious Narrators

Scott commonly uses third-person narrators, with a few exceptions. Scott uses a first-person narrator only in *Rob Roy*. Scott also frequently writes from the first person in introducing and concluding remarks. In these introductions and conclusions, Scott is mostly speaking on his own behalf, so when in the conclusion to his last rebellion novel, *Black Dwarf*, he writes, "I retire from the field," this is a direct statement that he is withdrawing from writing rebellion novels.[39] Scott clearly felt, at the end of the series, as if he was on the "field" himself and fought in the rebellions that he describes with such acute sympathy.

In the body of the other four rebellion novels, besides *Rob Roy*, Scott uses an omnipotent narrator, who frequently interjects on the actions to describe the just history of the currently related or prior rebellions. The narrator colors thieves and rebels with a positive glow, for example writing in the *Black Dwarf*,

> The spirit of adventure, which formerly led to raids and forays in the same districts, was still to be discovered in the eagerness with which they pursued those rural sports.... The more high-spirited among the youth were ... expecting, rather with hope than apprehension, an opportunity of emulating their fathers in military achievements, the recital of which formed the chief part of their amusement within doors.[40]

The youth in the above quote are not only planning raids but also an armed Jacobite attack on England to encourage a "separation of the two English kingdoms."[41] Scott refers to raids upon the cattle of border English towns as "adventures" and "amusement," as opposed to calling them "crimes," or at least using a dispassionate tone. Using an enthusiastic and supportive tone when describing the rebels is a common feature of Scott's narrators' voices.

The narrator in *Waverley* supports the motivations of Fergus Mac-Ivor, who is eventually executed, by explaining, "From his infancy upward, he had devoted himself to the cause of the exiled family, and had persuaded himself, not only that their restoration to the crown of England would be speedy, but that those who assisted them would be raised to honor and rank."[42] These explanations of Fergus's innocent trust in the right and eventual success of the Jacobite cause are what makes his failure at the end so tragic and sympathetic to readers.

Besides using pro-rebellion language when describing the intentions of the rebels, Scott's narrators typically also give political summaries of the conflict that is leading to a rebellion in terms that explain the justice of the looming revolt. "All Scotland was indignant at the terms on which their legislature had surrendered their national independence. The general resentment led to the strangest leagues and to the wildest plans."[43] This quote is especially telling because Scott refers to "all" of Scotland, and to "general resentment" of England, thus suggesting that every single Scot in Scotland was for the rebellion. These types of conclusions are not the work of a detached narrator but of a narrator that is helping readers to draw a conclusion that the rebellion depicted was judged to be fair by all Scots, and thus suggesting that the reader, if he or she is reasonable, should agree with this "general" opinion and side with the rebels.

Occasionally, when the rebels or those who associate with rebels are mistreated or falsely accused, the narrator jumps in to support their position. In *Mid-Lothian*, the narrator exclaims, "To be imprisoned, even on a false accusation, has something in it disagreeable and menacing" in it,"[44] referring to the sudden arrest of the preacher, Mr. Butler, when he attempts to receive an entrance into the prison to see Effie Deans, on whose behalf her sister later has to travel all the way to London, barefoot, to prevent her execution. Further, the narrator explains that "Butler avowed his involuntary presence at the murder of Porteous," making a legal case on behalf of, if not a rebel, somebody who was among rebels during the murder.[45] The narrator does not only insist that Butler is being falsely accused, he also calls the action "menacing," showing his discontent with the methods of those who are fighting against the rebellion. To return to Effie's sister, Jeanie's, bare feet — she makes the pilgrimage with bare feet because, "She was not aware that the English habits of *comfort* attach an idea of abject misery to the idea of a barefooted traveler."[46] When the narrator explains that Jeanie was not even aware of what the English considered to be "habits of comfort," he is inspiring sympathy for this sister of a rebel Scot by appealing to the readers' sense of decency, and to the readers' sympathy for those who are poor and in need.

The nature of Scott's characters, plots and narrators betray Scott's radical rebellious purpose in his rebellion novels. Overall, the similarities in epic character types, plot structure and other elements show a clear, repeating structural formula in Scott's rebellion novels.

9

Scott's Linguistic Features

The complexity of Scott's linguistics hides rebellious anti-empiric passages. In addition, the complexity of Scott's Scottish language is used to promote the Scottish language and the suppressed culture of the Scottish people. Scott typically uses subversive linguistics to carry hidden rebellious messages across the details of his rebellion novels. For example, Scott winks to his Scot readers by insulting the English in Gaelic or Scottish, a language that those who were insulted could not understand, and therefore could not censor as treasonous.

Scott's linguistic formula is more intricate than his structural formulas. The structure of a rebellion novel is similar to a cardboard model of what a finished building should look like. The linguistics of Scott's rebellion novels are the stones that he meticulously carved and placed in beautifully designed and calculated patterns along the entire length of his buildings. The basic formula for the linguistics of Scott's rebellion novels is:

> Rebellion Genre's Linguistic Formula = Epic Imagery and Techniques + Scottish Language and Allusions + Middle English and Renaissance Borrowings

All of these ingredients have specific political purposes that are connected to elements of Scott's structural formula. Epic imagery and literary techniques assist the grandeur of the epic rebellious heroes, whom Scott built up by putting epic allusions and words into their speech. Scott uses things like epic epithets, such as, "the mistress of the rolls,"[1] to add grandeur to the poor, struggling rebels and to the Scottish people who are struggling to survive despite their poverty. By raising his characters up to hero status, Scott makes their tragic ends appear more sympathetic and symbolically significant.

At the same time, Scott uses the Scots language and allusions to empower the Scottish nation and people by showing the beauty of their language and heritage. In *Rob Roy*, Andrew is particularly rich in Scottish sayings and "native songs." Early in the story, as Andrew is gardening and explains that he has also worked as a smuggler, he sings the following native song:

> Jenny, las! I think I hae her
> Ower the moor amang the heather;
> All their clan shall never get her.[2]

These native songs and sayings typically evoke beautiful images of the Scottish countryside, such as the mention of the heather and the moor above. The songs are commonly sung in the Scots dialect to promote the validity of using Scottish languages and dialects in literature.

Lastly, the use of Old or Middle English and Renaissance borrowings helps to counterbalance the use of the Scots. The similarities between Middle English and Scots also suggest that Scots and Gaelic are closer to Shakespearean, grand English than modern English. The parallels between Scots and Shakespearean English were used by Scott and other Scottish cultural revivalists as a reason why Scots should be more commonly used in literature. For example, Scott uses Old English grammar when he uses the archaic form of "thou for the second person singular pronoun."[3] Putting a Tudor-sounding *thou* next to a Scots *hae* shows that the two languages and cultures have common roots. The parallels make Scots seem more like the classical form of English, rather than a dialect of the poor people in a region of Scotland. Scots is similar to Middle English because both have elements in them from before the Great Vowel Shift, which accounts for many of the changes that distinguish these languages from modern English. Scots and English differ, in part, due to the "separate development of some of the Old English long vowels," so that those in southern England pronounce [ou] or *oak, home*, while Scots pronounce [e:] or *gae*, and *ghaist*.[4] Another similarity between the two languages is that Scots consonants retain Old English sounds, which have been "lost in Standard English," like [x] as in Scott's *cleugh* or [klu:x].[5] Scott mixed Old English, Modern English, Scottish English and Scots pronunciations and languages in his novels, while using a grand epic narrative and linguistic style, which gave an epic feeling to the Scottish national language and to Scotland's national image. In this chapter, I will give examples of how critics have interpreted Scott's linguistics, and I will explain how his linguistics delivers radical or nationalist messages.

Scottish Linguistic History

A brief history of language development in Scotland will explain the radical nature of Scottish linguistics. The language tree of Modern English and Modern Scots is connected through similar roots in Old English. English and Scots are two languages on separate branches of the tree. Old English split geographically into Early Northern English, Midland English and Southern Middle English. The Northern English developed into Modern Scots and Modern Northern English, with their various dialects. Midland English became Modern Standard English, with its various regional dialects. And Southern English became the current regional southern English dialects used today. The Stewart Scottish monarchy used Scots in Scotland; the English Tudor monarchy used Early Modern English in London and its surroundings. When the two kingdoms and parliaments united and made London their political headquarters, Scots faded out of use, while Modern English became the dominant language.

The relationship between Scottish fiction, nationalism and Scottish linguistics is closely linked with the rebellion genre. The link can be explained by looking at what Anne McKim has called "one of the very first books printed in Scotland," *The Actes and Deidis of the Illustre and Vallyeant Campioun Schir William Wallace* (1471–9) by Blind Harry.[6] The work is referred to by Scott and other classical writers as Harry's *Wallace*. William Wallace was a Scottish nobleman who was responsible for securing Scotland's victory in the Wars of Scottish Independence (1296–1357). The name might sound familiar to modern readers due to its reappearance in the film *Braveheart*. *Wallace* has a rebellion plot, and a heroic, epic rebellious central character, and was likely one of the generic inspirations for Scott's Waverley novels. Harry's contribution to Scottish linguistics and nationalism were similar to Scott's as well. Imitation was a large part of this Scottish genre derived from these roots. Harry acknowledged that he borrowed some of Wallace's history from John Barbour's epic poem *The Brus* (*The Bruce: History of Robert I, King of Scotland*) (1370s).[7] Barbour wrote this poem under the patronage of the Scottish king, a couple of decades after the king Bruce's victory in the Scottish Wars of Independence, to glorify the achievement.

> A! fredome is a nobill thing!
> Fredome mayfe man to haiff liking;
> Fredome all folace to man giffis:
> He levys at efe, that frely levys![8]

A similar outrage against invasion by the English, and a pride in the noble cause of the rebels, is expressed in *Wallace* in the following passage:

> Rebell renkis in mony seir regioun;
> Trubbill weddyr makis schippis to droune,
> His drychyn is with Pluto in the se;
> As off the land, full off iniquite,
> He waknys wer, waxyng off pestilence,

> Fallyng off wallis with cruell wiolence,
> Pusoun is ryff, amang thir othir thingis;
> Sodeyn slauchter off empriouris and kingis.[9]

Across the centuries between the Wars of Scottish Independence and the eventual union of the crowns in 1707, it was fashionable among Scottish writers who were noble or those who had royal patrons to publish poetic books that glorified and eulogized the Scottish nationalist victors in the those wars. Besides the nationalist topics that these Scottish works utilized, you can observe from the above examples that the languages used are early Scottish and Middle Scots. Shortly after the publication of *Wallace*, the language mutated into Modern Scots, an even heavier separation from English. Murison writes: "The years 1460–1560 can be considered the heyday of the Scots tongue as a full national language showing all the signs of a rapidly developing, all-purpose speech, as distinct from English as Portuguese from Spanish."[10] Murison explains that after this peak, the Scots language suffered from a series of blows that diminished its status, including the Reformation (with its use of the widely-read English Bible), then the Union of the Crowns in 1603, and finally the Parliamentary Union with England in 1707. In addition, "the spread of books in Tudor English" was assisted by the "setting-up of printers from England and France in Edinburgh in the late 1500s."[11] The last mentioned development is significant because Edinburgh has been the capitol of the Scottish publishing industry from the 1500s to the present day, and the fact that these printers and publishers used Modern English instead of Modern Scots meant that Modern English became the "standard" language of "intellectual" communication in Scotland.

Scott read *Wallace*, and various other books in Scots, Scottish and Scottish English. One of Scott's favorite books was the *Book of the Dean of Lismore* (1512–1532), which included poems by Ossian, Allan M'Rorie and Fergus the Bard.[12] Murison notes that *Lismore* "is written in a phonetic [English] script based on the pronunciation of Scots."[13] Scott's 1810 *Lady of the Lake* mimics Ossian's poetic style and is also on a "Highland subject."[14] The *Lady of the Lake* was Scott's first commercial success, and he decided on this Scottish subject upon seeing that Ossian's poetry was popular in Scotland. Scott was interested in Scottish folklore and epic poetry and collected it. Scott's breakthroughs in the fields of literary linguistics are due to this early research. Scott is credited for beginning a revival in Scottish folklore, Highland traditions, and the use of the Scottish English language in fiction. Use of Scottish folklore and epic poetry was familiar to Scottish readers in the 17th century and was revitalized by Scott's contemporaries Robert Fergusson and Robert Burns, as "popular [Scottish] culture kept faithful to the old tongue in ballads, folk-song and tales, in proverbs and sayings, and in comic verse,"[15] and these books were only a few centuries removed from Scott's period. The Scottish that Scott uses is a diluted dialect, in which Scots and English Scottish are primarily used amidst English words even in the dialogue of poor Scottish characters.

The legal and political language in Scotland was Modern English, but the nationalist and folkloric language was Scots and Scottish English. Scots and Scottish words were gradually deleted from the Scottish legal language with the grammarian writings by David Hume and others, who published lists of "Scotticisms" to be avoided.[16] The modern languages used in Edinburgh are similar in many ways to the languages that were used in Edinburgh at the beginning of the nineteenth century. The Edinburgh area has a distinctive "bi-polar continuum" phenomena among Scottish speakers, so that "each speaker has access to features of both linguistic systems [Scots and Scottish English] and possesses the ability to range from one to the other as occasion demands."[17] Scott could have easily switched entirely to the Scottish English or to the "standard" English continuum and could have written his novels entirely in these English dialects, but he made a conscious decision to use Scottish languages and dialects for much of the dialogue in his texts. In addition, when writing in Scottish dialects, Scott and Stevenson are frequently inconsistent, writing the same word, as pronounced by the same speaker, with a Scots pronunciation in one passage and then in a different passage with an English pronunciation. This inconsistency is present in Scottish speakers as well, as it's also a part of the "bi-polar continuum" of switching at random between the two dialects.

Because Scott and Stevenson, as well as other Scottish-revival writers, read and studied Scottish printed linguistics from many of the same above-mentioned classical Scottish works, there are several similarities in the linguistic features they use to stress the use of a Scottish dialect by one of the characters in their stories. Scott and Stevenson insert "a number of archaic features" that have survived in Scottish accents, such as the /x/ phoneme. As you'll see across Scott and Stevenson's linguistic sections in this book, these novelists frequently substitute vowel diversity for a few repeating vowel sounds when they are writing in one of the Scottish dialects or languages. There is a "smaller set of vowel phonemes in Scottish; therefore, "Scottish speakers do not make some vowel contrasts that English speakers do, thus e.g. *full* and *fool* are both [fʉl]."[18] Another distinctive feature is that there are more short vowels in Scottish dialects. Scott and Stevenson frequently insert an apostrophe in the middle of words; this typically identifies a "breaking" in the pronunciation of a word, which "typically involves the vowel in a syllable being followed by a brief transitional vowel glide of an [iː] quality, e.g. [tjeiːl] *trial*. Vowels exhibit this process only before /r, l/ and /n/."[19] The apostrophe to signify deletions of commonly pronounced vowels and consonants is a common technique for Scott and Stevenson, in deletions of letters like the "h" in *him*, leaving '*im*.

The use of Scots and Scottish linguistic features similar to classic Scottish texts like *Bruce* and *Wallace* helped Scott to connect, in the minds of readers, his Jacobite rebellion novels to the history of the successful Scottish Wars of Independence. Scott used a wide array of innovative linguistic tricks and a variety of different dialects and languages in his books; proof of this is in the fact that there is hardly a critical book out there on Scottish linguistics that does not include Scott's name in the index. He had more than a bipolar Scottish-English language, but rather a multipolar language of a highly educated Scottish lawyer.

Gaelic Poetry and Language

Scott studied Ossian or Gaelic poetry simultaneously with his study of epic poetry. Scott makes a natural leap between the two, and makes his Gaelic linguistic features appear as complex, unique and otherwise stylistically rich as his epic features. Thus, characters who speak in Gaelic gain depth, esteem, and multidimensionality, instead of appearing simply poor or unintelligent. One of Scott's letters in the memoirs, to Miss Seward, addresses the epic poetic elements in Ossian poetry, as well as in Homer and the other poets that Scott would later imitate in the Waverley novels. Scott explains that by merit alone Gaelic poems are not superior to something like the "Scandinavian Scaids," but because, like Macpherson, he is more familiar with the Gaelic tongue and manners, he is better equipped to write about this subject than about the Greeks or England. When Macpherson, a native Gaelic writer, tries to translate Homer, he loses the advantages of being born and groomed on Celtic poetry: "Few people wanted to see their old Grecian friend disguised in a tartan plaid and philabeg. In a word, the style which Macpherson had formed, however admirable in a Highland tale, was not calculated for translating Homer." Realizing these shortfalls in other poets from close critical study, Scott achieved what Macpherson failed to do by using the Homeric or mythic epic setting of his native Highlands.[20] Scott further confesses, "The Highlanders ... adopted the poems of Ossian as an article of national faith," perhaps more valuable than Scripture. Another reason Scott was interested in Ossian poetry was that the main funder of research into Scottish history, the Highland Society, was engaged in "investigating, or rather, I should say, collecting materials to defend, the authenticity of Ossian." The society was not successful in finding true originals that might serve as proof.[21] Scott wanted to further the nationalist cause of raising the status of Ossian and of Scottish poetry in general by utilizing Scottish settings and a Scottish poetic style in his popular rebellion novels.

Other Scottish Languages

Because Scott started a "revolution" in reading as well as in publishing with his enormous sales records, Scott's readers were located not only in Scotland but in large part in England. There are no concrete statistics on the number of Scottish versus English readers that read Scott's rebellion novels, but it is likely that it was a nearly even split. This means that a significant percentage of the readers understood Scott's Scots language and Scottish allusions, and another significant percentage did not understand many of these allusions and linguistic tricks. Even if some English readers missed many of Scott's meanings, most of them would have understood that *hae* means *have*, especially if they lived in northern England, or if they were poor, as the Scots language and the Lowland Scottish language had some linguistic similarities to these dialects. Wealthy English people were, in turn, likely to appreciate the Middle and Renaissance English allusions and linguistics, as they were likely to have read the major works from these periods. These points account for the popular appeal of Scott's rebellion novel, despite the heavy use of Scots and Lowland Scottish, as well as Highlander and Gaelic vocabulary. Scott succeeded in selling Scottish culture and language not only to the Scottish people, but also to the English people, thus achieving one of his chief nationalist objectives.

Scott's use of the Scottish language is subversive because it enriches Scottish characters and makes them more sympathetic and trustworthy than their English counterparts. The rebels use fancy linguistic tricks in Scottish that endear readers. Derrick McClure, in his "Linguistic Characterisation in 'Rob Roy,'" summarizes the scope and span of Scott's linguistics by focusing on the most positively critiqued feature of Scott's style, the "illusion of individual identity" created by Scott in his dialogues. McClure discusses dialogues of two characters in *Rob Roy*: Bailie Nicol Jarvie and Andrew Fairservice. According to McClure, these characters use: successive phrases with "parallel grammatical structures" (rhythmic/grammatical patterns, linking with alliteration, or by rhyme), have a "fondness for lists" (straightforward, synonyms, insults), "proverbs" (prolixity/aphorisms, for consolation, ironic euphemisms), "irony" (sarcasm, ironic understatements, exaggeration, heavy rhetorical irony, ironic emphasis to "twist" meaning, ironic wit/aggression, ironic replies/repetitions of interlocutor's speech, puns), "interpolated maledictions" on institutions, parenthetical critiques, physical imagery, jokes "at their own expense," "untranslatable polysyllables" (whigmaleeries, curliewurlies), and "onomatopes" (clinkum-clankum). This list includes a lot of coy, witty or potentially subversive elements, which D'Arcy and other recent critics have picked up on. McClure also briefly describes the linguistic elements employed by one of Scott's English-speaking characters, a speech McClure feels is inferior to the more individualized style employed by Bailie and Andrew. Diana Vernon, the English speaker, uses "irony, humour, apt similies and metaphors, neatly applied literary allusions, and other readily recognizable habits."[22] As one of the leading rebels, Diana Vernon's complex and multidimensional linguistic style attracts readers towards her, and in turn towards the rebellious Jacobite cause.

Scott's most common type of linguistic subversion is using the Scottish language to hide messages that Scott did not want English readers to understand. According to D'Arcy, Helen MacGregor was *raped* while her husband, Rob Roy, was away helping Frank (the main character). She appears savage, cruel and lawless to the English reader, and to the narrator, Frank, because they do not understand that she kills Morris partially to revenge the violation that she suffered by Morris and his men, not only to avenge her arrested husband. D'Arcy points to words such as "misguided," "sense of dishonor," "deep wrongs to avenge," "new insult and atrocity," "perturbation of mind," and "sair misguided" in Chapters 26, 34, and 35 of *Rob Roy*, which symbolize or imply rape to a Scottish reader.[23] This is one of the best examples of how the insider knowledge of these terms would have made Scott appear as a rebel to Scots, but as a loyalist to the English. Scottish readers see Helen MacGregor's savage violence or execution of her rapist, as a just and noble action; English readers see Helen MacGregor as somebody Scott is showing as unjustified in her extreme violence, as they do not see the justification that she explains only to readers who understand Scottish languages. English readers might have wanted to see the rebels as wrong in their actions, and Scottish readers wanted to find that the movement for Scottish nationalism was right and justifiable. By splitting the language of the rebellion novels in two, Scott frequently offers both perspectives. But, if one reads the novels closely enough, one sees clearly that the rebels are always justified by the narrator and with their own pro-rebellion speeches. Scott clearly is a radical nationalist, but he strived to dim his nationalist fervor so that his works would not be censored by his publishers or by his distributors. As I noted earlier, there were a few times when they were censored by both, but Scott bypassed these blocks by developing his subversive linguistics and structural methodologies.

Standard English versus Nonstandard

A discussion of the difference between standard and nonstandard English is highly politically charged. A Scottish person would be highly offended if one called the Scots or the Scottish languages dialects, instead of putting them into the "language" category. A dialect cannot be a national language or one that everybody learns in school. "Nonstandard" English is typically associated with erroneous or improper English, a language that is full of mistakes that should be corrected. By putting Scots next to his English vernacular, Scott separated the two further into separate languages.

Scott is frequently credited for the rebirth or even the birth of Scottish culture, as he popularized the kilt and other Scottish symbols when King George IV wore these symbols, and with epic grandeur these symbols are painted within Scott's Scottish novels. The influence that Scott had on the Scottish languages is equally significant.

The fight for the right of national languages like Scots to survive started before Scott's period. The fact that Scott was writing *Life of Swift*[24] during his composition of the first rebellion novel, *Waverley*, coincides with the fact that Scott utilizes some of Swift's linguistic tricks. *Gulliver's Travels*[25] can be viewed as a dystopian rebellion novel. I am excluding utopian and dystopian rebellions from the rebellion novel genre category for the purposes of this study. Still, Swift's use of an invented foreign language is similar to Scott's occasional use of invented words, as opposed to English or Gaelic words. In *Gulliver's Travels*, in the first land that Gulliver encounters, he meets with the Lilliputs, who attempt to teach him their language and manners. Jonathan Swift, born in Ireland, was also deeply concerned with linguistics of the "standard" English language. The emperor provides scholars for the task of teaching Gulliver the Lilliput tongue, and within three weeks, Gulliver makes great progress with acquiring the language: "And the first words I learnt were to express my desire that he would please to give me my liberty, which I every day repeated on my knees. His answer, as I could apprehend, was, that this must be a work of time..., and that first I must ... lumos kelmin pesos desmar lon emposo; that is, swear a peace with him and his kingdom."[26] The fact that the English or a standard language is necessary to appeal for "liberty," Irish or Scottish independence, is a key ingredient in many fictional and theoretical Irish and Scottish nationalist theories and tales. The emperor does not speak Irish or Scottish and cannot even understand the protagonists' desires or urgent appeals without them assimilating into his empire, by learning the empire's language and "uncommon"[27] manners. While the emperor begins by demanding that Gulliver should make a peace treaty with him, he is soon insisting that Gulliver should help him fight in his wars, as many Irish and Scottish men did for England. Lastly, at the end of the tale of the Lilliputs, Gulliver is accused of "high treason" and "makes his escape."[28] The accusation of rebellious activity implies rebellion without casting blame on the hero for committing it. There are similarities in pattern between the rebellions, linguistics and antigovernment propaganda in Swift's and Scott's works. George Orwell called Swift "a rebel and iconoclast ... he cannot be labeled 'Left.' He is a Tory anarchist, despising authority while disbelieving in liberty."[29] Regardless of whether Swift or Scott were on the left or on the right, they studied the rebellious and linguistic tricks their predecessors used and followed similar subversive nationalist strategies.

The most thorough study of Scott's language was made by Graham Tulloch in *The Language of Walter Scott*.[30] Tulloch writes, "Though others had used dialect and archaisms before, no one in English had used it so extensively and thoroughly" before Scott.[31] Scott, however, acknowledges that he was not the first to employ dialects: "when the success of Burns, writing in his native dialect with unequalled vigour and sweetness, had called from their flails an hundred peasants to cudgel their brains for rhymes."[32] Tulloch further claims that Scott "contributed to Modern English many words current in the Scots of his own time," including "awesome" and "gruesome" from *Rob Roy*, and "raid" from *Waverley*.[33] Scott's and the Scottish language's influence on modern "standard" English can be seen by comparing David Hume's mid-eighteenth-century list of "Scotticisms" to a modern English dictionary. Most of the Scottish words Hume references are now accepted as Standard English.

It is clear that Scott was more interested in promoting the Scottish language than in being understood by his English readers. The original English readers of *Waverley* would have missed the meaning behind the Scottish sayings and words. For example, *brought far ben* is translated as "made much of," and *flemit* is translated as "chased."[34] *Flemit* is not even included in the "verb" section of *Observations on the Scottish Dialect* by John Sinclair (1782).[35] Out of the following several Scottish words in *Waverley*: *umwhile* (late), *taillie* (agreement),[36] *gaed* (went), *tail* (tickle),[37] *lunzie* (wallet), *shilpit* (insipid),[38] only a word similar to *gaed* appears in Sinclair's list, and it is in a slightly different dialect, "*gang*," with a note that it comes from "Saxon, and Low Dutch." "Gang is an old word, says Dr. Johnson, not now used, except ludicrously."[39] Of course, it seems to follow that *gang* went out of style, and *gaed* became popular by 1814, when *Waverley* was published. Further still, it appears that the translator of the more recent twentieth-century *Waverley* edition did not translate some terms which are included in Sinclair's dictionary, perhaps because some of them are very familiar to modern English readers; for example, *to ken* or "to know" is listed in the dictionary as originating from the "Saxon" language,[40] and it appears in the modern *Waverley* without a translation.[41]

The first readers to purchase *Waverley* did not have the same grasp of some of Scott's Scottish words as we do today, as many of these words have now integrated into Standard English. Sinclair sent a similar list of Scottishisms to Hume in 1782, and these have now become a part of the standard American English. This list includes phrases or common sayings like "to want for any thing,"[42] "to open up a wound,"[43] "to profit from experience,"[44] and "to fall in the gutter."[45]

While today Scottishisms are a part of Standard English and linguistic diversity is supported by a majority of the world's population, Scott's linguistic turns were radical and widely criticized during his lifetime. Many 19th-century critics wrote essays for *The Critical Review*, *North American Review* and *Quarterly Review* complaining that Scottish made Scott's works unintelligible. D'Arcy cites J. W. Croker from the *Quarterly Review* writing that Scott's novel "would be on the whole improved, by being translated into English."[46] The first "translations" appeared when Scott added a glossary to *Rob Roy* in 1817, and then to *The Antiquary* in 1819, and they have expanded since that date. While the critics raged, major 19th-century authors picked up on the trend. The result was a linguistic fallout. It would be inconceivable to hear a similarly blunt critique of the heavy uses of foreign words today.

Sinclair even mentions on several occasions that Shakespeare ("have with you" in Act II, Scene I of *Merry Wives of Windsor*), as well as other English writers, occasionally use sayings that are similar to the Scottishisms that appear in Scott. There were and still are shared words and expressions in geographically neighboring northern England and in Scotland and Ireland. Because Shakespeare, Scott, Johnson, Defoe and others used these Scottishisms in world-wide classics, many words that were incomprehensible to Scott's readers are more commonly known today. In addition, we should keep in mind that Sinclair's dictionary was extremely limited, with under a thousand words in the nouns, adjectives and verbs categories. This also means that even if an English author had access to Sinclair's popular work on the Scottish dialect, he would not have been able to understand Scott's Scottishisms, and would have been bewildered and confused for large stretches of the book. This was probably the reason few other works were printed in the previous century that used an excessive quantity of foreign words mixed with the English language, but Scott managed to popularize the heavy use of dialects and foreign words in 19th-century novels across the world, as seen in Mark Twain, as well as the two other authors considered in this study: Charles Dickens and Robert Stevenson.

Scott clearly had a stronger grasp of the "standard" English of his time than most upper-class Englishmen. But Scott's linguistic tricks can also be seen as a nonstandard language, neither fully Scottish, nor fully English. Tul-

loch offers thousands of examples from Scott's unique use of linguistics. Scott frequently used:
1. Word borrowings from Middle English literature (Chaucer, Dame Juliana Berners), Renaissance literature (Shakespeare, Spenser, Jonson, Milton), as well as from many other works that Scott read
2. Cant terms from cant dictionaries (i.e., Francis Grose's *Classical Dictionary of the Vulgar Tongue*, 1796)
3. Foreign words (medieval and modern French, Latin, Spanish)
4. Oaths and exclamations ("Ninety percent of the religious oaths in Scott's novels mention God ... or the saints")[47]
5. Quotations from the classics
6. Artificial creation of Scott's imagined period (Old English) grammar, such as the use of the archaic "thou for the second person singular pronoun,"[48] and "use of *it* for *he* or *she*,"[49] by combining grammatical elements from varied periods and texts
7. Imitation of "real speech" used by Scots in Scott's own period

Thus, Scott's linguistics are significant because Scott utilized an incredible arsenal of complex multilingual strands, and also because Scott brought the Scottish language into England. Scott added many words to the English language, which prides itself on being a mixture language that adopts words into its vocabulary when they come unto be common use and the fact that many read Scott's novels meant that they started to use some of the foreign words that he was introducing.

Scott's desire to promote the validity of the Scottish languages can be better understood when we look at what critics have said about the Scottish languages. The most biting and direct critique of the Scottish language was written by Edwin Muir in his frequently cited *Scott and Scotland*. He wrote bitterly that the "Scottish writer" can achieve "completeness" only by absorbing "the English tradition," because Scotland did not have a "major literary tradition" for one to lean on, due to the "disintegration of the language of Scottish literature ... some time in the sixteenth century," or to the lack of a unifying "homogeneous language."[50] Both Rob Roy and his wife, Helen, occasionally speak English, which is "proper" or a close "mimicry" of English, unlike most of the other Highlanders and Lowlanders, who have thick Gaelic accents. When they choose to speak English, they are portrayed as attempting to "suppress" their Scottish idiom or dialect.[51] Scott shows that many of his characters feel ashamed about using the Scottish idiom, and thereby inspires sympathy in his readers with the beauty of this idiom. If Scott intended to explain the weaknesses of the language, he would not have consistently used it across large portions of his historical Scottish novels.

Scott is self-conscious and self-analytical of his use of Scotch colloquialisms, dialect, phrases and words, as well as Scottish manners. He frequently explains that his English characters have difficulty grasping what native Scots are trying to say when they give "rapid answers" with a "haste and peculiarity of the dialect," as he does in Chapter IX of *Waverley*, when readers first meet a Scottish character.[52] According to Scott, he wrote the chapters that proceed this one in 1805 and received a negative reception from a friend, but when he later showed the book with these sections with the Scottish dialect included, the reception from the same friend was positive. The elements of the "national tale," its exotic dialects and manners, only appear in these later chapters, so it is possible that the "national tale" formula is more endearing and sympathetic to readers who feel connected to and cheered by the "fool" of a guide that Waverley finds in the gardener, Davie Gellatley, the character that the protagonist has difficulty understanding.

In his book *Subversive Scott*, D'Arcy argues that the use of the unknown, to the English audience, Scottish language was a subversive tactic on Scott's part, used in order to argue for rebellion and nationalism, or for his "consuming passion for the survival of his native country of Scotland,"[53] right under the nose of English censors, without alarming them. While I could give examples of insults that Scott enclosed in the Scots language, which were missed by English readers, I believe that these insults were only minor elements of Scott's nationalist agenda. Scott wanted to promote Scotland and Scottish culture, and it was his radical, nationalist agenda to promote Scottish independence by supporting the validity of the unique Scottish languages.

In his memoirs, Scott writes that when he was studying in a day school in his fourth year, he "never acquired a just pronunciation."[54] We can clearly see from the study of Scott's dialects, foreign words and other rich linguistic features that Scott picked up not only a "just" English "pronunciation" by the time he wrote *Waverley*, but also learned to mine a variety of languages and traditions for the gold that he then utilized in his popular novels.

In order to develop a technique such as multilingual usage, writers have to keep some other elements constant, so that they do not have to worry about an unmanageable quantity of dimensions (plot, setting, characters, linguistics, etc.). By choosing to write five rebellion novels, all set in Scotland, Scott was allowed the luxury of performing acrobatics with mimicry of a realistic Scottish language, and was able to subversively criticize the English empire. Instead of spending time on developing new, original plot structures, most of Scott's energy was consumed in developing a single rebellion plot structure into a compelling, believable and realistic set of stories that attracted an enthusiastic worldaudience.

Epic Language and Allusions

The most complex and classically inspired trick in Scott's linguistic arsenal is his use of epic-like imagery, meter, rhythm and the like. Scott uses epic elements in order to elevate his rebellion plots and characters above common realities and to make the actions of the rebels seem more heroic and grand. A rebel who utilizes epic poetry to relay his rebellious message is more convincing than a rebel who uses common expressions. In her thoroughly researched *Epic Suggestions in the Imagery of the Waverley Novels*, Christabel Fiske identifies a number of epic-like linguistic features in Scott. These features are: ancient Germanic epic meter (unrhymed, four-accented, alliterative — similar to *Beowulf*), images and rhythms (similar to the ones used in the Old Testament), and figurative imagery (Greek metaphors, similes).[55] Fiske also gives numerous examples of Scott's use of epic epithets ("the mistress of the rolls" = a baker's wife), kennings (from Teutonic epics — an expression used for "a simple name of a thing") — handcuffs = "bracelets," gnomic wisdom (aphorisms and proverbs), rhetorical figures (litotes and euphemism), pattern phrasing, alliteration, personification, recurrent figures (tree, old song), pictorial quality, and revivification of faded figures or traditional figurative images/characters.[56] A few words above stand out as especially repetitive across various rebellion genre novels.

Carlyle referred to Scott as a "song-singer" and "pleasant tale-teller." Frequently, rebellion novels are melodious and soporific, as if to disguise the violence with pleasant music.[57] Songs and proverbs are similar in their concise and moralistic elements. According to *The Book of Proverbs*, in form, proverbs fall into the "wisdom genre," a category primarily for biblical works, but into which Scott clearly attempted to squeeze his novels. Proverbs are "terse" (concise), and include aphorisms ("formulation of a truth"), imagery, similes, metaphors, allegory, anthropopathism, anthromorphism, synecdoche, metonymy, personification, hyperbole, litotes, irony, parallelism, and "sound patterning" (consonance, assonance, alliteration).[58] The above list shows that Scott mimics many of the standard proverbial techniques in the Waverley novels. Proverbs and the epic are sister genres: one as short as a phrase or a sentence, the other epic in proportions, but both are concerned with divine wisdom and morals and both follow similar literary techniques. There is a sharp parallel between Scott's technique and the epic, even more so than with the national tale, because Scott memorized and read closely most of the classic epics in his youth, when the structural ideas behind them left the deepest impressions on his imagination. In his memoirs, he talks about reading the classics: Homer, Allan Ramsay's *Evergreen*, fairy tales, Shakespeare, Ossian, Spenser, Tasso, and Bishop Percy's *Reliques of Ancient Poetry*.[59] Scott was closely familiar with epic classics, and he worked to imitate epic techniques to give the history of Scotland an epic or grand flair.

Scott used Gaelic, Scottish English, Standard English, Scots, Middle and Old English and epic linguistic techniques and varieties in his rebellion novels. He made numerous strides into the development of complex literary linguistics. Some of these tricks were picked up by the rebellion novelists that followed him. The depicted rebellions are frequently cultural and national in nature. Therefore, the use of dialects and suppressed languages creates a strong subversive nationalist or radical undercurrent in rebellion novels.

PART III. CHARLES DICKENS: THE RADICAL SOCIALIST

10
Dickens' Socialist Purpose

Dickens' career started with the following series of events in 1835: he befriended Scott's old publisher, Hogarth, started developing an idea for a rebellion novel, *Barnaby Rudge*, and studied Scott's literary technique closely enough to mimic it. Dickens was first published by radical publishers, who expected social commentary and radical critique in his novels. Dickens was a radical from his youth to the end. He had a predominant radical, socialist purpose behind his writing, and especially behind his rebellion novels.

Charles Dickens' rebellion novels were *Barnaby Rudge* (1841) and *A Tale of Two Cities* (1859). Unlike the social novels that Dickens wrote between these two works, during the Great Famine, *David Copperfield* (1849), *Bleak House* (1852), *Hard Times* (1854), and *Little Dorrit* (1855), these two fit into the rebellion generic formulas that Sir Walter Scott developed. The divergences from Scott's formula I count as innovations that Dickens added into the pot to reflect his own individual novel-writing style and his own authorial purposes. Between these two rebellion novels, Karl Marx wrote *The Communist Manifesto* on the eve of the 1848 revolutions. The beginning of socialism, as well as the end of slavery and other movements, allowed radicals to speak more openly about their beliefs in the middle of the nineteenth century than Scott could have done at its beginning. Still, the English censorship machine kept its power, and Dickens was also "subversive," and did not make many open or direct expressions of his personal radicalism.

Dickens as a Radical in Pre–Cold War Criticism

The rebellion genre has not been discovered previously for political reasons. The conflict between socialism and capitalism from the eighteenth century to the present day has curtailed literary opinion and has left major gaps in research due to censorship. There have been periods when socialism was more and then less censorable. These periods are clearly distinguishable when one reads literary criticism. Charles Dickens has been called a "radical,"[1] a "Socialist," and an "apostle of the people"[2] by two of the most frequently cited Dickensian critics, T. A. Jackson and Edwin Pugh. Dickensian criticism leaned towards calling Dickens a socialist before the end of World War II, and started calling him a waverer, somebody who fluctuated between contradictory opinions after the Cold War started. With the Cold War, communism (frequently equated with socialism and radicalism) became a feared, censored and prosecuted topic in the West.

One of the earliest and best-known categorization of Dickens as a socialist was by a Frenchman, Louis Cazamian, in 1903, in the critical book, *The Social Novel in England 1830–1850: Dickens Disraeli Mrs. Gaskell Kingsley*.[3] It was first published in England in 1973, but it was read and cited by the critics mentioned below, who immediately followed it. Cazamian saw the pattern of imitations of rebellion and social themes between Dickens and earlier writers better than most of the critics that followed him. Cazamian concludes that Dickens was inspired to write a novel that followed *Tale* (1859), or *Hard Times*

Figure 18. "Charles Dickens in his study at Gadshill by Samuel Hollyer, ca. 1875" (Library of Congress, Prints and Photographs Collection).

(1854), by reading working-class novels and by following the news about mid-century worker rebellions.

> Disraeli's *Sybil* (1845), Mrs. Gaskell's *Mary Barton* (1848), and Kingsley's *Alton Locke* fired Dickens with an ambition to emulate these successful working-class novels. The great engineering strike of 1852 had just drawn public attention to industrial disputes once more; according to Sidney Webb [*A History of Trade Unionism*, pp. 196–97] the strike, which lasted from January until March, "interested the general public more than any previous conflict. The details were described, and the actions of the employers and the policy of the Union was discussed in every paper."[4]

Placing this group into a category of social novels is similar to what I am doing when I group rebellion novels into a genre. Among the above literary examples, *Alton Locke* nearly falls into the rebellion genre, but fails the genre test because it involves mostly a peaceful Chartist struggle, with a hero who is repelled by violent revolts, and after a few passionate pro-peace speeches, such as, "I cannot bear the thought of being mixed up in conspiracy — perhaps, in revolt and bloodshed,"[5] he dies in desperation, exile and poverty. Dickens wrote at least four novels that considered peaceful resolutions or moral rebellions, instead of the solely violent revolts that dominate all of Scott and Stevenson's rebellion novels. They are moral rather than violent rebellions, and as a result, do not fit into the rebellion genre.

The perspective of Dickens as a socialist that Cazamian planted was tuned to a more Marxist key in 1908, when Edwin Pugh wrote about *A Tale of Two Cities*, "Thus the French aristocracy sowed their seed of dragon's teeth; and inevitably, when the Revolution came, they reaped the predestined harvest"— the reference is to the scene when Monsieur the Marquis throws a coin for killing a poor child.[6] In Pugh's perspective, the violence during the revolution is interpreted as a threat against the aristocracy, unlike the Cold War Western view of the same scenes as portraying Dickens' "terror" of revolutionary violence, which mistakes sympathy for justifiable rage, with fear of a violent attack.

Because Pugh's perspective of Dickens is more accurate than Cold War misnomers, it is important to look closely at his definitions of Dickens' "socialism." Pugh concludes that Dickens "was a Socialist without knowing it," as the term did not become popular until 1883.[7]

> He was never false to this class: his class being, of course, the respectable, self-respecting poor ... Dickens, in short, knew the class — his own class — that he wrote about, as no other writer, before or since, has; and he pictured it faithfully, according to the light of his temperament ... Dickens aspired to be a savior.... He was so inflamed by his feeling of resentment against the confiscation by one small class of all power, all wealth, and all

the means of joy in life, whilst the rest of the race toiled and sweltered and agonized, from the cradle to the grave, for the bare wherewithal to prolong a life hardly worth living, that he could not, in his righteous anger, always be just and impartial.[8]

Dickens' purpose for writing rebellion novels was his desire to contribute to the "literary battle" for the poor against the bourgeoisie that exploited them. Dickens sympathized with the cause of the poor because after working as a laborer in his childhood and seeing his father go to debtors' prison, he identified with the poor class. Despite making a profit from his writing and editing, Dickens remained dedicated to the cause of rebellion against the bourgeoisie until his last days.

Rebellion novel literary warfare was effective because it convinced the novelists who read these works to join with this elite literary struggle. In the same year as the publication of Pugh's book, 1908, Bernard Shaw gave a speech comparing the communist Ruskin with Dickens at a book exhibition in Liverpool, where he said, "One of the greatest books in the English language is *Little Dorrit*, and when the English nation realizes it is a great book and a true book there will be a revolution in this country. One of the reasons I am a revolutionist is that I read *Little Dorrit* when I was a very small boy."[9] These sentences gain a more direct meaning when we think back to a quotation from a review of Arthur Conan Doyle that Shaw published in 1893: "My first acquaintance with the French Revolution was acquired at the same age, from *A Tale of Two Cities*; and I also struggled with *Little Dorrit* at this time."[10] Because Dickens was inspired to write about rebellion and to become a radical by reading Scott, Carlyle and other reformers, he might very well have taken comfort knowing that his rebellion and social novels would inspire many intellectuals, like Shaw, to become cultural revolutionaries.

The peak in radical Dickensian criticism occurred in 1937, during a decade when the West allowed the Soviet Union into the League of Nations, and they fought together against the emerging Nazi forces. Thus, in 1937, Jackson took the idea that Dickens was a socialist to the utmost extreme, summarizing Dickens as a pro-revolutionary radical. Jackson finds that *Barnaby Rudge* is a "burlesque of the 'underground' Radical clubs," and that Dickens shows his pro–"moral-force" Chartist and pro–"physical force" radical views.[11] In contrast to *Barnaby*, Jackson finds that *Tale* presents the uprising "with historical truth, as a just and necessitated uprising of people whose afflictions and privations had grown to be such as could no longer possibly be endured ... Dickens went to extreme length ... in vindication of the French Revolution."[12] Jackson concludes that both the Gordon Riots and the French Revolution are presented as "justly-deserved punishments inflicted upon Governments and ruling-classes in return for gross misrule."[13] Jackson sees the difference between the two novels in that "between 1839 and 1859 Dickens' Radicalism had modified in the direction of being much more ready to appreciate the need for a mass uprising and much more ready to tolerate the use of armed force."[14] Jackson is clearly stating that Dickens was radical and a revolutionary when he wrote the first rebellion novel, and became a more outspoken revolutionary by the second work.

Some ten years after Jackson, right after the end of World War II, in 1946, we can see the abrupt shift in perspective in the West of Dickens' political purpose. On the night World War II ended, the U.S. and England turned against the Soviet Union, depicting it as a party that was guilty of nearly joining Germany, before being betrayed by Hitler. In turn, the Soviet Union saw the U.S. use of nuclear force as a major threat, and felt compelled to immediately begin developing its own nuclear arsenal. These tensions and the build-up of nuclear arms comprised the Cold War, and during this time, socialist and communist ideas became taboo in the West.

How Orwell Mutated Dickens into a Capitalist

As a notable and recognizable literary and critical figure, George Orwell led the sudden shift from critically labeling Dickens as a socialist to calling him a capitalist. Dickens was on the pedagogic curriculum around the world in the middle of the twentieth century. It was important for ruling capitalists to stress that he was not on the side of the Soviet Union's communist politics. If Dickens was a communist, and America was opposed to all communists, especially during the McCarthy era, then he either had to be taken off reading lists or his political status had to adjust to the anti-socialist, Western political climate. And if there were some remaining undeniable radical elements in Dickens once he was reinterpreted, these had to be publicly ridiculed. Here is a summary of what Orwell said about him: "Dickens was a bourgeois, he was certainly a subversive writer, a radical, one might truthfully say a rebel.... In *Oliver Twist, Hard Times, Bleak House, Little Dorrit*, Dickens attacked English institutions with a ferocity that has never since been approached ... Dickens seems to have succeeded in attacking everybody and antagonizing nobody."[15]

Throughout Charles Dickens essay, Orwell argues that Dickens is "not a 'revolutionary' writer,"[16] even if he is a "rebel." Here are some of the points that Orwell uses to downplay Dickens' radicalism:
 1. Dickens "does not write about the proletariat" or the "working class," but instead about the "middle class."[17]
 2. The attacks on institutions are made without suggestions about what

would be "put in their places" or a lack of "constructive" radical "suggestions."[18]
3. Dickens makes "no clear sign that he wants the existing order to be overthrown, or that he believes it would make very much difference if it *were* overthrown."[19]
4. Dickens does not include diatribes that say exactly what is wrong with the system, but instead allows readers to "infer the evil of *laissez-faire* capitalism."[20]
5. Dickens includes the recurring figure of the "Good Rich Man," frequently a merchant, in his stories.[21]
6. "Dickens says very little about ... child labour."[22]
7. Dickens shows "that revolution *is* a monster" by portraying "the mass-butcheries, the injustices, the ever-present terror of spies, the frightful blood-lust of the mob,"[23] while "apologists of any revolution generally try to minimize its horrors."[24]
8. Even his poor characters have a "bourgeois exterior and a bourgeois (not aristocratic) accent."[25]
9. Dickens' happy endings include leisure, rather than work in the future of the main character. "The ideal to be striven after, then, appears to be something like this: a hundred thousand pounds, a quaint old house with plenty of ivy on it, a sweetly womanly wife, a horde of children, and no work."[26]

Lastly, Dickens is accused of being "Christian ... in his quasi-instinctive siding with the oppressed against the oppressors."[27]

From all this, Orwell concludes that Dickens is "pro-capitalist" because his "moral is that capitalists ought to be kind, not that workers ought to be rebellious."[28] The above points and this conclusion can be countered by the examples in Dickens' works that show the exact opposite of the points Orwell derives above. There are several passages in *Barnaby Rudge*, and in *A Tale of Two Cities*, as in all rebellion novels, which explain the reasons for the uprising and detail the ills and problems in the existing capitalist or aristocratic system. In addition, Orwell has a very hazy definition of the lower versus the middle class, and dismisses several of Dickens' impoverished characters as not truly being a part of the "working class." For example, anybody who has ever cleaned a house would probably call house servants a part of the working class, but Orwell dismisses them as failing to "work." Orwell begins his discussion about Dickens' two novels that "deal with revolution" by stating that *Barnaby Rudge* is really about "rioting" rather than about a "revolution,"[29] clearly stressing this point at the beginning to downplay the fact that Dickens wrote two novels about violent uprisings against the government — which by their sheer number should make a strong case that Dickens was indeed a "revolutionary" writer.

Orwell even explains that the Gordon Riots of 1780 were "little more than a pointless outburst of looting" with the "pretext" of "religious bigotry."[30] Religion is hardly "pointless" for those who are religious.

Orwell is twisting the facts and avoiding the obvious conclusions that the facts of the events point to. The Gordon Riots were a righteous rebellion for religious tolerance and liberty, and therefore they were not "pointless," having the point of obtaining religious rights. Orwell's argument similarly stumbles throughout this long essay on Dickens. He says that the actual numbers of executed aristocrats during the French Revolution was small, without quoting the actual numbers, but rather comparing it with modern battles in World War II. Orwell is using the political doublespeak in this essay that he himself criticized in his "Politics and the English Language." He uses language as a weapon to hide the simple facts of Dickens' revolutionary books. However, Orwell is not a politician, and so he frequently slips and gives the evidence to the contradictory argument, and even occasionally admits that his conclusions are flawed. For example, in his conclusion, Orwell expresses his respect and admiration for Dickens saying that he "fights in the open and is not frightened," and is "*generously angry*," and is a "nineteenth-century liberal, a free intelligence, a type hated with equal hatred by all the smelly little orthodoxies which are now contending for our souls."[31] Orwell sympathizes with Dickens because he is also an intellectual, who is "angry" and also feels the opposition of the "orthodoxy" to some of his "free" ideas, but at the same time, he feels that he can make more friends by writing an essay against Dickens than by supporting this dangerous radical who is so "hated" by all sides. Why would reading about the horrors of a violent revolution do anything but convince the aristocrats to give into revolutionary demands to avoid seeing those horrors in reality?

Point 8 (above), on the poor characters' "bourgeois accents" is crucial and misleading. Why do Dickens' main or "*jeune premier*" characters speak in an "upper-class English" accent instead of the "broad Essex," or "Lancashire accent" that their family members use?[32] For the same reason Stevenson's *David Balfour* was not as successful as the first book in that series, *Kidnapped*—the introduction of Catriona's (and most of the character's) thick or "broad" Scottish "accent" made the book harder to read. An "accent" is only an effective literary device if it colors the narrative, not if it overwhelms it, and so the characters who give long revolutionary speeches or who carry the majority of the plot have to speak in a BBC accent, as their message has to be understood by all of the book's readers. Rebellion novelists were after poor readers and middle-class readers. These readers were spread across the United Kingdom and spoke in various accents, and they were more likely to comprehend a "standard" English accent than a minor "Lancashire accent." Taking the approach of only using heavy accents in supporting characters is a trick that's common among rebellion novels, as it allows for those from a given region to sympathize with the regional or national character, without isolating readers from other regions. The main characters' Standard English does not diminish the radical content and accents used sparingly but effectively, in a rebellion novel.

What about the point that most of Dickens' novels' conclusions suggest his attraction to leisure as an ideal ending? Anybody who studies Dickens' biography will be assured that he did not rest. Among other things, his giant family, with about a dozen children, took up a significant portion of his working life. Even if the father is not actively rearing the children, having a dozen of them around is likely to give the hero a bit of work in his old age. Secondly, while the creation of art or literature, in the Marxist sense, is a form of "secondary production," when it is done in Dickensian quantities, when one simultaneously publishes several magazines, writes a book a year, does reading tours, and is also involved in political debates, it is likely that despite appearing to be sitting in one position at a desk all day, one is regularly hard at work. The production of both "art" and "propaganda" takes a lot of work if the creator wants to successfully sell his "message,"[33] because poorly composed art and propaganda would not lead to having "copies of one or two of his books lying about in an actual majority of English homes."[34] Further still, it's likely that every revolutionary looks forward to leisure and a restful home life once his or her revolution has been won; showing the happy ending for a rebel or a revolutionary with gifts of a good wife, money and a horde of children is a carrot-stick that encourages rebels to see the potential rewards of rebellious activity, rather than deterring revolutionary thought.

Orwell's final accusation that Dickens is a Christian moralist is perhaps the most absurd argument in this essay. Obviously, Dickens was a Christian and must have had a moral foundation, but this fact in no way prevented him from also being a radical or socialist. Dickens never read Marx or Nietzsche. He lived in an age when atheism was a pretty foreign concept and when the idea that a whole country would create a Robin Hood "give-to-the-poor" government was completely incredible. Dickens could not have been a communist in an age when only a very different brand of socialism existed. Dickens could not have been an atheist when there were still anti-blasphemy laws on the books that could send a writer to prison. Dickens was a Christian moralist radical socialist rebel — these terms are not contradictory, and are all true, and even Orwell himself concedes to most of them. Supporting the "underdog"[35] is not a Christian trait. When a murderer receives the death penalty, or when a rapist goes to jail, they become the "underdog," but few Christians would take their side in the battle for justice. The key is that Dickens supports the

Figure 19. "Mr. Pickwick and Sam in the Attorney's Office," *The Writings of Charles Dickens* Volume 1, *The Pickwick Club*. Engraving by Hablot K. Browne, 1894 ed. (Library of Congress Prints and Photographs Division).

"persecuted" in *Barnaby Rudge* and in *A Tale of Two Cities*, but Orwell twists Dickens' meaning when he says that in *Tale*, the persecuted are the aristocrats. In *Tale*, the "persecuted" are Madame Defarge and the other downtrodden poor and middle-class workers in France and England. Their rebellion against their oppressors is violent in both books. It is an illogical argument to say that in *Barnaby*, the "underdogs" are the Catholics, but in *Tale* the underdog is the aristocracy — just as saying that among two falling apples, one is falling up towards the ground, and the other is falling down.

Because so much of earlier criticism made the conclusion that Dickens was a socialist, in 1946, George Orwell still summarizes Dickens as a "subversive writer, a radical, one might truthfully say a rebel."[36] Orwell echoes earlier radical critics, writing that in *Tale*, "Dickens sees clearly enough that the French Revolution was bound to happen and that many of the people who were executed deserved what they got."[37] After Orwell, there was barely a single study that called Dickens a "radical," a "rebel," or a "revolutionary," without simultaneously calling him a conservative or a waverer. The turn towards seeing Dickens as betraying his terror of revolutionary violence in *Tale* and in *Barnaby* started with Orwell, who presented the above mentioned view of Dickens as a rebel but cushioned it by saying that Dickens was not a "socialist," but was instead "pro-capitalist, because its [*Tale's*] whole moral is that capitalists ought to be kind, not that workers ought to be rebellious."[38] This switch betrays more about the West's new fear of communism, socialism — and specifically of revolutionary violence — than any such fear in Dickens himself. The portrayal of violence that horrifies or terrifies readers does not prove that the writer was equally frightened of the scene he is painting. In fact, to portray revolutionary and rebellious violence with a steady hand that draws all of the miniature details of the scene means that the writer has to be emotionally detached from the passion that envelops the violent actions.

My argument is not that Scott, Dickens and Stevenson were pro-violence, insane madmen, but that they were supporting revolutionary movements with a detached, calculating eye, aware that the causes of the revolutionaries were typically justified and also frequently led to positive peaceful social reforms. Like Marx, these authors knew that only a "literary battle" was possible for them as semi-bourgeois, middle-class intellectuals, who were not willing or eager to risk their lives in lifting revolutionary weapons themselves.

Textual Evidence for Dickens' Radicalism

The proof that Dickens was a staunch radical lies in the fact that both *Barnaby* and *Tale* were poorly reviewed. *Barnaby's* sales were notoriously responsible for closing a magazine, *Master Humphrey's Clock*. In fact, it's likely that Dickens was more surprised than any of his readers that *Tale* outsold all of his other novels.

Thomas Hood in an 1842 review of *Barnaby* for the *Athenaeum* writes that the novel is a "well-built story," despite the fact that Hood also calls the riots a "storm" after an "overture."[39] In contrast, Wilkie Collins called *Barnaby*

Figure 20. "*Barnaby Rudge*: Joe trying to make up with Dolly." F.O.C. Darley; R. Hinshelwood, 1873 (Library of Congress Prints and Photographs Division).

"the weakest book that Dickens ever wrote."[40] *Barnaby Rudge* notoriously dropped the circulation of *Master Humphrey's Clock* by 70 percent from when it was first serialized on February 13, 1841, to the closing of the journal on November 27, 1841. In a study of Dickens' sales, Robert Patten writes that at the end of the publication of *The Old Curiosity Shop* (1840) sales of the magazine were up to 100,000 copies; but that the following novel, *Barnaby Rudge*, "failed to sustain this readership, plunging sales to around 30,000."[41] Henry Crabb Robinson kept a diary in 1841 as he read *Barnaby* and records that on September 4 he thought that the "picture of the riots of Lord George Gordon's mob is excellent and has poetical truth whether it be historical or not." But by September 5 he catches up to the last installment and decides to "read no more till the story is finished," to avoid exposing himself "to further anxieties."[42] There is plenty of exciting drama in the novel, as, for example, Dolly is in the air, as she "shook, and pulled and beat" Simon.[43] While many bourgeois critics were appalled by the violence and judged *Barnaby* harshly, other writers, who were on the same side in Dickens' "literary battle," were inspired by the book. For example, Edgar Allan Poe was inspired to write his applauded poem "The Raven" in 1844, based on Barnaby's memorable talking raven, Grip. Still, to put it simply, *Barnaby* was one of Dickens' worst flops, but it is important to keep these poor reviews and sales in mind when we question why Dickens went on to write so many moral and violent rebellion novels after it.

In contrast to *Barnaby*, *Tale* was serialized on a weekly basis in *All the Year Round*, a magazine that Dickens owned. *Tale* sold better than any of Dickens' other works. Still, there were some early reviewers who called *Tale* "deadly dull"; it lacked "Dickensian humour"; it "pleased nobody."[44] Surprisingly, overall, there were fewer early reviews of *Tale* than of *Barnaby*, or any of his other novels; and the two reviews of *Tale* that Collins includes are both by John Forster, a close friend of Dickens, who wrote his semi-autobiography, *The Life of Charles Dickens*.[45] Just as there are liberal and conservative parties, there are two camps on Dickens' rebellion novels. Carlyle, for example, thought that *Tale* was "wonderful!" The feeling was mutual as Dickens read Carlyle's *French Revolution* "forty times!"[46]

Madame Defarge, the notorious knitter of vengeance in *Tale*, makes only one crucial speech to explain her radical pro-violence stand towards aristocrats, "All our lives, we have seen our sister-women suffer, in themselves and in their children, poverty, nakedness, hunger, thirst, sickness, misery, oppression and neglect of all kinds?"[47] This outcry reflects several of Dickens' speeches and political opinions, so it can be taken as reflective of a radical authorial intent. There are clear parallels between Madame Defarge in *Tale* and Gashford in *Barnaby*, as both "never forgot, and never forgave," and wreak vengeance and destruction on their enemies.[48] A bit later, as the "revolutionary tribunal" is in its heat, Dickens writes with the voice of the narrator of "three hundred thousand men, summoned to rise against the tyrants of the earth."[49] Dickens is clearly showing enthusiasm for the multitude that is rising up against the corruption and depravity of the French aristocracy. "Looking at the jury and the turbulent audience, he might have thought that the usual order of things was reversed, and that the felons were trying the honest men. The lowest, crudest, and worst populace of a city, never without its quantity of low, cruel and bad, were the directing spirits of the scene."[50] While we can read into this quotation to see sympathy with the wealthy people on trial, it is more likely that Dickens had to include passages like this in order to lighten his radical message with subversive counter-messages. A book that openly supported revolutionary violence would not have been approved by the censors of the day. The most outspoken pro-revolutionary of the time was Karl Marx. He moved to London in 1849, after the 1848 revolutions. His first publication after his move was in 1852, in a New York German-language paper, *Die Revolution*, titled "*The Eighteenth Brumaire of Louis Napoleon.*" It is more a work of a historian, rather than a radical political thinker. Marx was writing revolutionary treatises like the *Grundrisse* in the decades right after his move, but the *Grundrisse* was not published until 1939. The first major revolutionary economical treatise that Marx published in English was in 1904 with another American publisher, in Chicago, Charles H. Kerr. *A Contribution to the Critique of Political Economy* was basically a critique of capitalism, which was later partially integrated into Marx's mostly highly regarded work, *Capital*. Another history book by Marx called *Writings on the U.S. Civil War* was published in 1961. I can give many other examples, but it is clear that Marx could not find a publisher in London for his pro-revolutionary, anti-capitalistic and pro-communist propaganda. If Marx was sending his manuscripts to America, one can logically conclude that he first tried sending the same works to publishers in London, where he lived. The quality of the writing style in *The Communist Manifesto*, which Marx published in 1848, before the move, shows that it is unlikely that any rejections he had from English publishers were because of any problems with his prose; therefore, English publishers had to have rejected his work because they had policies in place against publishing radical, socialist, and specifically pro-revolutionary manuscripts.

Jackson brings up the crucial term "subversive" when he writes that John Forster, Dickens' biographer, thought that Dickens' "opinions were much more 'subversive' than it was expedient to publish — that his hatred of social inequalities was, more than anything else, the reason why Dickens avoided, wherever possible, any sort of 'going into society.'"[51] Unlike Marx, who wrote direct attacks on capitalism and the aristocracy, Dickens' fictional or subversive rebellion novels were published, despite a few hurdles that he had to overcome to achieve these publications. Even Cold War critics, like Baldridge, write that the "vigor" of the revolutionary violence betrays Dickens' subversive "enthusiasm" for revolutionary actions, which is done through "thoroughly disguised and displaced forms," despite his "middle-class horror" of violent uprisings that threatened the middle or upper classes.[52] Any literary enthusiasm about violence against the bourgeoisie or the aristocrats had to be done subversively, to avoid censorship.

An example of Dickens' subversive techniques is that *Barnaby* begins with a rebellion against another rebellion. The riot begins when Hugh throws the first stone at Mr. Haredale, as he is making a speech in rebellion against the "No Popery" cries of the gathered crowd.[53] Mr. Haredale's peaceful rebellion on one side of the debate is met with a violent rebellion by the poor, who do not have the intellectual strength to engage in a political debate or in a literary battle. Dickens is siding with rebellion in general, no matter if it is for or against "Popery." There is justice and right on the side of Mr. Haredale's and the mob's arguments and rebellious actions. Speaking up and fighting against injustices is a responsibility, which Dickens shows is necessary for the progress of society. It was easy for Cold War critics to read into the passages where Hugh and other anti-papists are called "devils,"[54] "scum,"[55] who are out for "booty."[56] Critics point to Dickens' negative attitude towards rebels when they notice these phrases, ignoring the convincing pro-rebellion propaganda that accompanies these exclamations. These maddened rebels burn themselves and each other in the conflagrations of Mr. Haredale's house[57] and at the Newgate prison. The violence is a mad frenzy, but it is a frenzy that has a just cause as it is perpetrated by poor and desperate people. During the attack on the prison, Dickens explains that many in the crowd who set it aflame and burst in were family or friends of the convicts.[58] They charged in out of personal rather than religious or political motives. Only a few among the rioters are "honest zealots."[59] The fact that some of the rioters were "honest zealots" further betrays Dickens' radicalism, as he admits that even among a mad mob there are fighters who are there to right real wrongs that they have endured. A few characters openly hold socialist views and defend the rights of the lower class. Simon says that he is "not a workman, not a slave, not a victim of your father's tyrannical behavior, but a leader of a great people."[60] This, and other pro-rebellion diatribes, are more in tune with Dickens' radical political purpose than his outbursts that the rioters are "devils" and "scum." Dickens stresses the majesty and grandeur of the riots by the phrase, "great riots."[61] The Lord Mayor chirps in that there are "great people at the bottom of these riots,"[62] indicating the quantity and vigor of the rioters, rather than their status or superiority. Even if the riots themselves are devilish, evil, and pointless, Dickens repeatedly acknowledges that the people behind the riots and the riots themselves are great, or of historic significance.

Marxism and Literary Battles

"That Marx should have retired into relative seclusion to perfect his economic studies was in itself evidence that, at that time, 'only a literary battle was possible.'"[63] The full quotation on "literary battle" from Marx reads:

> III. Socialist and Communist Literature: I. *Reactionary Socialism*, (a) *Feudal Socialism*. Owning to their historical position, it became the vocation of the aristocracies of France and England to write pamphlets against modern bourgeois society. In the French revolution of July 1830, and in the English reform agitation, these aristocracies again succumbed to the hateful upstart. Thenceforth, a serious political contest was altogether out of the question. A literary battle alone remained possible.... In order to arouse sympathy, the aristocracy were obliged to lose sight, apparently, of their own interests, and to formulate their indictment against the bourgeoisie in the interest of the exploited working class alone. Thus the aristocracy took their revenge by singing lampoons on their new master, and whispering in his ears sinister prophecies of coming catastrophe.[64]

Why did King George IV meet with Walter Scott? Why were Stevenson and Dickens funded by aristocrats? Why did so many aristocrats turn to writing

Figure 21. "Charles Dickens as he appears when reading." Sketched by C.A. Barry, 1867. Illus. in: *Harper's Weekly*, Vol. 11, No. 571 (1867 December 7), p. 777 (Library of Congress Prints and Photographs Division).

rebellion novels, social novels or "pamphlets?" Marx explains that the "literary battle" initially began as a struggle for power between aristocrats and the wealthy businessmen, or the "bourgeoisie." The monarchy was not violently overthrown in England because the aristocracy gained sympathy by siding with the poor in a literary battle, against the businessmen class. The latter were guilty of creating difficult working conditions, polluting the industrial cities and other evils. The "sinister prophecies of coming catastrophe" were in part the rebellion novels that by describing past uprisings threatened the bourgeoisie with future unrest. Scott and Stevenson are not completely aligned with this particular literary battle because Scott and Stevenson's uprisings are frequently against the English aristocracy and Crown. Dickens is the author who best fits Marx's definition, as he targeted the French monarchy and English bourgeoisie in his rebellion novels, and primarily wealthy business owners in his social novels, like *Bleak House*. Still, Dickens is not merely a "tool" of the capitalists because he does occasionally ridicule them; he was frequently sided against the greater evil, or against the French aristocracy, when he had to choose between capitalism and the monarchy.

Throughout the manifesto and in other works Marx repeatedly and openly supports a "forcible overthrow" by "Communists everywhere" through "revolutionary movements against the existing social and political order of things."[65] Marx supported violent revolutions, but in reality actively participated in a literary revolution with his pen. One of the best examples of this is that before the 1848 revolutions, Marx married Jenny von Westphalen, a Prussian baroness, hardly an anti-monarchic or an anti-capitalist decision. Marx published with radical newspapers and presses in Paris, Brussels, and Cologne. There are allegations that Marx used his inheritance to fund the Brussels 1848 revolution, but these are not strongly substantiated. While he edited a radical paper, *New Rhenish Newspaper*, in Cologne, Marx was prosecuted and acquitted on charges of insulting the chief public prosecutor and inciting rebellion through tax evasion. Marx never picked up a weapon in any revolutionary cause.

Dickens and other rebellion novelists, fighters in the "literary battle," bloomed in England even though Marx did not think a violent revolution was possible on English soil. In a December 8, 1880, letter to Hyndman, Marx writes "On Violent Revolution," that in England, where he had lived for four decades by that point, "the party considers an English revolution not necessary." In contrast, in Germany, where he lived in his youth and succeeded in promoting the 1848 violent revolution, "the working class were fully aware from the beginning of their movement that you cannot get rid of a military despotism but by a Revolution."[66] While many social movements and poor laws were passed in England, a violent revolution did not erupt in the capital.

A year before the 1848 revolutions, Marx wrote in the *Communist Manifesto* that the bourgeois are "horrified" at the idea of the elimination of "private property."[67] Further still, he argued, in England, there is a "reform agitation," which cannot rise up to a "serious political contest." As a result, he concluded, "A literary battle alone remained possible," because the "aristocracy" was rallying the "people" by offering them "the proletarian alms-bag" or feudal or reactionary socialism.[68] In a climate of censorship and suppression of dissenting, anti-bourgeoisie and antiaristocratic opinions, rebellion novels were a significant tool in the subversive currents of this radical "literary battle."

Dickens' Political Activism

On at least two occasions, Dickens was personally caught in the middle of riots. He "took a prominent part in organizing a strike of the reporting staff of the *True Sun*—the first paper he worked upon—and ... he acted suc-

Figure 22. "Mr. Charles Dickens and his former American acquaintances 'not at home.'" Drawn by C. G. Bush, 1867. Illus. in: *Harper's Weekly*, Vol. 11, No. 573 (1867 December 21), p. 812 (Library of Congress Prints and Photographs Division).

cessfully as the spokesman for the strikers."[69] Decades later, during Dickens' visit to Ireland, as he was watching a play at the theater, he was interrupted by the breaking of glass, force and "violence" of the Dublin crowd. Dickens began writing *Tale* shortly after this incident, so it is clear that it inspired him to rejoin the rebellious literary battle.[70] Did Dickens join in and throw a few stones, siding with the crowd? Since it was illegal to participate in rioting, Dickens certainly did not confess to an active role in the event. Dickens' decision to go to Ireland during the height of the crowd riots shows a willingness to insert himself into scenes of mass uprisings. Dickens was also likely to have picked up radical views during his trips to Paris in 1847, through America, and in Scotland 1858–1859, all before he wrote *Tale*. Across his life, Dickens showed an interest in both peaceful and violent anti-establishment uprisings.

The friends and enemies who knew of Dickens' radical political agenda asked why he did not decide to run for Parliament, unlike Disraeli. When asked by yet another politician, late in life, about why he decided not to run for Congress, Dickens shot back, "The House of Commons and Parliament altogether is become just the dreariest failure and nuisance that ever bothered this much-bothered world."[71] Dickens felt that "any seat in the House can be bought for any candidate, even for an uneducated and untalented lout picked up off the street," as he wrote in various *Household Words* pieces.[72] Dickens was keenly aware that a political battle could not be won and that only his literary battle was likely to affect the minds and hearts of the populace with a sympathy for the poor and a desire for more rights for the disenfranchised.

While Dickens lacked faith in the ability of politicians to single-handedly make positive changes in peoples' lives, he did his best to actively campaign for reforms as a private citizen. Dickens was a political campaigner and a reform activist across his journalistic, parliamentary reporter and literary career. Goldberg wrote that Dickens "made all-out attacks on workhouses, debtor's prisons, the Poor Law, and the corrupt or delinquent officials who administered and supported them."[73] Monroe Engel wrote that Dickens campaigned on issues of: "representative government; class structure and English society; the poor, the Poor Laws, charity and self-sufficiency; money and speculation; industry and progress."[74] Engel wrote that Dickens was pushed towards being a revolutionary radical by developments like the cholera epidemic in 1854, and the "riots in Hyde Park against the Sunday Bill, which restricted the amusements of the populace on the Sabbath" in 1855 — both detailed in letters to Dickens from his friend Lady Burdett-Coutts, and both of which aggravated the class struggle in England.[75]

Carlyle, Bentham and other reformers inspired Dickens in his political and literary battles, in his "passionate revolt against the whole industrial order."[76] Many characters in Dickens' works echo Carlylean heroes, such as "young Evremonde in *A Tale of Two Cities* ... who repudiates aristocratic privilege in favor of work."[77] Goldberg states that Dickens read Jeremy Bentham's *Canada. Emancipate Your Colonies! Canada*, along with other arguments like it, began the anticolonial struggle as early as the eighteenth century. In this speech, Bentham addressed France's leadership in 1790. He had been awarded "the honorary distinction of Citizenship" a year earlier, after the French Revolution. Instead of congratulating France on a victory, Bentham argues that now the country has to show that the revolution was just by freeing Canada, one of France's colonies.[78] Bentham proclaims that to fail to do so would be a form of "despotism" and "tyranny," and would not reflect the pillars of the revolution, "fraternity ... liberty and equality."[79] Dickens was likely to have been affected by this argument, which asked France to go even further and to raise another revolt against remaining backwards practices even after the end of the French Revolution.

Another major inspiration for Dickens' rebellion writings was Chartism, which began with "The People's Charter," signed by twelve supporters on June 7, 1837. This charter, the original declaration of demands, asked for the vote, legislative representation, a decline in government corruption, and payment for government service for the poor. As Goldberg demonstrates, Dickens read Thomas Carlyle's *Chartism*, which was published in 1842, when the movement grew to a "million and half" supporters[80] and split into two sects, the violent "torch-meetings, Birmingham riots, Swing conflagration,"[81] and the nonviolent reformists. Carlyle does not focus on the right to vote or on parliamentary reforms. He only briefly touches on "Parliamentary Radicalism" and instead debates the "Condition-of-England Question," the "New Poor-Law," and "Laissez-Faire." The connection between *Chartism* and Dickens is strengthened by the fact that it includes an advertisement of Dickens' "Cheap Edition" of works on its last page. Clearly Dickens not only read but sponsored this Chartist publication by paying Carlyle for the advertisement. Many critics such as Mark Willis in his 2006 essay in the *Dickens Quarterly*, have noticed Dickens' sympathy to Chartism.

One of the objections that several conservatives raise against this idea that Dickens was a pro-revolutionary radical is that he had a Hobbesian view of human nature. Myron Magnet argues that Dickens believed that humanity needs to be restrained and controlled by society or it might erupt in rebellion and violence "against everything." In *Leviathan: Or the Matter, Forme & Power of a Commonwealth, Ecclesiasticall and Civill*, Thomas Hobbes wrote that with the goal of "atteyning of peace, and conservation of themselves thereby," men formed together to form a "Commonwealth," and "Artificial Chains, called Civill Lawes."[82] The Hobbesian view of human nature is typically summarized as being pessimistic, and expresses a belief that the world would erupt in violence and crime if there were no civil laws to control people's behavior. Dickens frequently argued on the injustice of English "Civil Laws," as shown by his continued campaigns for law reforms. Thus, it is farfetched to call Dickens a conservative, and the radical perspective of him as somebody who deplored unjust civil laws is more accurate given Dickens' biography and expressed beliefs. Dickens was not an anarchist, and he was not an anti–Hobbesian; Dickens believed in just civil laws, and argued against unjust civil laws.

Moore wrote: "In the 1850s, he became increasingly critical of *any* institution responsible for spreading misery anywhere; whether it was the appalling sanitary conditions of London or the rack-renting of the East Indian peasantry."[83] Amidst the Crimean War, the Indian Mutiny and the potato famine and mass emigration, Dickens published various radical and rebellious articles and books, including his novels, and his journal, *Household Words*. Not only Dickens' own works were radical, but many of the other writers published in *Household Words* were radicals. In 1854, it published Henry Morley's "A Home Question," which protested against government incompetence in handling the exploding cholera epidemic, which resulted in the loss of over 10,000 lives. In Moore's words:

> Morley ... took the radical and — as many saw it — irresponsible step of calling on the working class to rise up.... "We shall fare no better ... unless we take pains to help ourselves" ... Morley continues to list a new six-point "people's charter" for reform, for which he suggests the workers should agitate. By this point Dickens was keen to at least be seen to incite revolt.... Several pieces such as his article "To Working Men" called upon the disenfranchised masses to make their voices heard and call for basic sanitary reforms, suggesting to the workforce that it was their obligation and their right to do so.[84]

Dickens was willing to publish potentially seditious outcries against injustice in the publication that he edited, even in the first years of his editorship. Dickens was publishing pieces on behalf not only of the poor but also of colonized people. For example:

> When it became apparent — largely through the reports of his friend, the famous Crimean War reporter William Howard Russell — that the ghastly actions of the sepoys were matched by equally repugnant behaviour on the part of the British, Dickens's outbursts ceased abruptly.... In *A Tale of Two Cities* Dickens revised his attitude towards the sepoy soldiers and the rebels who joined them, by sympathetically aligning them with both the French third estate of 1789, and the English working classes.[85]

About a year later, Dickens repeated these concerns for the working people in a letter to Angela Burdett Coutts, "in which he charts his annoyance at the Government and its failure to take responsibility for the people." Dick-

Figure 23. "The London of Charles Dickens." Photograph by C. H. Graves, Philadelphia, 1900 (Universal Photo Art Stereograph Cards Collection: Library of Congress Prints and Photographs Division).

ens insists that the poor need "cheap pure water," and "wholesome air." Despite these dire needs, Dickens concludes, "that a worthless Government ... will never do these things for them or pay the least sincere attention to them, until they are made election questions and the working-people unite to express their determination to have them, or to keep out of Parliament by every means in their power, every man who turns his back upon these first necessities." He further states that the people should be led to understand that cholera is a "preventable disease," because upon understanding this, "you will see such a shake in this country as was never seen on Earth since Samson pulled the Temple down upon his head."[86] The symbolic image of Samson reappears in *Tale*, "to illustrate the strength of popular discontent and the devastation that the working classes could cause if basic social reforms continued to be neglected."[87]

One of Dickens' most politically charged and the most radical Condition of England novels was *Little Dorrit* (1855–57), originally titled *Nobody's Fault*. It was the culmination of Dickens' growing suspicion that the governing class was completely inert and unwilling to do anything or "to take responsibility for anything at all."[88] Moore explains that the original monthly installments that appeared in *Household Words* were much more politically charged than the book version of the novel because they were juxtaposed against "scathing and openly critical articles such as 'Nobody, Somebody and Everybody.'"[89] In that article Dickens lists the various crimes and negligence he feels the British government has committed and instead of naming the names of the administrators responsible, he blames "Nobody" and "Everybody." The use of indefinite pronouns is a form of subversion that avoids making seditious or libelous statements against specific officials, and thereby avoids potential censure. The simple radical statement made by *Little Dorrit* is that England's impoverished condition is "Everybody's" fault, and especially the slothful government that repeatedly fails to fix the blatant social ills.

Dickens' response to the Indian Mutiny was particularly emotionally charged because his son Walter, at age 16 joined the British ranks in India in 1857, right before the mutiny broke out, and Dickens never saw his son again. Walter fought with the 42nd Highlanders during the mutiny. As Walter was dying, Dickens' son Frank arrived in India and joined the Bengal Mounted Police. Dickens might have formulated an unusually negative denouncement of the "revolt" and called "for its violent suppression,"[90] when he temporarily suspected that his son Walter might have been one of the hundreds of victims of the Cawnpore massacre of surrendering British East India Company affiliates and their families. When the details of the dual situation in India became clear, "The violent upheaval thousands of miles away provided Dickens with a target onto which he would legitimately discharge his fury, without any fear of being labeled either a reactionary or a subversive — it was much easier to hit out at the sepoy rebels than the British government."[91]

Moore focuses much of his criticism on a short story by Dickens that is not a common topic of Dickensonian critical debate, "The Perils of Certain English Prisoners (1857)." "The Perils" is a story of a piratic attack on white settlers, and their eventual rescue. In contrast with *Barnaby* and *Tale*, this is not a rebellious work, but one that defends the "Empire" and its dominion. Dickens' view on Empire and rebellion remained steadily pro-rebellious and radical between 1840, when he wrote *Barnaby*, and 1859, when he finished *Tale*, with this exception. This sudden change of attitude can be explained by the fact that his son Walter left for military service in the empire's Indian colony in 1857, right before Dickens sat down to write "The Perils." Patrick Brantlinger was among the earliest critics at the end of the Cold War to see the revolutionary nature of *Tale* and to see the connection between it and Dickens' perception of the Indian Mutiny in "The Perils of Certain English Prisoners." Brantlinger writes about Dickens in *Rule of Darkness*, "'His Carlylean view of the Revolution as irrational, frenzied, and bloodthirsty is close to this view of the Mutiny. The coincidence of names between Captain Carton and Sidney Carton and some of the metaphors in the novel also suggest India.'"[92] Dickens based some of his research in *Tale* on Charles Ball's 1858 *History of the Indian Mutiny*, as seen in the similarity between Miss Pross' conduct and Miss Wheeler, depicted in both the history and in "The Perils."[93] In *Tale*, "The Parisian mob does not simply represent the sepoys in India, but also the working class in Britain.... The Chartist activity of the 1840s was displaced onto a depiction of the Gordon riots of 1780."[94] Dickens shows outrage in *Tale* that he did not display in some of his other works about rebellion. "A Tale of Two Cities shows that those who have been treated as animals (whether they be French peasants or Indian soldiers) by the class that should have been responsible for them can only be expected to respond as animals."[95]

Dickens had a radical rebellious purpose that stood on the shoulders of many of his radical predecessors and contemporaries. He had a strong radical support system in publishers who expected social rebellion, rather than punishing or censoring it.

11

Dickens' Structural Features

Genre Categorization, Mixture and Influences

There are epic, sensational, mystery, gothic and historical generic residues in Dickens' rebellion novels. The ingredients of Dickens' rebellion novel formula can be best understood by first isolating influences and elements from previous popular genres. Despite the noticeable differences, Dickens borrowed the core of Scott's technique, as did most other writers who wrote historical rebellion novels after Scott.

A rebellion novel has to include some epic or mythic details in order to heighten the significance of the antigovernmental violence that is portrayed. Without epic scope, the action would fall apart as pointless or melodramatic. Epic poetry, similarly to tragedy, is an "imitation of serious subjects in a grand kind of verse," and it differs from tragedy because it is written in narrative form, and takes more "time."[1] Dickens created "crowd fiction," which merged individual quests with panoramic historic events.[2] Dickens uses a simile to compare "settles" in the Maypole to the "twin dragons of some fairy tale," which "guarded the entrance to the mansion."[3] Simple descriptions of country life before the riots are made epic with many similar linguistic devices. And the momentous horrors of the escalating events during the riots are also of epic proportions. Iain Crawford wrote an essay studying Dickens' use of "classical myth" and epic elements in *Barnaby*. Crawford writes that the rebel, Hugh, is a "Dionysian character," as he is referred to as a "satyr," he drinks heavily, and he has an insatiable lust for Dolly Varden.[4] The Gordon Riots are also a reenactment of, or follow the "mythological patterning" of, the Prometheus myth, in which Prometheus rebels against Zeus and gives fire to humans. Among other parallels between the myth and the narrative of the riots, Crawford explains that "the element of fire" is "the central agent and symbol of their revolt."[5] Scott, Dickens and Stevenson use classical illusions or myths and epic structures to heighten the significance of the rebellious events they portray. *Barnaby* and *Tale* are epic because they depict a grand symbolic and mythic struggle of right against might or against the powerful aristocracy and capitalists. In *Barnaby,* the epic struggle is the Gordon Riots, and in *Tale* the epic struggle is the French Revolution. Hundreds or thousands of rioters flood the streets of these novels, and the scope of the violence and social unrest is epic in proportions.

Because *Barnaby* bankrupted one journal and *Tale* made Dickens rich, we should consider if one of these books is more "sensational" than the other. There is a parallel between Scott's sensational elements and inspirations for his rebellion novels, and the same inspirations that sparked Dickens. As George Augustus Sala wrote in his essay "On the 'Sensational' in Literature and Art" in the *Belgravia* in 1868, "Mr. Charles Dickens is perhaps the most thoroughly, and has been from the very outset of his career the most persistently, 'sensational' writer of the age." Sala specifies, "*Barnaby Rudge* begins with the sensation of an undiscovered murder, and ends with the sensation of a triple hanging and a duel *a' mort.*"[6] The mystery and the rebellion in *Barnaby* are connected by the fact that they are both sensational and exciting in their basic plot. The sensational spectacle of rebellions is the primary reason rebellion novels sold well in the 19th century. "Dickens had an eye to popular success, and was calculating on fashion" when he slowly strategized on how he would write *Barnaby*, both by leaning on the "quaint crutches of the post–Scott historical romance,"[7] and by including sensational elements in the first half of the book. Both *Tale* and *Barnaby* rely on sensational suspense; the latter novel was simply crafted with greater skill and achieved the trick in which the first novel failed. *Tale* was successfully sensational because it focuses on a far more outrageously sensational event, the French Revolution. This riskier choice of showing events from one of the most shocking and terrifying moments in history, for both the French and the English aristocracies, grabbed the attention of his audience better than the comparatively minor events of the Gordon Riots.

Some have speculated that Dickens was not as proficient in the mystery genre as Arthur Conan Doyle or the other sleuth detective story writers. In an 1842 review, Edgar Allan Poe points out the "mistake" that the elder Rudge's wife was not supposed to seize Rudge, based on the logic of the story, but was supposed to seize her by the hand at a crucial point in the murder plot. Poe concludes that Dickens did not have the "metaphysical art" necessary for executing well-crafted mysteries. The mystery aspect is further diminished by being mixed with the historical genre or with the rebellion theme. Collins wrote: "In the multitudinous outrage and horror of the Rebellion, the one atrocity is utterly whelmed and extinguished."[8] If Dickens intended for the murder mystery to take center stage in the book, he would have colored it with epic and dramatic imagery and actions. Instead, Dickens clearly, purposefully downplays the mystery, stressing and highlighting the rebellion plot. Dickens' attempt at splitting the plot in two, one with the mystery and the second half with the rebellion, is an example of one of his innovations in the rebellion genre. Neither Scott nor the rebellion novelists that published between Scott and Dickens made similar splits in plot and stylistics.

The gothic elements have been mentioned by several critics and should be explored here for us to have a fuller view of the novel. The gothic works mix horror and romance; Poe, and especially his poem "The Raven," is one of the leading representatives of the Victorian gothic. In contrast to Poe, and other well-known pure gothic writers, Dickens sprinkles gothic images, metaphors and details into his descriptions and dialogues. Adding words like "a night of horror"[9] heightens the suspense and drama of a scene. Suspense is also improved when instead of just telling Barnaby to stay in, Barnaby's mother warns him that, "There are ghosts and dreams abroad."[10] "Phantoms,"[11] "a phantom without shape, or form, or visible presence,"[12] "fiends,"[13] a "ghost!"[14] and a "ghostly rider"[15] describe the maddened rioters more graphically and intensely than calling them "evil" or "malevolent." Scott also utilizes elements of horror, mysticism and romance to make his rebellions more terrifying. Because direct support of rebellious actions with realistic depictions would have been directly threatening to the aristocracy and the bourgeoisie, rebellion novelists chose to use the gothic. The rebellion genre must have some gothic elements to avoid being a simplistic description of a brutal massacre of enormous quantities of innocent people. If the riots are not horrifying, they are only exciting, bloodthirsty adventure stories about mass murder.

The most important genre influence for this study is the overruling presence of the historical novel genre as the foundation genre that Dickens used to construct both *Barnaby* and *Tale*. Nicholas Rance best summarizes the mimicry that Dickens performed of Scott when he writes:

> In his first historical novel, *Barnaby Rudge*, Dickens eschewed the distant past and dealt instead with the era of the Gordon Riots of 1780, vital prehistory to him as 1745 was to Scott. The accidental involvement of the passive Barnaby in the Riots is like Waverley's in the Jacobite rebellion, and Dickens was both conscious of Scott's example and anxious to compete.[16]

The important part of this quotation is the fact that in a book called *The Historical Novel and Popular Politics in Nineteenth-Century England*, Rance recognizes that Dickens and Scott contributed equally to popular politics by depicting accurate histories of the near past or events that still had political significance in their own time.

While Dickens and Scott never met, there was a close indirect relationship between the two men. Three years after Scott's death and at the peak of his literary fame, in 1835 Dickens' journalistic employer, *Morning Chronicle*, launched the *Evening Chronicle* and hired for its editor George Hogarth, an Edinburgh lawyer and editor who previously helped the Tory Party in a political campaign. Upon taking the editorship, he commissioned Dickens' contributions. Hogarth was Dickens' first and most influential patron, as the articles Dickens published in the *Evening Chronicle* later became his first major literary success, *Sketches by Boz*. Hogarth "was related to Scott's publishers, the Ballantynes ... Hogarth had remained Scott's legal adviser and friend."[17] Ballantyne had succeeded in selling enormous quantities of Scott's books, but had been bankrupted due to the books' low prices. This bankruptcy had plagued Scott in his last years, as he worked to settle these debts and finally succeeded, despite litigation with the publisher over how the bankruptcy should be settled. Thus, the fact that he had remained friends with one of the Ballantynes and trusted Hogarth enough to take legal advice from him, despite being a judge himself, shows the strength of this connection. From the various references that Dickens makes to Scott in his letters and other works, it is clear that "Dickens revered Scott.... He owed much to Scott, for it was the literary influence of Scott that lay behind *Barnaby Rudge*, the novel that first emancipated Dickens from the loose-knit, wandering narratives he had inherited from his earlier gods, Fielding and Smollett."[18] Perhaps the best testament to the fact that Dickens loved Scott was that he married Hogarth's daughter, Catherine, twenty at the time, within a year of his first meeting with Hogarth.

In the year between Dickens' first meeting with Hogarth and the marriage, Dickens went from being a near-unknown journalist to a literary sensation. This progression was not accidental. Besides publishing Dickens himself, Hogarth put him in touch with the literary community, who were also Scott's literary associates, and who had the power to make literary bestsellers. For example, Dickens met Harrison Ainsworth through Hogarth, and Ainsworth in turn introduced him to Cruikshank, who illustrated *Sketches by Boz*. As you might recall from earlier in this book, Ainsworth's literary career was launched when Scott wrote a few positive reviews of his first historical novel, and Ainsworth then paid Scott a large sum of money for the short story "Margaret's Mirror." Dickens could not have been any luckier in literary terms than to be introduced into this pool of brilliant and best-selling novelists, illustrators, and more importantly editors and publishers.

Dickens had not moved into editing in his many years as a journalist, but suddenly he had a best-selling novel, and was offered an editorship of a new magazine, *Bentley's Miscellany*, which also succeeded. This spurt in success clearly resulted from his presence in this rich circle. Dickens solicited submissions from outstanding authors, including George Hogarth himself, who contributed "The Poisoners of Seventeenth Century" to Volume II of the magazine. "Poisoners" is a historical essay that includes a lengthy quote from Sir Walter Scott's *Kenilworth*, a historical novel about the courtship of Queen Elizabeth I in 1575 by a power-hungry, married earl (not exactly a rebellion novel). Hogarth might have honored Scott's *Kenilworth* in this essay because it started the three-volume-novel publishing trend, which, in turn, mutated into the periodical publishing scheme that Hogarth, Dickens and Ainsworth profited from as editors and writers. It's interesting to note that when Dickens quit this editorship at *Miscellany* in 1839, Ainsworth took over. As part of his editorship, Dickens published his own *Sketches by Boz*, and his second novel, *Oliver Twist*. This group of writers and editors went to great length to promote each other's literary careers, and they almost inherited the rebellion genre.

Was there a political reason Ainsworth and Hogarth might have encouraged Dickens to write a rebellion novel in 1836? Was there a Tory or a fictional radical pro-rebellion movement that Dickens joined when he married into this clique? Did they have a conversation about social rebellion, the Jacobites, and the French Revolution at the dinner table? Regardless of how contact with these radical writers, and Dickens' attraction to Scott's literary success, affected Dickens, in 1836 he made plans for writing a novel about the Gordon Riots, *Barnaby Rudge*, and spent the next five years intricately developing this work, unlike his other swiftly penned compositions. Is it more likely that Dickens simply mimicked the rebellion generic elements because of financial and literary ambitious concerns, "daringly looking to rival the great master Scott himself?"[19] Wilson writes that "in the final version there is only a skeleton of Scott's world surviving," such as the rioters storming Newgate Gaol, which is similar to the "outline" of the "taking of the Edinburgh Tolbooth in *The Heart of Mid-Lothian*."[20] The key word here is "outline"—generic formula for the rebellion novel that is carried down between Scott, Ainsworth and Dickens.

A major shift occurred in historical studies that changed the historical dimensions of Dickens' novels, as compared with Scott's. Carlyle pushed the nature of historical narratives beyond anything that Scott could have imagined a few decades earlier. Dickens mimics Scott's historical novel techniques, but also mimics the structure and details from Carlyle's historical depictions in *The French Revolution*. In the preface to the first edition of *Tale*, Dickens adds in the last line, "No one can hope to add anything to the philosophy of Mr. Carlyle's wonderful book."[21] This direct acknowledgment has led to dozens of studies on the parallels between Carlyle and Dickens. As Vanden Bossche points out in a short column, there are numerous striking similarities between Carlyle's *The French Revolution* and Dickens' *Tale*. For example, both end with a prophecy. Carlyle writes, "'All Dwellings of men destroyed; the every mountains peeled and riven, the valleys black and dead: it is in empty World! Woe to them that shall be born then!—A King, a Queen (ah me!) were hurled in; did rustle once; flew aloft, crackling, like paper-scroll...' This Prophecy, we say, has it not been fulfilled, it is not fulfilling?"[22] Similarly, Dickens concludes with a prophecy, also in quotation marks, that Sydney Carton would have said if he had given an "utterance" to his "thoughts," "'I see... The Vengeance, the Juryman, the Judge, long ranks of the new oppressors who have risen on the destruction of the old, perishing by this retributive instrument.'"[23] Dickens had *The French Revolution* and *Waverley* on his shelf as he wrote, and he consulted them frequently as he was making decisions about the different structural, theoretical and linguistic components of his rebellion novels. Overall, there is plentiful evidence that Dickens was an admirer of the Scottish historian Thomas Carlyle and his famous *The French Revolution: A History*, which was published in 1837, a year after Dickens began working on *Barnaby*. *The French Revolution* influenced both of Dickens' two historical rebellion novels. Dickens did not earn a doctorate to become a great novelist; instead, he learned about genre from the authors whom he read and communicated with. He learned about history from Carlyle and about the historical novels from Scott, and about the proper way of portraying rebellions from both of these established authors.

To summarize, in *Barnaby*, the rebellion is the primary dramatic action in the book. The mystery builds suspense and charges the first half of the book. The epic elements are present in the minor details throughout. Gothic elements add artistic horror to the scenes of brutal violence. Finally, details from history make the actions believable and make readers feel as if they enter the battlefields by Dickens' side.

Dickens' Rebellion Novel Formula

Great literature is based on great formulas just as great mathematics or great statistical analysis is based on formulas. Dickens clearly mimicked Scott, Carlyle, Gaskell and Disraeli, among others, in his rebellion novels. What are the details of Dickens' rebellion novel formula? Here is a summary formula of the structure of Dickens' rebellion novels:

Dickens' Structural Formula = C Many Characters + P 2 Main Plots + T 2 Main Time Periods + L Many Locations/ Places

Dickens' structural elements can be summarized by using Aristotelian unities of time, place and plot, adding in characters as a fourth dimension.

Imitations of Scott's Rebellion Formula

Dickens' rebellion formula differs from Scott's, as he consciously altered it to avoid being charged with mimicry. Dickens keeps many of the elements that Scott inserted into his rebellion novel structural formula. Scott's formula is:

> S (Sales) + P (Scottish Nationalist Propaganda) = J (Violent Jacobite Uprising) + T (Travel) + L (Love) + S (Success of Protagonist)

Editing Scott's formula to conform with Dickens' structural elements leaves the following new Dickens structural formula:

> S (Sales) + P (Radical English Propaganda) = R (Rebellion or Revolution) + T (Travel) + L (Love) + S (Success of Protagonist)

Elements of plot, time, location and characters are better descriptions of Dickens' formula because the love and travel themes fade in comparison to the grandeur of the rebellions themselves and the enormous list of characters and intervening plots in Dickens. It is difficult for an average reader to see a similarity between Dickens' and Scott's formulas because Dickens has split the plots, times and other elements in two, while Scott observes at least some unity of time, if not of place. Basically, Dickens took the mystery, gothic, rebellion and other genres, cut out parts from all of them, and created a brand new formula for a more complex and telling rebellion novel. Dickens was affected by spurts of realism, which was leading writers away from unified structures to more spread-out tales. Still, the primary foundation for imitation behind Dickens' formula is Scott, and *Tale* and *Barnaby* are clearly rebellion novels, as opposed to mysteries or gothic horrors.

Dickens follows many of the linguistic and structural rules that Scott set, such as placing the action sixty years in the past, using similar actions as in Scott's *The Heart of Mid-Lothian* (1818), making Barnaby similar to Madge Wildfire, the madwoman in *Mid-Lothian*, and using the same technique of jumping between domestic and national matters. *A Tale of Two Cities* and *Barnaby Rudge* were the "only two historical novels that Dickens wrote, despite the prestige and popularity of the genre."[24] From what Dickens wrote and what critics have said about his motivations for writing historical novels, it is clear that he wanted to "emulate the success and authority of Sir Walter Scott," after "avidly reading" Scott's novels and Lockhart's 1837 *Memoirs of the Life of Sir Walter Scott*.[25] Dickens read his friend Thomas Carlyle's essay "On Sir Walter Scott," written in 1838. Dickens' passion for Scott was so great that he visited Scotland as he was writing *Barnaby* and actively campaigned to erect a monument in Scott's honor in Edinburgh. Dickens' Scottish wife must have supported this noble campaign. In Chapter 17, "Philadelphia, and Its

Solitary Prison," of the *American Notes*, Dickens says that an imprisoned loom spinner calls a painting he made of a "female" "over the door," "'The Lady of the Lake,'"[26] a reference to Walter Scott's 1810 poem. Patricia Ingham, the editor of the *Notes*, refers in a note to a speech that Dickens made during his American visit, in Hartford, Connecticut, on February 7, 1842, in which he said that "if there had existed any law in this respect [copyrights], Scott might not have sunk beneath the mighty pressure on his brain, but might have lived to add new creatures of his fancy to the crowds which swarm about you on your summer walks."[27] The above quotations are examples of how Dickens felt he was aligned with Scott in financial, political and literary goals. Dickens deliberately imitated Scott for political and financial reasons.

Dickens' Structural Elements

Poe complained that *Barnaby* fails in "pure narration," in other words that it fails to follow the three classical Aristotelian unities of time, place, and action because it is spread out over two decades, spreads into the countryside around London, and includes two main actions: the murder mystery and the Gordon Riots. Aristotle was one of the first literary theorists, after Plato, and he was the first to talk about the formula under which different types or genres of literature should be constructed.[28] The unities are discussed in Aristotle's *Poetics*, in chapters 4–13. For Aristotle, the unity of plot means one main "action, a complete whole, with its several incidents so closely connected that the transposal or withdrawal of any of them will disjoin and dislocate the whole. For that which makes no perceptible difference by its presence or absence is no real part of the whole."[29] Unity of time means that a story should stay "within a single circuit of the sun."[30] Poe explains that Dickens' flaws in unity exist because Dickens followed a "novel path," and used a complex "style of narration," which missed the "ordinary sequence" of events, and tried to adapt two different genres in one book (mystery and historical); all of these innovations meant that the task of combining all these techniques was too great and left the obvious mistakes in basic plot and character construction.[31]

In an age when thousands of novels were published monthly and millions of copies were sold to the masses, it became essential to fluctuate formulaic rules to avoid creating a replica of an earlier novel. The rebellion novel was new when Scott wrote his works, but by *Barnaby*, in 1841, it had already been exercised, not only by Scott (six times), but also by Carlyle, Ainsworth, Barrow, Bray and others. If Dickens placed these volumes on his desk, he would have felt compelled to break away from the repetitive formula that these works utilized, but would also feel drawn to imitating a formula that worked for many great writers. Dickens decided, consciously or unconsciously, to break most of the Aristotelian rules, to stand out as unique in the eyes of critics.

Plot

When we consider the novelty of the argument that Charles Dickens mimicked the elements of Sir Walter Scott's rebellion novels, we are fighting against a tide of critics who have put Dickens on a pedestal of originality that is free from mimicry. Humphry House first explains that parallels have frequently been made between Dickens and industrial novels, such as Disraeli's *Sybil*, but he vehemently objects to these claims, writing, "But there was never any question of a conscious and deliberate imitation of her [Gaskell], or of Carlyle, or of anybody else."[32] The truth is that in both *Barnaby* and then in *Tale*, Dickens did consciously and deliberately imitate the generic formulas of not only Scott but also his close friend Carlyle's (Scottish) 1831 novella, *Cruthers and Jonson; Or the Outskirts of Life: A True Story* about the 1745 Scottish Jacobite rising, which, in itself, is a mimicry of Sir Walter Scott's *Waverley* (1814) about the same topic. In *Cruthers and Jonson*, Jonson joins the 1745 rising out of boredom and despite wavering or being dispassionate at first,

	Barnaby	*Two Cities*	*Waverley*	*Cruthers*
Plot:	2 Plots	2 Plots	1 Plot	1 Plot
1st Half	Murder mystery	Unlawful imprisonment & English corruption	Travel to periphery & preparations for rebellion	Biographical explanation for Jonson's decision to rebel
2nd Half	Rebellious violence	Revolutionary violence & trials	Rebellion, trial, acquittal, marriage in periphery	Rebellion, trial, acquittal, exile, marriage, return
Rebellion	Gordon Riots	French Revolution	1745 Jacobite Rising	1745 Jacobite Rising
Temporary Defeat	Murderer goes free	Darnay imprisoned	Rebellion fails	Rebellion fails
Final Victory	After the rebellion, Barnaby freed	Darnay freed	Waverley is not convicted & marries	Jonson returns wealthy & married

Figure 24. Comparative Plots of Dickens', Scott's and Carlyle's Rebellion Stories

soon is "mad" and dashes "against the enemy" in a "frenzy."[33] As in *Waverley*, the hero is captured, imprisoned and nearly executed but is then set at liberty. Let's look at a comparison table between the plots of *Barnaby*, *A Tale of Two Cities*, *Waverley* and *Cruthers*.

There are "two plots"[34] in both of Dickens' rebellion novels. In *Barnaby*, the plots are a mystery and a rebellion. In *Tale*, there is the mystery (who is "Recalled to life?"), and the revolution in the second half. In both novels, an individual man is imprisoned and in trouble with the law in the first plot. A giant mob that breaks into anarchic violence represents the second half or the second plot. This split is in contrast to the single-plot formulas that Scott and Carlyle employed, as shown above.

In theory, splitting the plot in two should have created a confusing and disjointed story, but Dickens makes up for this by inserting startling, shocking, violent and otherwise attention-grabbing incidents in these works. Most critics notice that *Tale* is "the most compact and plot-driven of" Dickens' novels, but that it also "lacks the expansive cast of Dickensian characters whose personalities are expressed in imaginative invented idiolects."[35] The plot in the second half of *Barnaby Rudge* depicts the Gordon Riots and is just as compact and invigorating as the pace of *Tale*. The murder mystery in the first half of *Barnaby* drags on, and does not include many exciting or unusual scenes. On the other hand, the riots are constantly suspenseful and dramatic. For example, there is an overabundance of exclamation points on almost every page in the second half of the book. The rebellion theme and plots are simply more exciting and allow for more dramatic tension than many other genres, including murder mysteries. There is a debate today about portraying too much violence on TV, but it cannot be denied that reading about thousands of executions, assassinations and murders in the French Revolution or in the Gordon Riots is more exciting and interesting than reading about a single "murderer," who commits a single bloody crime two decades before the riots in *Barnaby*. Thus, Dickens is working with both a criminal mystery and a rebellion plot in *Barnaby* and in *Tale*, but manages to display to his readers that the revolutionary and rebellious violence, while horrifying, is a more exciting read than twisted murder mysteries or criminal cases.

Time

To see a pattern in the timing of these novels, here is a comparison of the periods of action in *Barnaby*, *A Tale of Two Cities*, *Waverley* and *Cruthers*.

The arrows represent the peaks of an author's lifetime, or the peak of the rebellion depicted in a given novel's plot.

Unlike plot, Dickens stuck with the timing rules that Scott and Carlyle

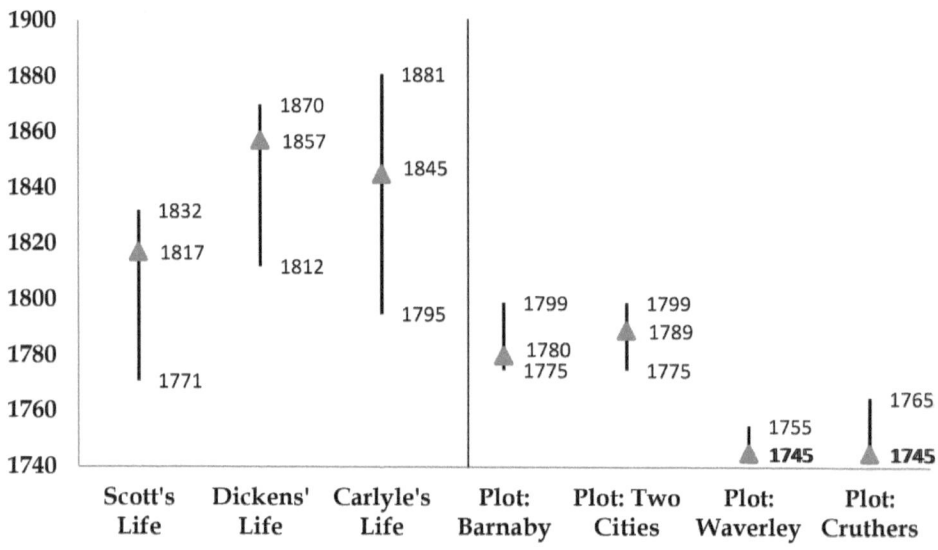

Figure 25. Comparative Times of Dickens', Scott's and Carlyle's Rebellion Stories and Lifetimes

set. The novels begin at least sixty years before the period when they were written, and there is a break of years or decades between the first and the last actions in the book. If one looks only at Dickens' two rebellion novels, one notices the fact that both *Tale* and *Barnaby* begin in 1775 and span several decades until the end of the 18th century. A few critics even go so far as to say that the "pivotal events of the Gordon Riots foreshadow those of *A Tale*."[36] It is not too farfetched to state that the events in one of Dickens' first novels "foreshadow" what would occur in one of his last novels. Dickens overindulged in foreshadowing in *Barnaby*. Here foreshadowing is occasionally as precise as a prediction by a man in a crowd: "To-night at eight o'clock.... The magistrate commits him to Newgate."[37] The narrator also foreshadows in the third person by saying that the rioters would "burn down the jail" later that night.[38] The narrator also writes that the rioters were "cruelly mistaken" in their expectations of what would happen later, at the end of the riots.[39] The main characters, such as the locksmith, use profuse foreshadowing that sounds more like a threat: "You'll want some coffins before long."[40] If *Barnaby* marked the "end of Dickens's apprenticeship,"[41] then foreshadowing is a technique that Dickens is clearly working to perfect. Foreshadowing a revolution with a rebellion is an interesting use of this tool. One can even go so far as to say that depicting the Gordon Riots was practice or preparatory research for depicting the French Revolution. Lastly, placing both works in the same period meant that Dickens already did a lot of the primary historical research on the manners, linguistics, customs, and political events in Europe at the end of the 18th century, before he took up the giant task of portraying the scope of the French Revolution.

It is still more likely that the timing of events in *Barnaby* and *Tale* is due to the fact that Dickens followed Scott's example of placing the events of his historical novels "sixty years"[42] into the past, as Scott tried to do with *Waverley; or 'T is Sixty Years Since*. There was a slight mix-up with Scott's calculations, and he ended up placing the novel more than sixty years since. *Waverley* is about the 1745 Jacobite uprising. Scott published it in 1814, which is sixty-nine years since 1745. Scott explains in the introduction that he started working on *Waverley* in 1805,[43] which would have summed up to sixty years, but he did not correct the date to match the actual date of publication. The year 1776 was sixty years before 1836, when Dickens started writing *Barnaby*. The French Revolution lasted from 1789 to 1799. The Gordon Riots took place in 1780. Despite slight differences in the time when the two uprisings took place, both novels start in exactly 1775. One way to explain the attraction to the number sixty is that sixty years is a good span of time to wait before writing about a rebellion because in sixty years all of the primary actors on both sides are usually dead and cannot object to the publication. Simultaneously, if only sixty years have passed, then the language, manners, clothing and other aspects of the characters' daily lives are similar enough to the present day that an enormous quantity of material research is not required.

Place

Splitting the setting of a rebellion novel into at least two locations has been a common practice in these novels since before Scott, as when in Irish national tales, an English hero traveled to the periphery of Ireland. Scott's characters spend most of the plots traveling from England to Scotland and between different locations in Scotland. The fact that most of the rebellion novels are already split in time and place is probably the reason Dickens felt it was consistent to also insert a second plot into the mix. Thus, it is only natural that Dickens also sends his characters traveling around England and abroad. O'Brien writes that having three settings (London, the Maypole, and

	Barnaby	*Two Cities*	*Waverley*	*Cruthers*
Locations:	London, Maypole, Warren	London, Paris	Scotland, England	Scotland, Jamaica

Figure 26. Comparative Locations of Dickens', Scott's and Carlyle's Rebellion Stories

Figure 27. Map of locations featured in Dickens', Scott's and Carlyle's rebellion novels (borders approximate).

the Warren) is handled badly in *Barnaby*, as the latter two are not essential to the story. However, O'Brien concedes that Dickens corrected this problem in *Tale* by spreading the action evenly and appropriately to only two settings (London and Paris). Still, two settings are not one, and Aristotle would not have been pleased. On the other hand, Dickens' readers and critics are frequently pleased by the changes in location, as a novel entirely set in Paris during the French Revolution would have been far more repetitive and dull than the galloping story that Dickens concocted.

Characters

Dickens talks about "insanity" where Scott talks about "wildness" because the definition of insanity and madness changed across the nineteenth century. Madness started out as a symptom of evil, and ended as a disease as the century progressed. Either way, the rebellious characters in most rebellion novels are typically not driven by reason, but rather by their wildness or madness. Dransfield explains that Dickens is deliberately portraying many of the characters, specifically, "Barnaby, Hugh, and Dennis," as "morally insane," or suffering from a "loss of self-possessed reason," and in need of "management" individually and also as a group. Dransfield concludes that Dickens is implying that the "mob" needs to be controlled and "managed" by a strong, but fair government and "discipline."[44] As I discussed earlier, the problem with the Hobbesian perspective of these scenes is that the mob is rebelling against unjust civil laws, and the government is not able to properly discipline the rioters before an enormous amount of damage is done. Control of the mob is nearly impossible, and the rebellion stops by itself. While some of the characters are clinically "insane," others are driven to mad actions by reasonable demands, such as better living and working conditions for the poor.

The foolish nature of a main character such as Barnaby is essential to the rebellion genre in general, and to Dickens' novels in particular. The most common insult in *Barnaby* is calling the rioters, and especially the main characters, "idiots." Fools have been present in literature across the ages. In Shakespeare, King Lear has a court fool who says some of the wisest passages in the play. In Act I, Scene 4, the Fool says, "I marvel what kin thou and thy daugh-

	Barnaby	***Two Cities***	***Waverley***	***Cruthers***
Characters:	Foolish Barnaby, mad mob	Mad mob	Wild Highland rebels	"Mad" rebel

Figure 28. Comparative Characters of Dickens', Scott's and Carlyle's Rebellion Stories

ters are. They'll have me/whipp'd for speaking true; thou'lt have me whipp'd for lying." In fact, "fool's literature" was a popular genre in Europe between the 15th and 17th centuries. As in *Lear*, the fool was typically a jester, and usually represented satirized "vice" and evil in a society.[45] In 19th-century novels the "fools" spread beyond these limitations, and Fyodor Dostoevsky even wrote *The Idiot* about Prince Myshkin, a royal personage, who made foolish, or rather mad (as "fool" became a term for a deranged person, rather than for a jester) personal and political decisions. In *Barnaby*, the fool is the main character, Barnaby Rudge, who foolishly jumps into being a leading actor in the riots. The fact that the man who jumps down to try and violate the proceedings of the pro–Catholic movement is mentally challenged suggests that Dickens (with or without humorous intent) is implying that rioters in general are mentally unstable. Barnaby is not called a fool with suggestions or hints, but rather directly. "An idiot, eh?" says a gentleman.[46] Dennis calls Barnaby his "dog."[47] Gashford smiles at the "simplicity of the poor idiot" because he knows he can and does use the idiocy to his advantage in the riots.[48] In Dickens' rebellion plot, "idiots" like Barnaby and poor men like Hugh commit the worst atrocities, so that Lord Gordon might escape execution or responsibility for the actions of the foolish members among the rioters. Because of his stupidity, Barnaby is "the only light-hearted, undesigning creature, in the whole assembly."[49] The last quotation suggests that the rest of the rioters were not fools, and were fully conscious of their actions, which contradicts the hypothesis that Dickens was calling all of the rioters fools. Instead, Dickens makes an intricate point on how a "fool" can be manipulated into joining a rebellion. But was Barnaby truly a "fool" or insane? Barnaby becomes "more rational" by the conclusion, gaining a "better memory and greater steadiness of purpose."[50] Facing the possibility of execution for his foolish participation in a rebellion sobers or enlightens Barnaby and he stops being the "idiot" who stumbled into associating with the wrong side of a political dispute.

How can the fact that Dickens called the rebels mad fools be reconciled with Dickens as a radical, who supported reform and even violent overthrows of a corrupt government? The drama of the rebellion and revolution that Dickens portrays is intensified when the characters acting in it are multidimensional or have some irrational or illogical motives. A purely logical explanation for the causes and outcomes of a rebellion would not have been as sympathetic or interesting for readers as the formula that Dickens came up with. Dickens' formula was to use multiple plots, multiple periods, multiple settings and mad or idiotic characters. If a person is driven mad by the English system, and then rebels, is he any less in the right?

Dickens' Methodology

The rebuttal to this idea is that Dickens was a meticulous editor and prepared detailed plots and plans for all of his novels. Dickens wrote many pages with "mems" and "chapter-notes" for his novels. A scan of these "mems" is given in Michael Slater's biography, *Charles Dickens*.[51] Slater explains Dickens' preparation process in detail, writing that even when he was writing his last novel, *The Mystery of Edwin Drood*, being deadly ill, he "got his number-plans organized in the usual way with 'mems' on the left-hand half of the page and chapter titles and chapter notes on the right hand. Among his 'mems' for the first number, noting the main characters to be introduced along with some important plot details, appears the phrase '*Cathedral town running through*.'"[52] After writing the last comment, Dickens ventured out into the city that he was describing, Rochester, went to the cathedral in question, and made detailed notes on how the cathedral and its surroundings looked. Slater also includes a scan of a page of the "reading text" of *Little Dombey*, "showing Dickens' emendations," which are thorough. Dickens energetically edits out a redundancy, "immediately in front of the fire."[53] Dickens was a very meticulous writer and editor. He was editing a weekly magazine amidst a reading tour, an illness that shortly led to his death, and his composition of *Drood*. Dickens did not have accidents. He did not create two plots instead of one in a novel because of a failure to plan out his design. Thus, Dickens' linguistic and structural patterns are intended and conscious decisions.

12

Dickens' Linguistic Features

The similarities between *Cruthers*, *Waverley* and Dickens' own rebellion novels indicate that he closely dissected the repeating elements of previous rebellion novels and followed many of these prescribed rules of his predecessors.

Gerson writes that "Dickens's mastery of dialogue is one of the primary reasons why his novels are so admired ... Dickens's own masterly gifts of expression and his interest in language as a means of communication make a study of his novels from the linguistic point of view more rewarding than is the case with, for example, Thackeray or Trollope."[1] Rebellion novels depict poor, dislocated, or "regional" characters. Some characters can't speak proper English due to a lack of education, or they are from Scotland, or the countryside, or France, so they must have some linguistic peculiarities to distinguish them from the establishment they are rebelling against.

Here is Dickens' rebellion novel linguistic formula compared with Scott's:

> *Scott's Linguistic Formula* = Epic Imagery and Techniques + Scottish Language and Allusions + Middle English and Renaissance Borrowings
>
> *Dickens' Linguistic Formula* = Epic Imagery and Techniques + English Regional and Class Dialects + Religious Allusions + Slogans + Idiolects or Invented Individualized Speech + French/Foreign Expressions

Dickens borrows several formulaic components from Scott, and makes a few of his own additions to the rebellion novel linguistic arsenal. Because, unlike Scott, Dickens grew up in London, he uses subversive regional English dialects, and attempts French and other foreign vocabularies. Dickens' allusions are frequently Judeo-Christian, and he typically inserts the standard slogans of the rebellious mob. The formulaic changes between Scott and Dickens are due not only to the differences in nation of origin but also to the political and religious climates in the different periods.

Varied Discourse: Allusions, Slogans, and Informality

Dickens' linguistic techniques included epithets, figurative language, class dialects, "minuteness" of detail, and historical language. Dickens' linguistic techniques frequently hide subversive rebellious sympathies. Dickens alludes to religious symbols to gain support for rebellious actions. He uses slogans to create a propagandistic backdrop for a rebellion. He uses class dialects to show tensions between classes. Dickens changes the dialogue of the simplest characters into grandiose style to show the grandeur of a rebellious action. If Dickens didn't have fluency in any regional dialect or foreign language other than standard London English, he made up for this deficiency by making up idiolects that created sympathy for uneducated characters. On several occasions, Dickens also attempted foreign languages and regional dialects to create depth in his characters, showing his unique linguistic skills and using these to make radical political statements.

Allusions

Rebellion novelists, including Dickens, frequently use proverbs, psalms, songs and other folk, religious and mythical allusions, quotations and asides. The proverbs are frequently used by the poor rioters to summarize their plight. For example, as they are deciding on continuing the riots, they use the proverb, "Being hung at all, they might as well be hung for a sheep as a lamb."[2] As Mr. Willet is sitting in stupefaction amid the wreckage of his house, he says distractedly, "Let us sing to the praise and glory of—"[3] Because the stated cause behind the riots is religious, even if bigoted, it is only appropriate that the rioters sing hymns or psalms.[4] Proverbs and other religious symbols and sayings are used both to excite rebellious feelings and to comfort people as they try to make sense of the violence and destructions of the riots. The same pacifying and enlivening technique is used by Scott and Stevenson to excite and then soothe readers before and after descriptions of revolutions, assassinations and other social disturbances.

Slogans

Dickens carries many of his linguistic and structural tricks over from *Barnaby* to *Tale*, making radical and interesting innovations to these tricks. One of these is that the raven, Grip, in *Barnaby* begins by repeating "I'm a devil,"[5] and is then trained by Barnaby and the "gentry," the rioters, to repeat the slogans of the rebels, "I'm a Protestant, No Popery!"[6] By having the raven repeat the slogans, Dickens makes fun of the repetitive nature of the rioters' cries, without making a long speech about how repetitive those types of slogans usually are. The raven is nearly executed as it starts shouting, "No Popery" in the "guard-house," where Barnaby is kept before trial for rioting.[7] Dickens refrains from repeating the same slogans in the lips of the rioters, writing instead that they are shouting, "repetitions of the usual cry."[8] As an editor, Dickens felt repulsed by repetitions, and some of the strongest socialist or radical criticisms in the novel come in the form of sudden outbursts by the main characters, rather than as slogans of the multitude. In *Tale* the revolutionaries keep shouting on every other page that they are fighting for "the Republic of Liberty, Equality, Fraternity, or Death."[9] Some repetition might help to stress a point, as when Dickens writes "Dig — dig — dig," when talking about Doctor Manette being "recalled to life."[10] As every editor knows, too much repetition is a grammatical mistake that is distracting and annoying to readers. The raven's repetitions are more sympathetic and innovative than the repetitions in *Tale*, which are flat and do not fluctuate between their uses. While the repetitions in *Tale* hurt the readers' ears, they are more innovative as this pain is an intentional technique that awakens readers to the repeating waves of anger that the mob is expressing.

Formality and Informality

In rebellion novels, the way lower and upper class characters address each other, with or without respect or honor, is essential to portraying the relationship between the struggling classes. Therefore, another key element in both *Barnaby* and *Tale* is how "appropriate" the language is for the person addressed, or if it includes the "right degree of formality."[11] Brook writes that Dickens used two absurd extremes when his characters stress their standing in relation to their hearers. One is the extreme of respect and flattery, or sycophancy. The second is an arrogant condescension, overbearing or patronizing behavior and language. An example of extreme flattery is a quote from Stagg in *Barnaby*, who speaks in the "third person, as though the object of his admiration were too exalted to be addressed directly."[12] While Brook only fits in a quote from Stagg, the surrounding passages are also essential to understanding the class-relations linguistic technique that Dickens is using. The flattery does not just fly out in a brief quote, but saturates everything Stagg says to Mr. Tappertit. Stagg calls Mr. Tappertit a "noble captain" and "illustrious general," and even exclaims that Mr. Tappertit has "precious limbs!" Then comes one of the longer examples of Stagg's use of the third-person voice in addressing his captain, Mr. Tappertit: "My captain *flies* at higher game than *Miggses*. Ha, ha, ha! *My captain is an eagle*, both as *respects* his eye and soaring wings. My captain *breaketh* hearts as other bachelors break eggs at breakfast." To this bowing exclamation Mr. Tappertit replies with the extremely condescending, "What a *fool* you are, Stagg!"[13] The italics in this passages are mine, used to stress words that best demonstrate this. The tension, conflict and drama of class struggle in Dickens' novels is partially built on the linguistic tricks and techniques Dickens puts into his characters' dialogues. The reader sympathizes with the underdogs and with the poor servants, and is repelled by the condescending rich, so that when the houses of the wealthy are burned in the riots the reader does not lose all sympathy for the mob. While the fun that Dickens pokes at the speech of his poor characters suggests a lack of sympathy for them, the condescension expressed for them by the rich restores the reader's sympathy, creating a more unbiased, less wavering Dickensian perspective.

An element of Dickens' linguistics that is the most frequently criticized or mentioned is the creatively contrived nature of the proper names that he gives to characters and places. The names rhyme with the symbols of what a given character represents, or are parodies of existing names. For example, Sir John Chester in *Barnaby* is similar to Lord Chesterfield, an author that Sir John states he admires in a passage in the novel. The frequent use of "surnames without any prefix by a wife in referring to her husband" is "now thought of as characteristic of servants in large households where husband and wife have the same employer," but is instead used by Dickens' poor characters who do not have servants. Mrs. Varden addresses her husband as "Varden" in Chapter 13.[14] This pattern is significant because it also helps to agitate class tensions. The repetition of the sycophant last name when addressing a husband has the same subconscious effect on the reader as the sycophant adorations that servants such as Stagg, offer their masters. We sympathize with the underdogs, the rebels, and the servile wives, and not with those who are being flattered.

Multilingual Elements: Class Dialects, Idiolects, Old English and French

Dickens used language that "suits the occasion," class dialects that stress the class struggle, idiolects (made-up linguistic elements), different foreign and archaic languages, and, in particular, the French language. The language that poor and rebellious characters use subversively excites sympathy for them.

Linguistics That "Suit the Occasion"

Dickens frequently uses linguistic characteristics that "suit the occasion." Unlike Scott, Dickens does not use specific lingual elements depending on a character's profession, but instead uses them to fit the needs of a given situation. For example, "euphemistic oaths," or substituting a mild expression for an offensive one, are "used by people who have little interest in etymology," the study of the history or derivation of words.[15] The lower-class servant Miggs is not a likely candidate to be a linguistic scholar, and yet when she sees her beloved Simon Tappertit trying to sneak out of the house, instead of screaming something like, "Damn!" she exclaims, "'Gracious!' again, and then 'Goodness gracious!' and then 'Goodness gracious me!'"[16] Similarly in *Tale*, a "vexed coachman" "ejaculates," "My blood!" in response to hearing the dangerous late hour it is to be leading the Dover mail.[17] This linguistic complexity is somewhat exhausted by the end of *Barnaby*, when in reply to Simon trying to sneak out of the house to join the rebels, Miggs, with one more "Oh goodness gracious!"[18] jumps on him and tries forcefully instead to make him stay home with wild and distracted screams. Exclamations that are appropriate to the drama of the occasion help Dickens in several scenes to intensify the energy of the rebellions.

Class Dialects to Portray Class Struggle

One key difference between Scott's and Dickens' linguistics is that Scott was careful to use vocabulary and grammars that were appropriate to the professions of the specific character that he was describing. If Scott were drawing a fisherman, the man would use similes that mentioned or related to fishing, hooks, poles, types of fish and the like. In contrast, Dickens was less concerned with stressing characters' profession in their dialogue, but instead focused on portraying their class and age. As Brook concludes, "People of the same age and social class tend to talk alike, whatever their occupation." Dickens makes "fun of grandiloquent phrases encouraged by the societies which young men founded or joined"; thus, for example, Tappertit is called a "mighty captain" of the "secret society of 'Prentice Knights."[19] Only people in specific professions are especially sympathetic in Scott, such as herders or Highland militimen. Dickens focuses the reader's attention on the class of his characters, instead of separating them into linguistically competing professions.

The French Revolution and the Gordon Riots, as described by Dickens, both include lower- and upper-class characters, as they both depict a struggle between those who are impoverished and those who are in power. All of the novels discussed utilize class dialects to some degree. Members of the upper class have a unique dialect, so much so that they have to translate their vocabulary to lower-class characters, as Sir John Chester does for Haredale in *Barnaby Rudge* when he explains, "You will be *hipped*, Haredale; you will be miserable, melancholy, utterly wretched."[20] The linguistics of the rich in Dickens is pompous, pretentious and difficult for the poor to comprehend. If the upper-class character is also a member of a dissenting religious sect, Dickens has him use frequent "archaisms and ... not very appropriate quotations from the Bible."[21] For example, Lord Gordon exclaims that a "vineyard" may be "menaced with destruction."[22] Unlike Marx, who described the theory and philosophy behind the antagonism between the rich and the poor, Dickens portrays this antagonism through the malevolent linguistics used by the two opposing camps.

Barnaby and *Tale* are filled with "substandard speech," "vulgarisms" and other deliberately grammatically erroneous phrases and words commonly misused in Dickens' own time. One example Brook sees in *Barnaby* is Dickens' use of "malapropism," or "confusion with a word of completely different meaning, where amusement is caused by the inappropriateness of the word in the context in which it is used,"[23] as when John Willet says *patrole* instead of "parole" in Chapter 29. To deliberately create humorous and quirky grammatical mistakes, Dickens also distorts parts of words, such as putting in "a different prefix or suffix,"[24] as when Miggs mixes up *relude* with "allude" in Chapter 41, or *repeal* with "appeal" in Chapter 19. Miggs makes more grammatical mistakes than most of the other characters in both *Barnaby* and *Tale*; her mistakes frequently appear at the peak of suspenseful riotous action as a comic relief from the madness that is going on in the streets of London during the Gordon Riots. Another substandard flaw in Miggs's speech is adding an -*s* ending to adverbs that do not have an -*s* in Standard English: "*otherways* than" for "unless" in Chapter 7. The stutter that the toll keeper develops as Mr. Haredale tries to convince him to come with him — "No-n-no"[25] — is another example of vulgar or mutated speech, though it is due to the character's mental state or fear, rather than to his class status.

Dickens utilizes the lower-class characters' linguistic mistakes "always with humorous intent,"[26] a trick that only an editor can fully appreciate. Thus, many critics see Dickens as a waverer or not fully in support of the socialist causes, as he is not always sympathetic, and frequently degrades his impoverished characters. But I believe that the mistakes clearly inspire sympathy for the poor characters. Even if readers is laugh at the mistakes, they simultaneously realize that the mistakes originate in the unfair lack of education the poor characters received. Miggs shows her lower-class lack of an education when she uses erroneous word substitutions, as in *aperiently* instead of "apparently," *practicable* for "practicing," and *pretensions* for "pretense." Miggs mixes up prefixes and suffixes when she uses *constrain* for "restrain," or *reduce* for "seduce," or *repeal* for "appeal." The use of "prolongation of sounds" with hyphens is another form of an idiolectic feature, as in *ye-es* by Cruncher in *Tale* to depict his "dogged manner," and, when a man shouts, *spi-i-ies*. One of the most common mistakes in spelling or pronunciation that is still made today is the use of "abbreviated verb forms," which are not supposed to be used in Standard English. In Dickens, the mistake can be made by those who are either lower or upper class, as upper-class characters can be using archaic or an out-of-date abbreviations, which are no longer in use. In *Barnaby*, the simple Hugh uses *who're*; a gentleman uses *thou'st*; and John Willet uses *Barnaby's*, when he is trying to say "Barnaby is," and *many's* when he wants to express "many is."[27] Stressing linguistic or grammatical errors in poor characters is a continuation of Dickens' campaign for education reform. If a direct appeal does not work, perhaps reading grammatical errors in the speech of the impoverished will prompt powerful or wealthy readers to act in support of education reform.

Idiolects or Made-Up Languages

Due to the fact that Dickens did not natively know a dialect and did not spend a substantial quantity of time in one particular foreign region, he makes up for his multilingual shortage by making up "special languages" for his characters. Brook calls the outcome of devising a made-up language for a character an "idiolect," or the "speech-habits of an individual, in contrast with a dialect, which describes the speech-habits of a group."[28] One technique for creating an idiolect is by creating an "eccentric pronunciation," which is used in *Barnaby*, as Dennis repeatedly says *Muster Gashford*, instead of "Mister Gashford." A character can also use "accidence of syntax, like Miggs's plurals of abstract nouns, which come in bursts in moments of excitement." For example, in Chapter 41, she has, "satisfactions, dispositions, in the rights, to go that lengths, separations, endings."[29] Looking at a long passage from Miggs in Chapter 63, where she uses the same *-s* additions, shows how the artificial idiolect starts to sound like a lyrical, linguistic way of stressing the unique nature of Miggs's character. The outburst comes after one of the longest speeches Miggs makes in the novel, in which she explains that she is not a Papist and why she just "poured a mug of table-beer right down the barrel" of the old locksmith, who was trying to defend his house against the rioters: "My sentiments is of little consequences, I know ... for my positions is but a servant, and as sich, of humilities; still I gives expressions to my feelings, and places my reliances on them which entertains my own opinions!"[30] Miggs' use of *gives* and *sich* in this passage is clearly a made-up or a class dialect. The heavy use of the technique in this passage makes it very noticeable to the point of being absurd, and helps to add humor to the absurd situation comedy of the ale going down the barrel of the locksmith's gun. In fact, the heavy use of Miggs' *-s* additions to various types of words points to the *s* that is tagged onto her own name. Perhaps Dickens decided to make up her idiolect when he made up her name.

All of these invented and devised linguistic quirks are used to stress the lower-class elements of a character. Without constantly describing the mire, mud and rags, as Dickens does in *Bleak House*, he repeatedly stresses the poverty and lack of education in his poor characters in *Barnaby* and *Tale* with the use of subversive or microscopically detailed linguistic quirks.

Use of Foreign and Archaic Languages

Brook explains the cause for the chief difference between Scott's and Dickens' use of regional dialects. Dickens "spent much more of his life in London than in any country district"; in contrast, Scott spent most of his life in the countryside of Scotland. Therefore, while Scott uses an abundance of Scottish words, phrases and even whole paragraphs, Dickens sprinkles a few words or a few phrases occasionally (i.e., the Scottish doctor in the *Bleak House*), similarly to how he utilizes foreign words and phrases. Despite this deficiency, Brook writes that Dickens researched dialects closely, and names four exceptions for when Dickens relied heavily on four particular English regional dialects: "East Anglia in *David Copperfield*, Yorkshire in *Nicholas Nickleby* and Lancashire in *Hard Times*" and "the dialects of the United States ... in *American Notes* and in the American chapters of *Martin Chuzzlewit*."[31] Unfortunately, this list does not include *Barnaby* or *Tale*. Still, Dickens does use numerous brief words and phrases in nonstandard dialects in both of these novels. For example, in *Tale,* a guard who is transporting Mr. Lorry suddenly breaks into archaic Middle English, or more likely a Scottish dialect (as the latter is close to Middle English), with words like, *d'ye, o', yourn, nigh,* and *'em.*[32] In other words, if Dickens was not trying to bring in a time traveler from the Middle Ages, these words are meant to imply a northern or Scottish dialect.

The East Anglia dialect is characterized by its rhythm or the lengthening of stressed syllables, and therefore the shortening or loss of unstressed syllables. East Anglia English is an early form of the Norwich dialect of northern England. The East Anglia dialect has a seventh vowel, due to its close relationship to Middle English, which existed before the Great Vowel Shift. Dickens used Middle English classical spellings to create the East Anglia atmosphere in the language of *David Copperfield*. Here are some examples of words deliberately misspelled in *David Copperfield* to create the East Anglia dialect: *obleeged, Em'ly, partic'lers,* and *a'n't.*[33] The use of apostrophes to contract words and to lengthen or shorten vowel pronunciations are the most common tricks used to create the East Anglia accent.

The Yorkshire dialect covers Yorkshire County in northern England, and has been used in several classic British novels, including *Wuthering Heights*. Some of the characteristics of this dialect are very strong contractions, like saying '*int*, instead of "isn't." Many of the vowels have a slightly different pronunciation, as the language has roots in Old English, and once again Dickens could have relied on classic Old English literature to guide him in building this accent in *Nicholas Nickleby*. Here Dickens used several repeating slanted words when portraying characters with a Yorkshire dialect. *Demd* appears twelve times, and is used by Mr. Mantalini when he is upset, instead of "damned." He occasionally also uses its variation, *demit*, which appears nine times; *demnebly*, which appears four times; *demnition*, which appears nine times; and the short *dem*, which appears eight times (once three times in a row). These repetitions point to a lot of cursing in this novel. Also, the word "idiot" appears five times. But besides these phonetic variations there isn't much of a Yorkshire dialect in this novel. It's possible that the spelling changes hide the obscene repetitive cursing to make it more appropriate for the general public. Of course, this is also a linguistic glitch that might have occurred because of Dickens' relative youth as an author, as *Nickleby* was his third novel after *Pickwick* and *Oliver Twist*.

Lancashire is a county adjacent to Yorkshire County, at the top end of northern England. The dialect is currently undergoing rapid extinction, so if you speak with somebody from Lancashire today, they might sound about the same as people from London. But back in the nineteenth century, someone who had a heavy Lancashire accent would have sounded more like somebody from Scotland, as the Scottish English and the Lancashire English dialects have similar Scandinavian or medieval Norse roots. In *Hard Times*, Dickens could have used vowel-shift tricks similar to those Scott used. Here is an example of the use of the Lancshire accent in early nineteenth-century literature, from Elizabeth Cleghorn Gaskell's 1815 poem "The Oldham Weaver":

> I Oi'm a poor cotton-weyver, as mony a one knwwaa,
> Oi've nowt fort' yeat, an' oi've wotn eawt my clooas,
> Yo'ad hardly gi' tuppence for aw as oi've on,
> My clogs are both brosten, an' stuckings oi've noae,
>   Yo'd think it wur hard,
>   To be browt into th' warld,
> To be-clemmed', an' do th' best as yo con.[34]

Dickens does not attempt the above style of a heavy Lancashire accent in *Hard Times*. At one point, he uses the slurred speech of a man with asthma, Mr. Sleary, whose name suggests his pronunciation, having him say things like *thquire, thervant, thith, ith* and *hith*.[35] The pronunciation colors the dialect and adds humor to Mr. Sleary's story. Once again, Dickens shows his tendency to reuse dialect words, in this case, *ma'am*, used forty-three times, and most frequently used by Bounderby, Mrs. Sparsit and Stephen. The contraction *wi'* appears twenty-nine times. Contractions, in general, are the most common type of accent change in *Hard Times*. Here is a string of repeated contractions used in one paragraph by Stephen: *'em, o',* and *th'*.[36] In the same passage, Stephen also uses a few mutated vowel and consonant pronunciations, such as like: *amoong* (repeated), *monny, yo, riven,* and *ere*.[37] Several of these words also appear in Gaskell's poem, including *yo* and *th'*, and even a different version of *mony*, which possibly suggests that Dickens might have based his spellings on her book. This is a radical change from his earlier linguistic attempts in *Nickleby*, as he uses an accurate, rich linguistic language for a significant part of the novel's dialogue.

Like Scott, Dickens occasionally uses alternative spellings or pronunciations for words that stem from Middle English, or pronunciations that existed before the Great Vowel Shift. Miggs is once again the most frequent offender. Miggs has strongly stressed vowels, similar to those that were used in "Middle English dialectal variants," the ones that were used before the Great Vowel Shift, as in *twenty-sivin*,[38] or *mim* for "madam,"[39] *Simmun* for "Simon."[40] Unlike Miggs, Dennis uses lightly stressed vowels, particularly in words of two or more syllables, which are "printed with a hyphen after the first syllable," as in *gen-teel* and *dex-terity*.[41] In addition, Dennis uses substandard vocabulary like "work off" instead of the verb "to hang."[42] Because of the similarities between Middle English and many northern English dialects, such as north English, Irish and Scottish dialects, Middle English can frequently be used by an educated author who wants to show regional diversity and class distinctions.

Use of French

One of the most criticized flaws in *Tale* is Dickens' use of "stage" French. Colin Jones remarks that in *Tale*, "The French in particular are depicted as melodramatic types who speak in a predictable stage French and lack the linguistic inventiveness usually associated with Dickens' characters."[43] Brook wrote that avoiding "predictable stage" dialogue was one of Dickens' chief goals in his linguistic innovations.

However, if we return to the fact that Dickens spent most of his life in London, we can understand why Dickens focuses on adding hyphens and -*s's* and avoids lengthy dialogues in foreign dialects or languages. In *Tale*, Dickens calls a French male character "Monseigneur,"[44] and frequently repeats the term "La Guillotine,"[45] but he makes few attempts at long conversations in French. The stage-like nature of the French might be due more to the limitations of Dickens' multilingual abilities than to a lack of desire to make the

French as realistic as he could. Jones wrote that *Tale* is "an icon of English national identity."⁴⁶ He adds that *Tale* is not popular in France because the French believe that it equates "French popular political radicalism with terroristic and bloody violence."⁴⁷ Jones' logic is that Dickens' French is intentionally dull and is meant as a critique of the French national character. But the latter option seems more absurd than a more realistic assumption. Dickens simply did not have enough knowledge of French to practice the linguistic tricks in a foreign language. This view is confirmed by a quotation from Volume 5 of Dickens' *Letters*, originally written in French on February 29, 1848, from Paris, to his close literary friend, John Forster: "My friend, I find that I like the Republic so much that I must renounce my own language and only write in the language of the French Republic — the language of gods and angels — the language, in a word, of the French people."⁴⁸ If Dickens hated the French language and people, he would not praise them and their tongue so highly. The truth is that Dickens tried to write in creative French, but all great writers have their Achilles' heel. In an 1842 review of Dickens, Poe brings up an interesting quotation from Talleyrand about "some cockney's bad French," *que s'il ne soit pas Français, assurement donc il le doit être*, which Google Translate renders as, "If it is not French, so he must assuredly be."⁴⁹ If Dickens wasn't French, how could he have written in good French? For, despite the difference in gender, as Dickens wrote himself, Miss Pross "is an English lady, and knows no French."⁵⁰

Dickens developed unique and sympathetic poor characters through his use of innovative dialogue. Dickens enriched the dialogue by using unusual vocabulary and grammar. Various dialects and linguistic quirks are present, primarily in the rebels' or the mob's speech. In Scott, the rebellious Jacobite Highlanders as well as the wealthy Lowland Baron Bradwardine (who in Chapter Thirteen is said to have read Harry's *Wallace* [1477], written in traditional Scots about a Scottish freedom fighter) have thick Scottish accents. In Dickens, Miggs and even the wealthy Lord Gordon have particularities or oddities in their speech patterns. Scott used subversive tricks when he used a foreign to English ears Scottish dialect. Dickens was similarly subversive by soliciting sympathy through the poor character's poor grammatical skills. There are also numerous parallels between the structure of Dickens' rebellion novels and those of his predecessors Scott and Carlyle. Dickens also followed Carlyle's historical and political example and portrayed the plot and actions of the French Revolution as well as of the Gordon Riots as explosions of justifiable violence against a corrupted aristocracy and the bourgeoisie. Dickens developed a "willingness to accept the right of revolution in certain conditions."⁵¹

Dickens' Linguistic and Structural Radicalism

The focus on breaking or editing the rules of Aristotelian unities is what separates Dickens' rebellion novels from Scott's and Stevenson's. For example, Dickens splits the plot in two, one half rebellion, and the second half mystery. This splitting of the plot in two is one of the reasons fewer critics notice a similarity between Dickens and Scott, while most notice the mimicry between Scott and Stevenson. This duality of plot can best be described as a break with Aristotelian unity of plot, thereby showing Dickens' deliberate disfigurement of his rebellion novels. Placing the rebellion and the revolution into the second halves of these rebellion novels meant that the radicalism and the violence of these uprisings was hidden away. It is a well-known rule in screenwriting that producers usually read only the first ten pages of the script. Similarly, Dickens probably hoped that by placing the violent rebellions at the end of these two novels he would dodge post-publication censors.

The plots of rebellion novels are radical because they inspire sympathy for the cause of the poor or periphery people. In *Tale*, Madame Defarge cries out against "poverty, nakedness, hunger, thirst, sickness, misery, oppression."[52] While the revolutionaries are bloodthirsty and crazed, they are shown to have a just cause, and to have just reasons to desire vengeance against the aristocracy. The aristocrat who throws a coin after killing a child with his horses at the beginning of *Tale*, is only one plot detail that suggests to readers that the revolutionary military and violent actions are justified.

Dickens set his rebellion novels at least sixty years in the past, following Scott's example in order to distance the events described from his present. Thus, Dickens could criticize social ills, such as poverty, hunger and thirst, which were still plaguing England during his time, and could show the violent rebellions and revolutions that were perpetrated to resolve these problems in the past. In so doing, Dickens was avoiding making a direct threat of revolutionary or rebellious violence against the aristocracy and the establishment of his own day, as he was covering past historical events.

Dickens split the locations of his rebellion novels into England and France in one and London, Maypole and Warren in the other. This split is different from the more common locations that Scott and Stevenson use, England and Scotland, but it would have been odd if Dickens chose to focus on a Scottish rebellion, having grown up near the center of London. The radical or subversive reason for the split in location in most rebellion novels is that Dickens and the other rebellion writers strive to show the existence of social problems in several different areas to make the members of these regions sympathize with each other, instead of assuming that those problems are only present in an isolated geographic area.

While Scott primarily uses tragedy to make his rebellious characters sympathetic to readers, Dickens employs the technique of making them appear "mad" or "insane" due to the poverty and want that they have experienced in their miserable lives. Scott's Fergus is passionate and a bit overly enthusiastic in his desire for a successful Jacobite rebellion, but Dickens' Barnaby is downright insane or mad. Of course, after the end of the Gordon Riots, Barnaby miraculously regains his sanity, and is no longer as mad as he was when he stumbled into participating in the riots. This change suggests that Barnaby's madness was partially caused by the problems that existed in his society, which were partially resolved by the riots. Thus, Barnaby becomes a symbol or a reflection of the poor people in England, who regain some of their communal stability after they express their madness or rage against the injustices they are suffering through violence. Dickens shows rebellions where the mob kills many more people than those that are killed in Scott's or Stevenson's rebellions. Dickens makes an "insanity" plea for these mobs, claiming that they act violently because they are crazed by the injustices they suffer.

Dickens' linguistic techniques are radical for most of the same reasons as Scott's. Dickens also mixes together epic imagery and techniques with regional and class dialects to show the similarities between the two, or between regional particularities, such as regional imagery and allusions, and epic imagery. In addition, epic techniques give grandeur and epic proportions to the lives and conditions of the poor people in England and France. Religious allusions help to support the radical and violent actions of the rebels. The slogans the rebels use are similar to those in Scott's rebellion novels, inserting pro-rebellion propaganda. Because Dickens spoke and wrote in London English, he occasionally settles for making up idiolects, inventing individualized speech for his poor characters instead of using actual regional dialects. Dickens' idiolects achieve the same purpose as Scott's regional Scots and Lowland Scottish languages, as both empower poor or regional people who are struggling to obtain equality. The primary radical purpose of Dickens' linguistics is to show that the poor characters are undereducated or uneducated and that they deserve to be educated. The debate for the education of the poor raged across the 19th century, and only quieted towards its end, so it would have been a radical political statement for a writer to use substandard English to show his sympathy for the linguistic difficulties of the poor people.

PART IV. ROBERT LOUIS STEVENSON: PATRONAGE AND REBELLION

13
Stevenson's Radical Political Purpose

Stevenson spent his writing life inciting rebellion and revolution against the empire, tyranny and corrupt judicial systems with both literary and political battles. He succeeded in promoting colonial rights, renewing the argument for Scottish nationalism and language, and various other radical and socialist issues. Stevenson was the most radical socialist in the rebellion novelists group. He published the most works about rebellions as a percentage of his combined works. Stevenson's list of rebellion novels is longer than Scott's. Stevenson began publishing rebellion novels in 1866, when he was sixteen, with a fictionalized historical novella, *Pentland Rising*. His first mature, popularly distributed rebellion novel was *The Black Arrow: A Tale of Two Roses*, first serialized in *Young Folks* in 1883 and then published as a book in 1888. He then wrote four more historical rebellion novels: *The Dynamiter* (1885), *Kidnapped* (1886), *The Young Chevalier* (1892, unpublished), and *David Balfour* (or *Catriona*, as it was known in England) (1893). It is possible that critics have missed the obvious repetition of the rebellion theme in Stevenson's works because four of the above have not been widely reprinted since the 1880s and 1890s, when they were first published. Today they are all accessible through Google Books and Project Gutenberg, and the lesser-known works can finally be readily examined in comparison with *Kidnapped* and *Balfour*, so that one can form a fuller picture of Stevenson's rebellion genre linguistic and structural features. Many early and later critics noticed that Stevenson openly mimicked his predecessors, including Scott and Dickens. The statements made by critics about the existing mimicry will show the influence of Scott and Dickens in Stevenson's rebellion novel formula.

Stevenson's radicalism was succinctly summarized by one of his major biographers, Ian Bell. "The verse R.L.S. was composing in youth gives a clue to the thinking of the 'red-hot Socialist.' 'White neck-clothed bigots' were being

Figure 29. From *Dr. Jekyll and Mr. Hyde*: "Great God! Can it be!!" Chicago: National Prtg. & Engr. Co., [188-?] (Library of Congress Prints and Photographs Division).

exposed, militarism confounded — though he had spoken against communism in a debate at the Spec. The next year he was writing to his father from France (at his father's expense, naturally) to rail against proposed income-tax cuts and anti-trade-union laws.... In the Pacific he was to see the destruction wrought by imperialism and commerce, and come to admire the communal life of the people ... [He was] accepting all the while that the majorities in 'the lesser nations,' Scotland and Ireland, found the Union 'obnoxious.'" In 1887, at the beginning of his literary peak, Stevenson commented in "The Day After Tomorrow," in the *Contemporary Review*, "We ... all know what Parliament is, and we are all ashamed of it.... There are great truths in socialism, or no one ... would be found to hold it; and if it came, and did one-tenth part of what it offers, I for one should make it welcome."[1] There is clear proof of Stevenson's radical socialism in both his biography and his literature.

Marxism

By the end of the century, Marxism and socialism became popular. Stevenson frequently used Marxist terms like "bourgeoisie." Many critics and readers have noticed Marxist influences on Stevenson's works. Here is an example from a 2007 critical study: "*Treasure Island* may be read as a rejoinder to Marx's political philosophy, which was variously disseminated in England from the late 1840s, and influential by the late 1870s and early 1880s, when working men's political groups, notably the Social Democratic Federation, were active in London and the Northern industrial cities."[2] Stevenson was heavily influenced by Marxist ideas and he can justly be called a socialist rather than a radical. At the end of the nineteenth century, rebellions started to be known as "terrorist" acts, as explosives allowed even individuals to engage in major violent rebellions. At the same time, modernity and absurdity started seeping into fiction. and we can see these elements seeping into the rebellion novels, on top of the romanticism and realism that preceded them. Stevenson's rebellion novels offer some new innovations in the rebellion genre as they are heavily influenced by Marxism, modernity, absurdity as well as the romanticism, realism and historicism that came before this period. Despite these drastic social and cultural changes, Stevenson's rebellion novels were as poorly received by most of the early critics. as was Dickens' *Barnaby Rudge*; and, yet like Dickens, Stevenson continued to write more and more rebellious novels.

Anybody who doubts that the author of *Treasure Island* is a socialist radical need only consider that the communists have come to claim Stevenson into their ranks. The Tenth Young Communist League of Great England National Conference ran a demonstration in Glasgow, in 1938, which featured Stevenson's image right beside those of Marx and Lenin.[3] The league would not have used Stevenson's flag if they did not consider him to be one of their major idols or supporters. Socialism and Marxism spread exponentially at the end of the nineteenth century, taking the place that Chartism held in the middle of the nineteenth century. A liberal, highly educated Scottish writer was bound to have been exposed to socialist ideas, and to have had opportunities to participate in both political and literary socialist movements.

Stevenson's Subversion

One of Stevenson's critics, Menikoff, concludes that Stevenson, like Scott, used "subversion" to depict the defeat of the rebellious clans, while simultaneously criticizing "the law of the state," personalized in the Advocate, as corrupt and out to preserve their own "power," rather than acting in the people's interest.[4] Stevenson inspired sympathy and empathy with the dying rebels in his rebellion novels. Stewart is wrongly hanged for a crime he did not commit. Stevenson highlighted that the legal system in Scotland is corrupt and criminally guilty in both *Kidnapped* and *Balfour*.

Another form of subversion that Stevenson practiced is hiding "secret lessons" inside of the plots and messages of his rebellion novels. Some of these "secret lessons" were not very secretive, the point being not to disguise the moral implications but simply to cushion their force to make them more digestible for the censors. Stevenson depicts the violent Appin assassination, but cushions it with an explanation of the effect it had on many suspected rebels in Scotland, some of whom were executed or otherwise disgraced or ruined. In May 1887, Stevenson explained in an *English Weekly* article, "Books Which Have Influenced Me," that he was writing for the "genuine reader," so that his words are "weighed and winnowed," in order to have "only that which suits ... be assimilated."[5] Stevenson anticipates that if his stories fell into the hands of a reader who lacked the ability to read intelligently, the same novels will stay "silent and inarticulate," and the secret lessons they hold would remain as if they weren't written.[6] Enclosing "secret lessons" inside of the subtext of his novels is similar to Scott's subversive use of the Scottish dialect and other tricks to make sure that his rebellious novels are somewhat incomprehensible or unclear to unintended readers. These secret or subversive lessons are only a part of Stevenson's rhetoric. The majority of Stevenson's radical and socialist opinions in his rebellion novels and in his theory and history are made as direct radical political statements.

Patronage and Political Independence

Stevenson's relationship with his patrons, the funders for his "scribbling," affected the rebellion novels that he wrote while under their funding. Stevenson was especially dependent on patrons due to his extraordinarily bad health. His father's opinion prevented him from taking almost any radical or socialist political actions early in life. When his father did not leave Stevenson a sufficient inheritance for him to become independent, Stevenson went directly from one patron to another in June 1887, when he won funding for his travels and talks in America from an American millionaire, Charles Fairchild, who was also John Singer Sargent's patron, and whose wife was a fan of Stevenson.[7]

Stevenson's dependence on patrons meant that his primary goal was to please his readers, to build a fan base that would support his literary endeavors. At the same time, Stevenson's constant suppression of his urge to be more honest about his socialist or radical beliefs, and his need to rebel against wrongs that he was seeing, led to outbursts such as writing numerous novels about violent rebellions. In "Letter to a Young Gentleman," Stevenson recommends to new writers that their primary end should be "to please," explaining, "It is doubtless tempting to exclaim against the ignorant bourgeois; yet it should not be forgotten, it is

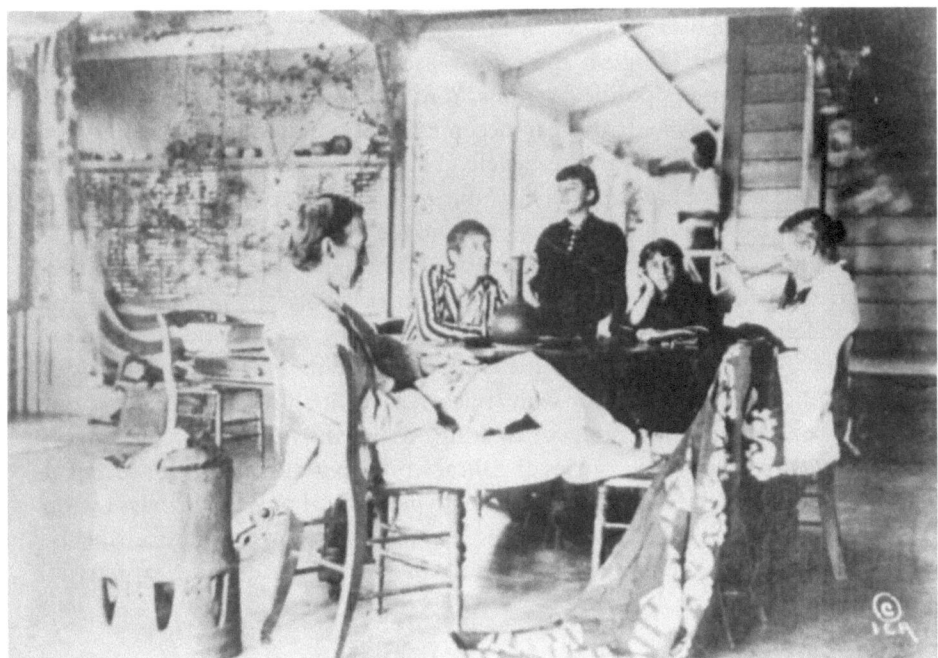

Figure 30. "[Robert Louis Stevenson with his family sitting around table at home in the Hawaiian Islands.]" Hawaii State Archives Digital Collections, 1889, published 1921 (Library of Congress Prints and Photographs Division).

he who is to pay us, and that (surely on the face of it) for services that he shall desire to have performed."[8] Once a writer supports himself by other means than his writing, he can write about whatever he wants. "Till then, he must pay assiduous court to the bourgeois who carries the purse." Stevenson goes so far as to compare the "patronage" that writers covet to degradations suffered by "dancing girls."[9] Stevenson writes that he feels he cannot fully revolt against the rich while he is accepting their charitable support of his literary efforts. He confesses that he didn't make any profits on writing or any other craft until after he turned thirty-one. His wealthy family, friends and patrons supported him throughout his life with money. Stevenson was aware that as a semi-bourgeois himself, he could offer only fictitious rebellions, and financial need preempted any willingness to make an outright political attack on the English government.

Socialism and Radicalism in Stevenson's Biography

While Stevenson stopped publicly confessing to his socialist views after the end of his youth, he became more radical and reactionary in his deeds and fiction. The idea that a major English author was a revolutionary or practiced radical "anti–English rhetoric,"[10] seems absurd until one rereads the details of Stevenson's political actions. Youthful writers frequently don't realize that even their private letters can become public, so they are frequently more outspoken about their sincere beliefs. Thus, it is significant that Stevenson confessed he was a radical "socialist" during his college days, but later became more guarded even in his private correspondences.

At the end of the nineteenth century, although slavery was outlawed and there was wide-spread literacy across the British Isles, the poor still suffered horrid living conditions, women didn't have a right to vote, and Scotland and Ireland were still subsumed by the United Kingdom. There were many available radical causes, and those who attacked social ills also attacked the empire that they felt was responsible for creating or ignoring these problems. Popular publishers censored many types of radical works to avoid offending the monarchy. Stevenson could not easily publish hyper-radical political articles in popular newspapers. But he did show numerous strands of radicalism and socialism across his life, which help to explain the radicalism he expressed in his rebellion novels.

A Life of Rebellion

At one point, Stevenson temporarily joined a socialist commune in Paris. How did Stevenson join this group of radical intellectuals that went as far as condoning violent attacks on the aristocracy and the bourgeoisie? What was it that put him on this course in his youth? Stevenson's socialism began in the same way as it did for many other wealthy youths, when he observed poverty and felt a desire to right the wrong. His early sympathy for the poor can be seen in details such as a description from a letter he wrote to Frances Sitwell on November 16, 1874: "I crossed the streets and made the fiddler very happy, and me 'poor indeed.'"[11] While a single charitable act does not prove that Stevenson was a socialist, it does signal that he had some sympathy for the poor, as opposed to a cold detachment from the struggles of the downtrodden. Stevenson was experimenting with refraining from accepting charity from patrons, and especially from his family, and giving his money away to the poor. On July 9, 1876, at the end of what might be called his "socialist" period, he wrote, once again to Frances Sitwell, that he was working on "A paper called 'A Defence of Idlers' (which is really a defense of R.L.S.)."[12] Marx considered writing to be a form of secondary production, or work that was inferior to factory or farm production of "more useful" or practical goods and services. Stevenson was thus making a satirical or perhaps a frank defense for his choice of a writing career when he wrote "A Defence of Idlers." This essay shows that Stevenson was aware that his actual life choices and his family's standing in capitalist society made it difficult for him to be a "socialist" in the traditional sense, especially when he was frequently too ill to do any other type of productive work besides his "idle" writing endeavors. Earlier critics have come to the conclusion that these words and others around them end the "socialist" period because Stevenson infrequently made similar charitable remarks in his later writings. Stevenson's radical socialism found other outlets, which are less visible to the critics who stop at Stevenson's journals, when searching for the progression of his political beliefs. By 1877, from his journals alone, Stevenson appears to have surrendered to the fact that his passion for writing or "idling" was far stronger than his desire to give his money to the poor, even if they were fiddlers.

Family Allegiances

While the cause of the Irish nationalists and farmers seems irrelevant at first, it was actually a family matter for Stevenson. When he thought of joining the Irish Curtin family, he "tried to arrange a meeting with the Chief Secretary for Ireland, Arthur Balfour (with who he could claim a distant blood tie, and whose brother, Eustace, was a fellow member of the Savile Club)."[13] Balfour was a name common in Stevenson's family tree, and Balfour is the name of the main character in both *Kidnapped* and *David Balfour*. Therefore, the affairs of the eighteenth-century Jacobite Balfours and the nationalist Irish Balfours were of direct personal significance to Stevenson.

Stevenson had other family-related motivations for writing *Kidnapped* and other works about Scotland and about rebellions. One of the best recent biographies of Stevenson, by Claire Harman, explains that Stevenson wrote *Kidnapped* because, "The evocation of the West Highland coastline was to be an oblique homage to the Stevenson family firm.... All this must have mollified the ailing old man's [Stevenson's father's] anxieties."[14] Honoring his Scottish heritage and the landscape of Scotland was a nationalist exercise that Stevenson's father would have approved of. Winning approval and financial support from his father for his "scribbling" was responsible for Stevenson's "limited ability to act out his political principles in life." Stevenson "died to politics," which was "a source of profound frustration and shame to him."[15] Stevenson finally broke his restraint while his father was on his deathbed, by supporting the "boycotted" Irish family, as will be described in a later section.

Stevenson used his family's history and biographies in his Balfour novels, so it is only natural that he sympathized with the cause of the Jacobites and nationalists described in these novels. In a letter to Alison Cunningham on July 16, 1886, as he began writing *Kidnapped*, he writes that Alison Hastie, a girl who rows Alan Breck and David Balfour across the Forth River in order to help them escape prosecution for the Appin murder at the end of the novel, is based on "an ancestress of yours," meaning Alison Cunningham. He continues: "David was no doubt some kind of a relative of mine," as Stevenson had dozens of relatives whose last names were Balfour (Sir Graham Balfour [Stevenson's biographer], Hanrietta Scott Balfour, Jane Whyte Balfour, Lewis Balfour, Rev. Lewis Balfour, and Mackintosh Balfour).[16] Stevenson gives his characters this name because he feels that the story of the failed rebellions affected his family personally and financially. It is a fact that most prominent Edinburgh families were affected by the Jacobite rebellions and their aftermath in one way or another. Unlike with Scott, there is not enough proof that Stevenson's family was directly involved in the Jacobite uprisings, but there were few middle-class Scots in Edinburgh, during the risings, who were not affected by the risings. Most middle-class families indirectly assisted the Jacobite and nationalist cause. In an essay titled "The First Biography," Michael Balfour talks about how his father, Louis (later knighted), Robert's second cousin, "came to be the official biographer" for Stevenson. In this essay Balfour also explains that Stevenson's family was wealthy and benefited financially from the Act of the Union.[17] However, it is unlikely that Stevenson's family supported the union, as the majority of wealthy and impoverished public opinion in Scotland was against the union. Balfour could be using politically correct rhetoric to avoid a touchy political subject, as the United Kingdom still includes Scotland to this day.

As early as 1607, although King James "liked the way the English did things," and "favoured a union" between the two kingdoms, so that he could hold two crowns on his head, originally neither the Scottish people nor their northern neighbors wanted to join identities or a joint Parliament.[18] Before a Treaty of Union could be signed, a great deal of work had to be done to stamp out "vestiges of resistance,"[19] and more suppression was necessary to crush the Jacobite risings that followed the union. MacLean summarizes that "the Union was from the start unpopular."[20] The Scottish rulers felt wronged to be considered as only a "county" of England. Presbyterians felt that their religious rights were violated. MacLean wrote: "Discontent with the Union permeated all classes and all parts of the country and when in 1713 a motion to repeal the Union was submitted to the House of Lords ... it was only defeated by four votes."[21] These were the tensions that brought about repeated Jacobite rebellions in 1715, 1745, and other years, after the union in 1707. Discontent with the union and the depression it had caused was partially quenched when Scotland started to struggle out of the economic depression by producing first tobacco, then cotton. In 1860, Stevenson was ten. His famous lighthouse engineer father, Thomas Stevenson, was forty-two, and at the peak of his career.

Stevenson's more famous engineer grandfather had been dead by this point for ten years, dying in the same year as Stevenson was born. The year 1860 was the peak of the Industrial Revolution in Scotland, when Scotland started relying mostly on the production of "iron, steel, coal, [and on] engineering and shipbuilding."[22] While Scotland developed more roads, railroads and other industrial elements across the nineteenth century, it is likely that the same changes would have occurred without the union. It is more likely that in an independent Scotland, Stevenson's father and grandfather would have benefited more financially from their engineering innovations than they did in the union. Most of their contracts were in Edinburgh and the surrounding region, not in England, so they were not economically tied to a unionist position. Still, it is likely that their government contracts and their reliance on English building laws made Stevenson's family hesitant about expressing anti-unionist opinions in public. Because Stevenson's father was his major artistic patron, the affairs of the Balfours were a matter that Stevenson felt indebted to protect and defend in his writings. Thus, Stevenson refrained from speaking directly against the union or for socialist causes while his father was alive. Instead, Stevenson relied on subversive expressions of his radical socialism and anti-union sentiments. For example, he discovered that his father and grandfather were fans of Scott and believed in the preservation of the Scottish national heritage, and so he stressed these elements in his Scottish novels.

Irish Nationalism

By 1885, Stevenson was blamed for "condoning the campaign of agrarian violence launched by the ... Land League" and the "Irish M.P.s,"[23] in the content, plot and details of *The Dynamiter*. If his other rebellion novels were similarly scrutinized by the press, he would have been found guilty of repeated offenses of inciting various types of rebellions. These details show that, in contrast to the common view that Stevenson turned apolitical, he actually became more radical and pro-revolutionary later in his career.

Stevenson's interest in Scottish nationalism gradually spilled into a concern for all nations that were disempowered by the empire. The closest colonial national neighbor to Scotland was Ireland. When the public activities of the violent Irish nationalists started taking a leading role in the news, Stevenson felt compelled to respond. Harvie wrote: "In 1887 he dreamed up a crazy scheme of moving his whole family to Ireland to take the place of a boycotted Tipperary family."[24] A few other radically inclined critics besides Harvie have mentioned this detail. Here is a more detailed version of the events from Sandison:

> Some eighteen months after the appearance of *The Dynamiter*, he took up the cause of the Irish Curtin family, whose head — a farmer — had been

murdered and the survivors condemned to the dreaded "boycott." Outraged at this, Stevenson proposed moving in with the family even though he might have ended up a martyr to their cause. Only the death of his father put an end to the quixotic scheme.[25]

Aspects of the above quotations maybe cryptic to modern readers, so I will provide some historical background. Irish politics turned especially bloody at the end of the great potato famine, when, in 1867, there was a "series of bomb explosions" at Clerkenwell Prison in London, and elsewhere. A decade later, these terrorist schemes organized into a more specific agenda with the Land League, "which sought personal ownership of the land for the peasantry," or a revolutionary overthrow of the landed aristocracy and bourgeoisie. The Land League had two factions, similar to the Chartists in England, those for "physical" and those for "moral" force. Tensions exploded when the league fought a "Land War" against evictions in the period 1879–82. The league boycotted those who were forcing evictions of peasants.[26] Stevenson proposed going into a war-torn country to move in with a family "called Curtin in County Kerry,"[27] against whom a terrorist organization announced a boycott. The fact that Stevenson was not, in fact, siding with the Land League shows the extent of his rebellious, anti-establishment beliefs. He even wrote "'I won't like it,'" in the same letter to Anne Jenkin where he introduced the idea of supporting the Curtin family[28]; clearly he felt split on the politics of the situation. Stevenson was not a radical who simply sided with the majority of the Socialist Party, but argued for standing up against totalitarianism, no matter at whose hands the unjust actions were taking place. Going against the tide of the rebellion can be a more rebellious action than joining the tide of the mob. It is also likely that Stevenson was more interested in seeing for himself what was happing in Ireland right after the Land War than in standing up for one particular family. It would have been a form of "war tourism" or "poverty tourism" for him to have gone to Ireland in 1887. His numerous novels about rebellions confirm that he was curious to see real rebellions in action, as much as he felt compelled to travel by ship before writing about pirates in *Treasure Island*. More significantly, Stevenson felt compelled to die actively in the middle of a violent action, "like General Gordon," rather than waiting for an "inglorious death by disease."[29] "The likelihood of getting killed doing this seems to have been the main draw of the plan; 'a writer being murdered would attract attention,'" as Stevenson explained in a letter.[30]

Samoan Civil War

Stevenson's latent desire to jump into active combat eventually led to Stevenson's move to Samoa in the middle of a civil war, in part a suicidal act.

Figure 31. "Jim Hawkins watching pirates coming ashore in canoes," by George Edmund Varian. *Treasure Island*. Robert Louis Stevenson. New York: Charles Scribner's Sons, 1918 (Cabinet of American Illustration: Library of Congress, Prints & Photographs Division [reproduction number CAI - Varian, no. 4]).

It was as if he hoped that if he was a casualty of the fighting, his death would be more glorious than slowly fading away in Scotland. Because of his daring, Stevenson was the first to write a historical depiction of a rebellious civil war on an exotic distant island. Neither Dickens nor Scott wrote a purely historical depiction of a rebellion similar to *A Footnote to History*.

An American millionaire picked up Stevenson with a patronage in 1887 after the death of Stevenson's father. Similarly, on the first day when Stevenson arrived in Samoa two years later, an American trader, Harry Jay Moors, embraced Stevenson and insisted on sponsoring the building of Stevenson's Vailima plantation, which led to the writer deciding to settle there and spend his last years on this tropical island. The project quickly became enormously expensive, so that Stevenson acknowledged it was his version of Scott's Abbotsford — an estate that drove both writers onto the ambitious "treadmill" of needing to produce novels at a very fast rate to be able to afford their households.[31]

The politics in Samoa were boisterous when Stevenson first arrived, and quickly turned to war in the years when he was settled there. Two years prior, in 1887, Germany carried out a "deposition ... of the Samoan King, Malietoa Laupepa," and put in place a "pro–German puppet ruler, Tupua Tamasese." As a result of this action, English and American warships were sent into the Samoan harbor. Then, Mataafa Iosefo "led a violent insurgence against Tamasese," with the patronage of none other than Stevenson's American friend Moors. The trouble was that when Mataafa Iosefo won, the Germans tried to reintroduce Malietoa Laupepa, the king they originally threw out. The civil unrest and warfare that occurred in Stevenson's time was between Mataafa Iosefo and Malietoa Laupepa factions of the Samoan population. Naturally, Stevenson was on Mataafa Iosefo's side, not only as a supporter of rebellious action, but also because he was benefiting from the financial support of the same American and English funders that sponsored the insurgent.[32] The trouble was that Stevenson was overly eager in his support for Mataafa Iosefo. He published a dozen articles in *The Times* expressing his radical beliefs. Stevenson argued against "petty corruption, tax avoidance, non-payment of rent among government administrators."[33] Harman argues that Stevenson was barely spared from deportation because Lord Rosebery, the Foreign Secretary, "was a great admirer" of Stevenson's books. There were rumors that Stevenson was a "troublemaker" who "was personally trying to engineer a war." In response to these rumors, instead of stopping his commentary, Stevenson wrote *A Footnote to History*.[34] Not surprisingly, instead of applause, Stevenson was met with a threat of a libel lawsuit by a Samoan "missionary," who felt that the above-mentioned corruption allegations were injurious to his character.[35]

Only a radical socialist could have moved to Samoa in the middle of a civil war and anti-empire stirrings. Here, unlike earlier in life, Stevenson openly supported the anti-imperialist rebels, once again showing his increasing socialism. Stevenson's interest in Samoa's rebellious politics is obvious, not only from the fact that he wrote *A Footnote to History*, but also because the High Commissioner of the Western Pacific, Sir John Thurston, nearly ordered him to be deported from Samoa for being "meddlesome and seditious."[36]

To explain why the high commissioner considered Stevenson to be seditious, one has to consider the history of English colonialism and the anticolonialism movement. The end of the nineteenth century not only saw a flourishing of Marxism, but also was rife in anti–European–colonialism sentiments. The term *anti-imperialist* became a political symbol with the creation of the American Anti-Imperial League around 1898, a couple of years after Stevenson's death. The anticolonialism movement was not only concentrated on Third World occupied territories or countries such as Samoa, but also on nation-states like Scotland and Ireland. Stevenson's passion for the Samoan cause was not only out of concern for the Samoan people, but was also a venue for him to express his anticolonial feelings against England occupying and ruling over Scotland. McCracken refers to "cultural colonization" of Scotland in her comparison of Scott and Stevenson's Scottish nationality.[37] Alan Breck is the leading proponent of pro–Scottish cultural rights in *Kidnapped* and *Balfour*; for example, he says that after England imposed new oppressive laws on Scotland, "it's now a sin to wear a tartan plaid." Of course, the colonization of Scotland was not merely cultural, but also political and economic. Alan complains against the Highlanders' "powers," "clothe," the right to carry arms, and lands being "stripped."[38] The idea that the cultural elements of the oppression were more important for Stevenson comes from passages such as the one where David says that the Act of Parliament was more severe "against those who wore the dress than against those who carried weapons."[39] There are many parallels between Stevenson's sympathy for the rights of the Samoan chiefs and his equal sympathy for the rights of the Highland chiefs, as well as for the rights of both indigent populations to preserve their cultural identities and national independence from colonial control.

A Footnote to History was Stevenson's contribution to the anticolonial and anti–European sentiments that were rife at the end of the nineteenth century. This is evidenced by the book's content. In "Chapter 1: Elements of Discord: Native," Stevenson explains that on the surface, there was infighting or civil conflict between Samoan factions or between "two royal lines,"[40] which Stevenson points out were both foreign to Europeans because they were in a "period of communism"[41] and extreme poverty and political chaos. In "Chapter

2: Elements of Discord: Foreign," he points his finger at those (German, English, American) who started businesses in the area but left the country so poor that what looks like "miserable villages" actually hold the residence of "Samoan kings."[42] Stevenson uses a striking simile to explain that the European and American businesses were robbing the Samoans: a dead German businessman's house "remains pointed like a discharged cannon at the citadel of his old enemies."[43] While *A Footnote* is a history and not a rebellion novel, it is an important document for understanding the motivations for Stevenson's writing of his rebellion novels. Buckton wrote:

> Stevenson used his Scottish fiction — specifically, *David Balfour*— not as an outlet for nostalgia, while he resided abroad, away from his beloved Scotland, but to develop a critique of the colonial conditions on Samoa. As such, *David Balfour* belongs in the company of *A Footnote to History*, a nonfiction text in which he developed his most scathing dissection of the impact of European colonialism on his adopted country.[44]

Stevenson blurred the line between fiction and history and between rebellions that occurred in Scotland and those that occurred more recently in Samoa. Stevenson wrote political pro-rebellion treatises with his fiction as well as in his histories and essays. From the more direct political attack on colonialism in *A Footnote*, it is safe to say that by the end of the 19th century, writers like Stevenson who wrote about rebellions were not as subversive. They did not hide their pro-rebellion sentiments as well as those who wrote at the turn of the 19th century, like Scott. A few decades after Stevenson's death, Lenin and other Marxist theorists claimed that imperialism was the worst form of capitalism. But before Stevenson, Marx barely mentioned colonialism in his anti-capitalist writings. It is likely that Stevenson's outspoken critical "appeal" "to the sovereign"[45] against the colonialism practiced in Samoa, his adopted country, in *A Footnote to History: Eight Years of Trouble in Samoa* (1895) was read by Conrad and later anticolonial writers, who can frequently be quoted as having learned from and admired some of Stevenson's works. The fact that Conrad wrote a work that meets many, but not all, of the criteria of a rebellion novel, *The Secret Agent*, is one example that connects later socialist thinkers with Stevenson. Another example of how influential Stevenson was on colonial politics is Brunsdon Fletcher's 1920 book called, *Stevenson's Germany: The Case Against Germany in the Pacific*, where Fletcher used Stevenson's theory, fiction, history, and biography to make a political case against Germany's colonial influence and settlement of the Pacific. Stevenson's history of Samoa was a significant historical reference and theoretical work for later anticolonial writers.

Evidence of Radical Socialism in Stevenson's Rebellion Novels

As in Scott's and Dickens' rebellion novels, the majority of the radicalism, socialism and nationalism in Stevenson come from remarks by the narrator, remarks by the characters and from the rebellion novel's rebellion theme and plotline.

The Dynamiter

Alan Sandison defines and classifies the dynamiter and the anarchist theme in late nineteenth century fiction in his 2003 essay "A World Made for Liars: Stevenson's *Dynamiter* and the Death of the Real," and in chapters "4: *Prince Otto*: To Write and Obliterate" and "5: *Kidnapped* and *Catriona*: The Missing Storey" of his 1996 book, *Robert Louis Stevenson and the Appearance of Modernism*. Sandison explains that the dynamiters or anarchists in English fiction reflected the times when these works were written. "The last quarter of the nineteenth century was distinguished by ... the number of bombs thrown. A popular target was European royalty, which appears to have dashed from one ceremony to another under a veritable hail of explosive missiles, mostly the violent expression of distaste by one group of anarchists or another."[46] Because of the frequency of attacks on royalty and other European institutions, "influential opinion," (i.e., intellectuals) started to regard "continental anarchists" with "relaxed detachment."[47] Sandison explains that Stevenson, Wilde and Conrad were members of this "influential opinion" and wrote works that satirized, modernized, and made "burlesque" and "absurd" dynamiters and terrorists. Sandison calls *The Dynamiter* "destructive irony," "an anarchic text,"[48] and an "absurdist tragic-comedy," full of "incoherence and meaninglessness."[49] This is a long step from Scott's romantic moral meaningfulness and Dickens' pointed social realism. The goal for the modernizing later writers, including Stevenson, was "to frighten H.M. Government and England's ruling class."[50] To achieve this terrorization of the bourgeoisie, or the "class ... that is primarily concerned with property values,"[51] Stevenson and others made their characters resemble historically based revolutionaries and terrorists. For example, Sandison explains how a character, Zero, in *The Dynamiter* and a professor in Conrad's *The Secret Agent* are both similar in appearance and habits to a well-known dynamite maker and pro-anarchist lecturer of their day, Mezzeroff.[52] In Stevenson's rebellion novels, the rebels become absurd and comedic, but their cause is still justified and supported. While Scott and Dickens relied on gothic horror to frighten the aristocratic and bourgeois readers with the rebellions, Stevenson increases the pitch from

Figure 32. "Robert Louis Stevenson House, 530 Houston Street, Monterey, California" (Historic American Buildings Survey: Library of Congress Prints and Photographs Division).

horror to absurdist terror. Stevenson's purpose in portraying dynamiters or Jacobite rebels is to threaten the English government with a violent overthrow, if the demands of the underdogs for social reform and independence are not granted.

At first, Oscar Wilde looks oddly out of place between hyper-political writers like Stevenson and Conrad, but he did write at least one drama with a dynamiter/rebellion theme, *Vera; Or, the Nihilists*. There was a correlation between the rebellion genre and the launching of spectacular literary careers — Vera; or, *the Nihilists* served the same initial catapulting purpose as *Barnaby Rudge* for Dickens and *Waverley* for Scott. While the play failed, closing after initial runs in the United Kingdom in 1881 and in America in 1882, it was a line on Wilde's dramatic resume, and it made it easier for him to sell future plays and to become a theatrical success. The play is set eighty-six years in the past, in the period 1795–1800, and covers a story about the Russian Nihilists' attempt to assassinate a new czar. The dialogue is thoroughly rebellious. A professor has published an article on the topic that assassination should be "considered as a method of political reform."[53] The nihilists are "preach[ing] socialism"[54] and communism. They are staging a revolution against the abuses of their government.[55] Wilde is frequently sarcastic, showing his typically dramatic wit: "Tragic, but they always end in a farce," says Baron Raff.[56] The play clearly failed because the language is flat, the actions are melodramatic, and the plot was too complex for a formulaic rebellion genre work. The czar at one point joins the nihilists, while he's still a prince, and nearly dies for the cause of the rebels. On the other hand, several rebellion genre formulaic devices are kept. There is a *Romeo and Juliet*-style scene at the end, where the czar proposes that he and Vera die together while Vera is dying, but she misleads the rebels and keeps him from death. The sacrifice of one of the rebels to elicit sympathy for the rebellion, and the use of a love connection to further this sympathy, is a technique common to most other rebellion fiction writers. In addition, there is travel between a periphery and the capital, adventure, a rebellion plot, and the other makings of a rebellion genre work. But the attempt to portray the czar as a rebel himself is not convincing, and as a result the reader's or viewer's suspension of disbelief fades away. The story is partially based on the life of Vera Zasulich, a Marxist revolutionary who was imprisoned for her revolutionary actions, and made a significant impact on the socialist and nihilist movement that eventually led to the assassination of Czar Alexander II in 1881, just as Wilde's play was finished. Of course, it's absurd to think that Vera and Czar Alexander II could have had a love affair between his assassination and her imprisonment for sedition. Wilde simply didn't think his plot through, a common mistake for a great writer picking up steam. The fact that even Wilde wrote a dynamiter rebellion play as early as an 1880 shows that the dynamiter rebellion was a familiar dramatic formula by the time Stevenson wrote *The Dynamiter* in 1885.

In the plot of *The Dynamiter*, M'Guire, an Irish terrorist, prepares for a bombing with some support from an Irish terrorist organization, then travels to and arrives at the square where the bombing is scheduled to occur. However, he faints instead of depositing the bomb, when he suspects that the police are watching him. After this failed attempt, M'Guire tries to find another place to deposit the bomb, but his paranoia takes over and he cannot settle on a good place. Then he is kicked out of a cab that he hoped would take him to a good destination. Finally, M'Guire attempts to throw the bomb into a river, but falls into the river with it, dying an absurd death after a nearly comedic absurd struggle to rid himself of the bomb that was supposed to cause harm to civilians, rather than himself. The descriptive details, that the terrorist dies after a long unsuccessful struggle, and is so frightened that he faints and cannot think logically, make him sympathetic to readers and also absurd. The fact that M'Guire tries to give the bomb to a little girl in the street at one point and almost blows up many people in a public square is, simultaneously, terrifying to readers. While the Jacobites, in *Kidnapped* and *Balfour*, had a justified moral nationalist and socialist purpose, the terrorists are less justified

Figure 33. "Kalakaua, King of Hawaii, with Robert Louis Stevenson and Lloyd Osbourne" (Hawaii State Archives Digital Collections, 1889).

because they act as if they do not know what their purpose is. At the same time, of course, the larger purpose of Irish nationalists was very similar to the purpose of Scottish nationalists, though the Irish nationalists were extremists. Their purpose was, and, for some, still is, to gain national independence and rights for the people living in their respective nations. It is clear that many elements in the *Dynamiter* story are absurd. Through absurdity, Stevenson shows detachment from the terror of the event. Overall, Stevenson is detached, rather than purely sympathetic with the dynamiter's actions, as he is in *Kidnapped* and *Balfour*.

Out of Stevenson's five rebellion novels, the most troubling, both because of its potential ultra-radical sentiment and because of the contradictions that its plot, narrator, and characters present, is *The Dynamiter*. The first-person nationalist extremist narrator in *The Dynamiter* story "Zero's Tale of the Explosive Bomb" comments as the dynamiter is about to be sent off on his deadly errand that despite pleas from the dynamiter, M'Guire, that he might be "arrested," "I was not to be moved, made a strong appeal to his patriotism, gave him a good glass of whisky, and dispatched him on his glorious errand."[57] The use of the first-person voice humanizes the extremist narrating the story, and makes his command less distant or foreign to readers. At the same time, the mixture of "whisky" and "patriotism" is absurd and has a modernist tint. The narrator then explains why the public square was chosen, saying that it has a lot of "unfortunate young ladies of the poorer classes ... all classes making a direct appeal to public pity, and therefore suitable with our designs."[58] Stevenson explains that the terrorists hope to inspire sympathy by harming innocent people, but in the end they instead achieve this sympathy by having the dynamiter himself killed by drowning. Zero, the narrator of the dynamiter tale, exclaims in the dynamiter's support, "There he was, friendless and helpless, a man in the very flower of life, for he is not yet forty; with long years of happiness before him; and now condemned, in one moment, to a cruel and revolting death by dynamite!... It is probable he fainted."[59] Zero inspires readers with sympathy through this and other appeals to the unfortunate state of the dynamiter, and to his semi-tragic and semi-absurdist demise. For example, the dynamite is called "tragic cargo."[60] Of course, calling the dynamite "tragic cargo" can also be a warning against the dangers of using dynamite, but the term "tragic" does suggest that a human "tragedy" is also afoot. Stevenson also returns to a favorite term of Scott's, "wavering," writing that M'Guire was "wavering like a drunken man" from his "terror and horror," as he was unsuccessfully trying to think of a way to rid himself of the bomb.[61] Just as Scott criticizes his wavering characters by showing their insanity and lack of courage, so does Stevenson show that M'Guire's drunken "wavering" is his primary mistake in the terrorist undertaking. Once again, I am not saying that Stevenson supported terrorism, but only that *The Dynamiter*, in particular, portrays a hopelessness and absurdist despair that sympathizes with the dynamiter as well as with the children in the square whom he might have killed if he did not waver. To inspire further sympathy for M'Guire, Zero exclaims, "Even your brutal Government, in the heyday of its lust for cruelty, though it scruples not to hound the patriot with spies, to pack the corrupt jury, to bribe the hangman, and to erect the infamous gallows, would hesitate to inflict so horrible a doom,"[62] referring to the dynamiter killing himself with his own dynamite. Stevenson explains and in part excuses the actions of the dynamiters by stating that they are actions directed against a "brutal" and unjust government for the greater good. If the government is "corrupt" and "brutal," this, in Zero's eyes, excuses the terrorists' "brutal" response.

Kidnapped

In comparison with *The Dynamiter*, *Kidnapped* and *David Balfour* follow Scott and Dickens' purpose, structure and linguistics far more closely. *Kidnapped* and *Balfour* were nearly called plagiarisms of Scott's Jacobite Waverley novels by early critics. The purpose in these rebellion novels is clearly to express support for Scottish nationalism, and for literal radical politics.

Stevenson uses the first-person voice in three out of his five rebellion novels. In *Kidnapped*, Stevenson frequently introduces socialist and radical views through his first-person narrator, David Balfour. When David is first kidnapped, he worries that he will be sold into slavery in the United States, as "in those days of my youth, white men were still sold into slavery on the plantations."[63] David makes an anti-white-slavery statement, and it is especially convincing coming from a sympathetic child who is being taken into slavery, without breaking any law. After David rescues himself from his captors with Alan's help, he overhears many conversations by Alan and his Jacobite friends about the injustices the English and Scottish government is perpetrating against the Scottish people. When David begins to encounter the term "Jacobite," a Jacobite asks him if he is "'of the honest party?'" David explains in parentheses after this question that "each side, in these sort of civil broils, takes the name of honesty for its own."[64] Similar explanations across the text explain that David is neutral in the Jacobite struggle. But his actions clearly side with the Jacobites, as, for example, in the second half of the series, in *David Balfour*, David tirelessly tries to rescue James, one of the leading Jacobites, from false imprisonment. Balfour's statement excuses both sides of the rebellions that Stevenson portrays, thereby equating the Jacobite rebels with the government that they are rebelling against. The idea that the two are equally just is in itself radical. The voice in *Kidnapped* that is the strongest supporter of the Jacobite cause is Alan, who makes frequent propagandistic speeches, such as the following.

> They stripped him of his powers; they stripped him of his lands; they plucked the weapons from the hands of his clansmen, that had borne arms for thirty centuries; ay, and the very clothes off their backs — so that it's now a sin to wear a tartan plaid, and a man may be cast into a gaol if he has but a kilt about his legs. One thing they couldnae kill. That was the love the clansmen bore their chief.[65]

Alan passionately defends the rights of the Highlanders to their culture and national traditions, and in practice fights for these beliefs, assisting the Jacobites in Scotland and in France. Many parallels can be drawn between Alan's speech above and similar speeches made in *Waverley* and *Rob Roy*, as the problems they discuss concern the same historical period, when the Highlanders right to their kilts and tartan" was one of the points of dispute between Scotland and England.

David Balfour

The political language in *Balfour* is a bit tamer than what is used in *Kidnapped* in part because, after James went on trial, Balfour and the Highlanders become a bit shyer about expressing their rebellious beliefs in public in front of a self-titled Whig like Balfour. When there are propagandistic, political, pro-rebellion statements, they focus on injustices among Scottish clans, rather than pointing the blame at England. The unjust trial of James for the Appin murder is called "a clan battle between savage clans."[66] In addition, most of the active maneuvers in *Balfour* are not violent attacks against representatives of the corrupted Scottish-English government, as David attacks the shipmates that kidnap him. In *Balfour*, we see a "peaceful revolution," where Balfour attempts, without success, to gain justice for Stewart and for other Jacobites by working through the legal system, instead of taking violent actions.[67] When James is found guilty and condemned to death, the duke, the "chief of the Campbells, sitting as Justice-General ... addressed the unfortunate Stewart" thus: "If you had been successful in that rebellion you might have been giving the law where you have now received the judgment of it ... and then you might have been satiated with the blood of any name or clan to which you had an aversion."[68] The justice who rules against the Jacobite is shown to be at fault of convicting a man simply because of his "aversion" to a rival "clan," rather than for any moral or justifiable reason. The government, and specifically the legal system in Scotland, is shown to be corrupt, and this is telling given Stevenson's legal background.

Pentland Rising

In *Pentland Rising*, Stevenson begins with a long speech on the injustices that led to the rising, which outruns Scott's propaganda in length. The speech's primary position implies that Stevenson was less afraid that censors like his publisher might stop the book from being published due to the radical nature of the following diatribe from the third-person narrator, who complains that "mean" "preachers" had so many "prejudices against the Episcopacy, that they took bribes from them, and that:

> when the fines could not be paid at once, bibles, clothes, and household utensils were seized upon, or a number of soldiers, proportionate to his wealth, were quartered on the offender. The coarse and drunken privates filled the houses with woe; snatched the bread from the children to feed their dogs; shocked the principles, scorned the scruples, and blasphemed the religion of their humble hosts; and when they had reduced them to destitution, sold the furniture, and burned down the roof-tree, which was consecrated to the peasants by the name of Home.[69]

This long explanation of the crimes committed by those that the rebellion was perpetrated against is an example of how Stevenson uses the narrator's voice to give his socialist or radical perspective on the ills he sees in society, which, as in this case, he indicates are severe enough to have brought about a justified rebellion. Stevenson shows a radical, socialist and actively propagandistic purpose in all of his rebellion novels and in the life he led as he wrote them.

14

Stevenson's Structural Features

Genre Categorization, Mixture and Influences

Residues from Other Genres

It is typical for critics of rebellion novels to state that they cannot easily place the rebellion novels into a single genre category. In fact, the writers themselves typically did not know how to classify their works. In an 1883 letter to Henley, Stevenson concludes that in his first rebellion novel, *Prince Otto*, he sees that "the whole thing is not a romance, nor yet a comedy; not yet a romantic comedy; but a kind of preparation of some of the elements of all three in a glass jar."[1]

W. W. Robson pinpoints the main problem when he writes that *Kidnapped* defies existing genre classifications: "Is it a travel book, or an adventure story, or a historical novel? It seems to be all these things, and yet not precisely any of them." He continues that when applied to Stevenson's novel, "the guidance we get from the concept of 'genre fiction' ceases to be helpful."[2] Susan Gannon explains that Stevenson is frequently placed into the children's fiction genre because he has simple plots and characterizations, relies on "formulaic plots," uses an "interpreting narrator," and includes "illustrations."[3] Rebellion genre novels are frequently misplaced for having parallels with fairy tales, children's stories, epics, gothic horror and adventure "quest plots," and in this respect Stevenson is no different.

This inability to define Stevenson's work has led critics to unsuccessfully try to assign links between his novels based on traditional genre designations. Hence Robson, for example writes, "His interest in the Appin murder may well be the generic explanation for the difference between the two books," (*Kidnapped* and *Treasure Island*).[4] Robson notices that the uprising or the assassination[5] separates the two works, both with historical and adventurous genre elements, but he does not conclude the thought by pinpointing and defining a rebellion genre because he is comparing the wrong set of Stevenson's novels.

Mimicry of Scott, Dickens, James and Other Writers

The evidence in support of Stevenson's open mimicry of Scott and Dickens is overwhelming, as seen by the sheer size of this section. But before discussing textual and critical evidence that Stevenson mimicked prior writers, and especially Scott, it is important to establish that Stevenson grew up listening to his well-known grandfather, the famous engineer, telling stories about how in 1814, when Walter Scott published *Waverley*, the famous author visited Bell Rock, the lighthouse that Robert Stevenson engineered, and wrote "upon deck" his preparatory notes for *The Pirate*. Stevenson's family admired and honored Scott decades later, not for his artistic merit, but for his "work ethic," Scott's ability to keep writing while on a tour of a lighthouse.[6] Thus, mimicry of Scott's method, in terms of Scott's generic rules as well as writing speed, was a primary measuring stick for Stevenson as he was developing his own writing. Mimicking elements of Scott's rebellion novels would have been as natural as following the steps of a tutor.

Most readers and critics know the formula that makes great literature. Most writers prefer writing according to this formula, as it helps them to alleviate writer's block associated with the possibility that they might write something that is incomprehensible or disordered. Stevenson wholly confesses that he has frequently dipped into the "old stock incidents and accessories, tricks of workmanship and schemes of composition (all being admirably good, or they would long have been forgotten)" because they offered him "ready-made but not perfectly appropriate solutions for any problem that arises" in literature. He also stresses that he has always worked to find "fresh solutions" and has worked to involve his art beyond the "academic" repetition of the same old tricks.[7] Stevenson settled on mimicry after he spent over fifteen years between ages fifteen and thirty-one in writing unsuccessful or financially unprofitable works, and writing nearly twelve unfinished novels.[8] Stevenson makes one of the most frank and humorous confessions about his mimicry in an essay he published near the end of his career, in 1894, in the *Idler*, called "My First Book: 'Treasure Island.'" He begins by confessing that it is "painful" for him to admit that the "parrot," in his *Treasure Island*, "once belonged to Robinson Crusoe," and that the "skeleton" was "conveyed from Poe." He excuses this weakness with, "No man can hope to have a monopoly of skeletons or make a corner in talking birds." Stevenson frequently cites his sources in his texts, without making formal notations. For example, in *Kidnapped* Stevenson provides an indirect reference to *Crusoe*, "In all the books I've read of people cast away, they had ... their pockets full of tools."⁹ In the same critical piece as the above, Stevenson explains another of his borrowings: "The material detail of my first chapters ... all were the property of Washington Irving." For Stevenson, Poe, Irving, Dickens and Scott were "useful writers" who left "Footprints" that he joyfully "plagiarized," a term he himself uses. Stevenson exclaims, "I believe plagiarism was rarely carried further." Yet, at the same time, "it seemed to belong to me like my right eye."¹⁰ By mixing together tricks and bits of so many great works, and by stirring in his own imaginings and drawing his own maps and his own plots, Stevenson created works that have independent literary merit from the giants that he originally mimicked.

It might not be too farfetched to claim that a majority of literary critics mention Scott when they discuss Stevenson's Scottish novels. Many say that Stevenson mimicked, if not plagiarized, Scott's novels, especially so in *Kidnapped* and *Balfour*. One of the best and earliest examples of this is an unsigned review in *St. James's Gazette* on July 19, 1886, days after *Kidnapped* was first published:

> Mr. Stevenson has boldly and even wisely ventured into the field of Jacobite romance which has already been occupied by the genius of Sir Walter Scott. Different as is the character of his book, we feel that indirectly Mr. Stevenson owes a little of his general idea to the author of "Rob Roy" and "Waverley." But although there is a perceptible parallel between the adventures of David Balfour and those that have immortalized the names of Osbaldistone and Bailie Jarvie, the parallel is too slight to be insisted on. The story of the Jacobite times is an inexhaustible mine for the writer of fiction, and the originality and literary skill of Mr. Stevenson is doubly welcome for this addition to the number of Highland stories. "Rob Roy" is inimitable; but it says much for Mr. Stevenson's powers that "Kidnapped" seems none the less charming for the very reason that it recalls the masterpiece of the greatest story-teller of our century.¹¹

The above review is very telling as it points out a similarity in "character" between Scott and Stevenson's rebellion novels, lightly hinting that Stevenson used Scott's formula. The critic claims that he is not insisting on the similarity, and yet continues to argue his case, clearly simply being nice to soften the blow of ridicule. But he also explains that if Scott's formula works and the finished products are pleasant to read, he does not see a problem with this type of mimicry of prior great authors.

Another unsigned review, written a month later, in the *Saturday Review*, stated that, "If Sir Walter Scott could revisit the glimpses of the moon, and read 'Kidnapped' by their light, that great man would acknowledge, with his characteristic excess of generosity, that David Balfour [in Stevenson's *David Balfour*] was worthy to rank with Alan Fairford [in Scott's *Redgauntlet*]."¹²

Here again the critic points out that the mimicry of the formula for two of the leading characters in the books is acceptable because Stevenson achieves mastery of the writing craft. When done professionally and with artistic skill, mimicry becomes a tool of a seasoned artist and not a fault of a hack.

Some critics point out that it is acceptable for Stevenson to mimic Scott because Scott in his turn mimicked historical accounts of actual characters and events. If two novels by two different authors discuss the same historical event, such as a Jacobite rising, it is impossible and undesirable that the finished product should have differing plots or other elements from those that were present in the original historical situation. T. Watts-Dunton notices in an 1886 review in the *Athenaeum* that, "of both 'Guy Mannering' and 'Kidnapped' the main action was suggested by the Annesley case, that marvelous romance of real life which, in 'The Wandering Heir,' not even Charles Reade could effectually vulgarize and spoil for future use." Watts goes on to explain the historical similarities between the historical Annesley and his likeness in the fictional character of Balfour.[13]

Reviews of Stevenson's novels, when read in great quantities side by side, almost seem like imitations of each other, as they convey very similar messages. Of course, similarly to Stevenson, each reviewer adds a new dimension to the general understanding of why and how Stevenson mimicked Scott. For example, in a review in the *Spectator* in 1888, R. H. Hutton writes that *The Black Arrow* does not only mimic the Jacobite plot of Scott's *Ivanhoe*, but that these two works also share an anti-feudal political agenda.

> The "Black Arrow" is the name given to an association of yeomen who combine against the exactions and tyranny of their feudal lords. It is an association not unlike that of which Sir Walter Scott has given us so brilliant a sketch in "Ivanhoe," in the picture of Locksley and his followers, though Mr. Stevenson's story is supposed, of course, to be a couple of centuries or more later.... The art of making outlaws impressive, and of so interweaving their feats with the feats of feudal oppressors as to excite sympathy for the outlaw without entirely destroying the charm of the feudal order to which he was opposed, seems to have been reserved for Scotchmen.... If "Ivanhoe" be the most brilliant tale for boys which genius ever penned, "The Black Arrow" certainly deserves to be mentioned next to it as one which, without even suggesting an imitator, displays a master-hand in the same field.[14]

One of the funnier criticisms of Stevenson's mimicry of Scott was written by Andrew Lang in an unsigned article, "Modern Men: Mr. R. L. Stevenson" in the *Scots Observer* in 1889, a year after the publication of *The Black Arrow*: "As an illustration of our author's popular success, it is told how a small American lad was once induced or compelled to read 'Rob Roy'—a romance by one of our forgotten old novelists. On finishing this fable, the American youth remarked that it was 'not bad, and rather like Stevenson.'"[15] The seventy-five years between *Waverley* and *The Black Arrow* meant that most people outside of Scotland were reading only the new works by Stevenson, with only a tiny portion of the population was still able to recall Scott's masterpieces. However, if Stevenson wrote his first rebellion novel hoping that Scott was forgotten and that the plotline would not seem too familiar, it is odd that he did not stop writing rebellion novels after numerous reviews started appearing, all mocking the mimicry in the plotlines. On the other hand, it is possible that more and more reviews appeared because numerous critics simply had to speak up and comment on the somewhat outrageous similarity. If Stevenson coveted the press, which would have helped his sales, then it might have been of benefit to him to repeat the same mistake again and again. If this was the case, he certainly received positive encouragement, as can be seen from the fact that reviews on the topic of mimicry of Scott kept appearing across Stevenson's five attempts at the rebellion novel.

Criticism of Stevenson's works was revived in the middle of the twentieth century by Daiches and other Scottish nationalists. Stevenson was abandoned for a few decades because he became stigmatized as a children's writer, and worst as a "hack" writer. A hack writer is typically known as such because he mimics previously used plots and generic devices to write books quickly for financial rewards. In a 1951 Memorial Lecture at Yale University, celebrating the acquisition of Edwin Beinecke's Stevenson collection, David Daiches, also an Edinburgh Scot, said about Stevenson "that even in his immature and imitative work we can see ... [the] desire to ring in the human implication through style and allusion which is the marl of a major writer."[16] Daiches was reacting to recent criticisms he read that objected to calling Stevenson a major writer, and rather saw him as a hack who closely imitated his predecessors or committed "plot clichés." Daiches' objection is that there is a paradox when most critics see mimicry and previously used plot patterns, and still call certain works classics. As most writers who try to evolve their craft soon learn, without imitation it is impossible to create "great" fiction because critics evaluate fiction based on criteria of elements that have been called "great" in the past, and a completely "original" piece is more likely to be incomprehensible than anything else.

While the most frequent comparison drawn by recent and earlier critics is between Scott and Stevenson, a few critics have drawn far more complex parallels between Stevenson and his predecessors. Edwin Eigner, explains that Stevenson took or borrowed elements from "such masterpieces as *Wuthering Heights, The Marble Faun, Huckleberry Finn,* and *Crime and Punishment....* And while it is perhaps improper to regard Stevenson as having improved on these books, it is just as wrong to dismiss him as a mere copier of the ideas he took from the great masters of his tradition. Always ... he modified their themes with his own insights and concerns, and he made their ideas fitter to be transmitted into our own [20th] century."[17] Eigner sees parallels between Stevenson's works and Scott's *Rob Roy*: in the appearance of Rob Roy's son in *Kidnapped*[18]; *Waverley,* in the depictions of Highlander culture[19]; *Redgauntlet,* because Stevenson is also a Jacobite sympathizer[20]; and *The Heart of Mid-Lothian,* because of the "light and dark sisters'" "dualistic psychology" technique.[21] Eigner also explains the parallels between Stevenson and Dickens' *A Tale of Two Cities* because this book also uses elements of "mesmerist" or "abnormal psychology," and attacks the established legal system.[22] It is amazing that, despite repeating comparisons between Stevenson, Scott and Dickens, none of the prior critics explained the similarities between this set of novels as all being members of the rebellion novel genre. Of course, one can see how the parallels can be blurred when one puts *Huckleberry Finn* in the middle of *Waverley* and *Kidnapped.*

One of the odder borrowings that Stevenson performed when he wrote rebellion novels was mimicking Henry James. This is odd because James made an uncharacteristic divergence when he wrote rebellious novels at the same time as Stevenson was at the peak of his rebellious writings. The correspondences between Henry James and Stevenson started around the time both published novels on rebellion themes, May 9, 1885, shortly after their first meeting. James published two rebellious or radical novels. There are several generic dimensions in these works that exclude them from falling into the parameters set in this study for membership in the rebellion genre. These two works are *The Princess Casamassima* (1885–86), and *The Bostonians* (1886). The first work is excluded because it is about a fictional, rather than historic, assassination by a Londoner of an aristocrat, which ends with the would-be assassin's suicide. Here is an interesting summary of the socialist and revolutionary politics in *The Princess Casamassima* by James in a 1908 preface to the work:

> He [the main character, Hyacinth Robinson] has thrown himself into the more than "shady" underworld of *militant socialism*, he has undertaken to play a part—a part that with the drop of his exasperation and the growth, simply expressed, of his taste, is out of all tune with his passion, at any cost, for life itself, the life, whatever it be, that surrounds him. Dabbling deeply in *revolutionary politics* of a hole-and-corner sort, he would be "in" up to his neck, and with that precarious part of him particularly involved, so that his tergiversation is the climax of his adventure [my italics].[23]

The above preface was shocking to its readers, despite the softening words that James uses, like "out of all tune with his passion" when referring to "militant socialism" and "revolutionary politics."

The Bostonians is excluded from the rebellion novel genre because it is about radicals and feminists, but does not include any violent revolts; thus, *The Bostonians* can be counted as a socialist or a radical political novel, but not as a rebellion novel. Henry James and Stevenson exchanged letters about their first rebellion novels. The two met shortly before they both wrote rebellious novels. After this meeting, James wrote to Stevenson upon seeing the first somewhat positive review of Stevenson's *Dynamiter*. The influence they had on each other is obvious, as even the titles echo each other: James' is called *The Princess Casamassima* and the second of Stevenson's rebellion novels is called *Prince Otto*. Further still, *The Princess Casamassima* was "inspired by the same recent political events, bombings and assassinations, as *The Dynamiter*."[24] While both were inspired by the same events, Stevenson's work is more historically accurate and includes rebellious violence, rather than just violence turned on the rebel himself. Still, the similarities are significant. The parallels between Stevenson and James are certainly not accidental; James also frequently admitted "his need to appropriate others' work."[25] Beattie explains that there were several parallels in the biographies and actions of the revolutionary characters in Stevenson's rebellion novels and earlier short works from the *New Arabian Nights* and James's *Princess Casamassima*. The two remained close friends over the next ten years, as Stevenson continued writing other rebellion novels.

While some critics see *Kidnapped* and *Balfour* as mixed-genre creations, or as works of uncertain generic identification, most explain them as Stevenson's imitations of Sir Walter Scott's "historical romances."[26] Stevenson did not hide his admiration for and mimicry of both Scott and Dickens. He put Scott on a pedestal as the first great historical writer, the one who "inaugurated" the use of "detail" in literature.[27] Stevenson viewed Dickens as a writer who, in his later years, mastered the most advanced literary technique or "tricking,"[28] as Stevenson called it. Stevenson frequently referred to both of these giants; for example he wrote "An Old Scotch Gardener" in honor of and upon reflecting on "Andrew Fairservice" from Scott's *Rob Roy*. Stevenson taught himself the rebellion novel formula through studying the formulas that Scott and Dickens used.

Stevenson's Structural Rebellion Novel Formula

While the Aristotelian unities were a major concern for Dickens, they were not as significant for Stevenson. Stevenson's formula is closer to Scott's, especially as both returned frequently to the Scottish nationalist theme. Here are the two formulas side by side:

> Scott's Structural Formula = **S** (Sales) + **P** (Scottish Nationalist Propaganda) = **J** (Violent Jacobite Uprising) + **T** (Travel) + **L** (Love) + **S** (Success of Protagonist)
>
> Stevenson's Structural Formula = **S** (Sales) + **P** (Scottish Nationalist and Socialist Propaganda) = **R** (Rebellion) + **T** (Travel) + **A** (Adventure)

The goals that Scott and Stevenson set for themselves in writing rebellion novels were very similar. Both writers wanted to promote the Scottish national identity and to support the economic growth and enrichment of Scotland. Both were concerned with producing novels quickly to pay their enormous bills. To achieve these goals, Stevenson mimicked many aspects of Scott's formula, but also added innovations and alternations to these elements. Both writers depicted at least a few Jacobite rebellions. But while Scott focused solely on Jacobite rebellions, Stevenson also depicted an Irish dynamiter and other categories of rebellious events. Travel by the main characters is an important ingredient that moves both writers' novels forward and adds a frequent change of scenery to the novels. One of the changes in Stevenson's model, which has been most criticized and examined by literary critics, is Stevenson's avoidance of the love story to instead focus on the adventure of a busy plotline. Of course, in *Catriona* and other works Stevenson makes some attempts at portraying love, but it is usually notoriously badly done, so that it is not a major ingredient of the formula, but rather an add-on that he occasionally sticks into his plots.

Another way of calculating Stevenson's rebellion novel formula is by looking at the "five movements" of plot[29] in Stevenson's six rebellion novels.

> Stevenson's Five Plot Movements: 1) Exposition + 2) Threat or Conflict Begins + 3) Rebellious Attack + 4) Rebels are Defeated and Run + 5) Varying Resolution for the Main Character (marriage/ inheritance/ death)

The plots of Stevenson's rebellion novels follow similar roads, with the same major acts or plot development points. The five movements are: the introduction to the characters and their motivations or political views; the main character faces conflicts and trials and struggles through them; the rebellion occurs amidst other adventures; flight away from the rebellion or the continuation or decline of the rebellion; the hero recovers an inheritance/marries or otherwise wins over his adversaries and major challenges/simultaneously the rebels guilty of murder, or suspected of murder are executed. Robson explains the existence of five plot movements in fiction in general, but does not apply it specifically to the types of developmental points that exist in rebellion novels.

While the plots are occasionally split in two, typically there is a single plot around a single rebellious movement or event. The endings are frequently tragic for some of the minor rebels but happy for the main character. There are a few exceptions, such as *The Dynamiter*, when things end badly for the main character. The following sections will detail the structural ingredients of Stevenson's rebellion novels.

Plot

To better see the similarities and differences between the plots of Stevenson's six rebellion novels, a table is needed.

The same author who talks about the "five movements" of plot, W. W. Robson, finds that Stevenson's narrative does not have "clear-cut plot-outlines."[30] This objection can be countered by studying the methodical patterns of similar rebellion novel plotlines that are listed in the table above. The threat of rebellion or build-up always comes before a violent rebellious action. There are always expositions and resolutions. The criticism originates from the fact that Stevenson crams a lot of travel or adventurous incidents into his rebellion novels, and these numerous actions make the main plot seem less connected.

Stevenson began developing his rebellion genre techniques in his youth. The seeds for *Kidnapped* were planted when Stevenson, at 16, published his first book, *The Pentland Rising* (a short novella of 22 pages), using material from histories to create a historical fiction based on the 1666 Edinburgh rebellion or "rising." In a letter to Theodore Watts-Dunton in 1886, Stevenson wrote, "*Kidnapped* was doomed, while still in the womb and while I was yet in the cradle, to be the thing it is."[31] Stevenson's desire to become a fiction writer went hand in hand with his designs for his first rebellion novel. Across the three major authors discussed in this book, it is clear that writing rebellion novels is a life-long obsession and dedication.

In Part I of *Pentland*, Stevenson explains the "causes of the revolt": the preachers were scandalous and had "violent tempers"; so "the country-folk refused to go to the parish churches"; the preachers raised funds against those who didn't attend of "twenty shillings"; and these debts piled up until it was impossible for the poor to pay them.[32] Part II describes "The Beginning" of the revolt as three soldiers threaten to "thresh" the corn of an old man; folks hear the news that an old man is about to be roasted "naked, on his own girdle"; when the people arrive on the scene, John M'Lellan of Barskob draws a pistol and shoots a corporal, thus rescuing the old man.[33] Just like the chapters in *Waverly* on the march of the Scottish troops, Part III is titled "The March of the Rebels." In Part IV, as usual, the rebels are crushed and many die in the cause of "life and liberty."[34] In Part V, the remaining thirty rebels are hanged, two of these being first "tortured with the boots"; then the goods of those blamed are confiscated and the dead bodies are dismembered.[35] The

	Pentland Rising	*Black Arrow*	*Dynamiter*	*Kidnapped*	*Young Chevalier*	*Catriona*
Plot Movements:						
1st: Exposition	Corruption among the preachers	Richard struggles as a dependent	M'Guire, an Irish terrorist, prepares attack	David goes on a quest for inheritance	Prince Charlie drinks & argues in a wine-shop	David attempts stopping Stewart's execution
2nd: Rising Action & Conflicts	Rebels defend old farmer, about to be roasted	Richard joins the Black Arrow rebels	M'Guire arrives at the Square, but faints instead of depositing bomb	David's uncle has him kidnapped, but David escapes with Alan (Jacobite)	Prince contemplates a Jacobite resurgence	Lord Advocate kidnaps & maroons David on island with Highlanders
3rd: Peak of Rebellion	Rebels march on the authorities	Rebels attacks Richard's guardian	M'Guire tries to deposit the bomb in other places	David witnesses the Appin Murder/assassination	There is a fight/quarrel in the wine-shop	David escapes & argues for Stewart's innocence at his trial
4th: Flight & Loss of Rebellion	Rebels lose the fight; 30 hanged	Rebels lose & are imprisoned	M'Guire is kicked out of a cab	David is suspected & flees through the country with Alan	The Prince contemplates his sad Jacobite fortune	Stewart is executed, but other rebels (David) are freed
5th: Resolution for the Main Character	Narrator supports the cause of the dead	Richard marries Joanna	M'Guire attempts throwing bomb in a river, but falls with it	David & Alan arrive at safety & reclaim inheritance	Fragmented book: ends abruptly, without a resolution	David marries Catriona & runs his wealthy estate

Figure 34. Comparative Plots of Stevenson's Rebellion Novels

separation of *Pentland* into five parts makes it easier to see the major plot movements at work in it.

Stevenson's next rebellion novel is similarly titled to Dickens' *A Tale of Two Cities* or Disraeli's *Sybil: A Tale of Two Nations*. Duality is an important element in the plots of these books. The haves are cruel and corrupt, and the have-nots are forced into violent rebellions. It is difficult to separate the *Black*

Arrow's plot from its hackish formula and the resulting high sales of the book. Even if early criticisms of this and other rebellion novels were negative, *The Black Arrow: A Tale of Two Roses* "sent sales through the roof," as the circulation of *Young Folks* rose enormously.[36] The plot of the novel follows Richard Shelton, or Dick, as he joins a band of outlaws as their captain in the second half of the book and fights against the man who assisted in killing his father to access his fortune, gained by acting as his guardian. Dick sets out to avenge his father.[37] One critic, Paul Maixner,[38] referring to the highly hackish style, wrote that in this novel, "The hero's ups and downs recur at intervals of five pages or so until the oscillation between triumph and despair becomes positively ludicrous." These abrupt plot turns are also the element that makes the plot seem disjointed. The civil war is in the background of Dick's rebellion. The *Young Folks* "hack" writer whom Stevenson mimicked, Phillips, used the "historical cast" or formula by utilizing "high-sounding titles," "swordplay, derring-do and tushery."[39] The novel was written in a short period, "galloping only a few days ahead of weekly deadlines."[40] Stevenson claimed at first that he didn't write it, and that instead "George North" wrote it.[41] In January 1888, McClure paid Stevenson $11,000 to print the book in America — this was the largest sum Stevenson was ever paid for his fictions.

Dick fully joins the Black Arrow in Book III (out of five), where in Chapter 1, three months pass after Book II, and Dick is by then the leader of the "outlaws." Duckworth is the founder of the "fellowship of the Black Arrow," which he started as "a ruined man longing for vengeance and money."[42] The outlaws are so poor that Lawless, a sea captain who is Dick's primary assistant in his rebellious attacks, says, "This is my native land, this burrow in the earth!"[43] referring to a dugout hall with some wood and straw in it to keep them warm from the snow, as they run from their pursuers. The rebels assist Dick, killing Joanna's husband-to-be, whom she is forced to marry. At an earlier point, Dick pirates a ship, trying to rescue Joanna from the same marriage and from a kind of imprisonment. Dick and Lawless are seized for killing Lord Shoreby, the groom. Dick accuses Sir Daniel of being "the murderer of my natural father and the unjust retainer of my lands and revenues."[44] Dick explains that he was forced to join the Black Arrow because he was "helpless and penniless" due to Sir Daniel's crimes against him.[45] After Dick and Lawless' capture, they are taken to Earl Risingham's cabinet. He lets them go for political reasons because Sir Daniel is on the other side of the War of the Roses.[46] In the end, Lawless dies in an abbey as a "friar." Dick and Joanna are married, with the help of Lord Foxham, who earlier helped in the theft of the ship and was injured. While the personal lives of the rebellious heroes end well, the Black Arrow "flieth nevermore — the fellowship is broken," as Ellis Duckworth, the founder, declares.[47] As you can see, this is a rapid story with many plot twists, and with the main five plot movements that are summarized in the table above.

The Dynamiter was original published by a London press (Longmans, Green & Co.), in the same year, 1885, as *Kidnapped* and *Prince Otto*, both also with London presses (Chatto & Windus, Piccadilly). *The Dynamiter* is the second part of his *New Arabian Nights* series; it focuses on the Irish, anti-English and anti-union rebels, or terrorists, labels depending on the perspective of the reader. The book is addressed, in an introductory note, to "Police Officers," and mentions the horror the public has of "political crime."[48] As the title suggests, unlike the gun that is used in *Kidnapped*, the primary weapon of choice for these Irish rebels is dynamite. Several short stories about their political crimes are related. The most direct story about a bombing is a chapter titled, "Zero's Tale of the Explosive Bomb," narrated, as a note indicates, by an Arabian author, and only translated by Stevenson and his wife. The first-person "I" in the narrative is an Arab friend of a man, M'Guire, who attempts to bomb a public square in London, but fails when he becomes paranoid upon seeing a police officer at the scene, and suspects a government conspiracy against the rebels. In a modernist twist, he faints instead of depositing the bomb in the crowded square and then runs around the city trying to find a little girl, a woman or a taxi driver who might deliver the bomb for him. The story ends with M'Guire flinging the bag with the bomb into the river and falling "headlong after it."[49] The tale is comically and lightly told, with a few strokes of gothic horror in the elements of terror of death (similar to the gothic horror or "superstitious fear" in "Black Andie's Tale of Tod Lapraik" in *Balfour*) by explosion on the part of the man carrying the bomb. It is likely that Stevenson read many novels about rebellion in preparation for this work, and the polished stylistics in *Kidnapped* are clearly the result of these early experiments.

After the above experiments, Stevenson wrote his most tightly constructed and best-loved rebellion novel, *Kidnapped*. Despite contrary opinions, Stevenson made detailed outlines before he began writing a new novel and he stuck to them. He even included a summary of *Kidnapped* on the first pages:

> KIDNAPPED: Being memoirs of the adventures of DAVID BALFOUR; in the year 1751: how he was kidnapped and cast away; his sufferings in a desert isle; his journey in the Wild Highlands; his acquaintance with ALAN BRECK STEWART ["a rebel and a smuggler"[50]] and other notorious Highland Jacobites; with all that he suffered at the hands of his uncle, EBENEZER BALFOUR OF SHAWS, falsely so-called; written by himself, and now set forth by ROBERT LOUIS STEVENSON.[51]

The most pivotal point of the plot is not named in this summary. This missing plotline is the assassination at Appin of Colin Campbell, the "Red Fox," who collected King George's taxes, and the subsequent accusation and arrest of James Stewart, a member of a rival Scottish clan that opposed the Campbells, for the act. If Stevenson wanted to fool the censors, leaving the assassination out of the book's summary would have been a great trick. The fact that the main character was friends with a Jacobite simply places the novel in Scotland; it does not advertise it as a rebellion novel to the English boys, who were the primary buyers of Stevenson's fiction.

The Young Chevalier is difficult to test for the five common rebellion novel plot movements because it is only a segment and does not even reach a climax or a rebellion. In the table under this title, I expanded the short actions into the basic exposition, rising action, and climax, but it is obvious that with only two chapters to go on, this work cannot be properly tested for genre rule adherence. *Chevalier* only went as far as being an unpublished short story with the same title, partly set in Scotland, about "Prince Charlie about the year 1749."[52] There is no doubt that Stevenson read Dickens closely, as he writes that he hopes that what turned out to be one of his last works, *St. Ives*, is like Dickens' *Dombey and Son*, to be followed by better and better works, and likely to culminate in his own equivalent of *A Tale of Two Cities*.[53]

The beginning of the end of Stevenson's *The Young Chevalier* experiment starts when Stevenson, as the narrator, asks, "A king at all?" Then Stevenson has Prince Charlie exclaim in a drunken stupor, "The weaver ... he died for my papa [King James]! All died for him, or risked the dying, and I lay for him all those months in the rain and skulked in heather like a fox." After that, Prince Charlie exclaims that he is now "the only king in Europe," and finally drinks to King Louis of France's "damnation."[54] Stevenson probably wondered why neither Scott nor Dickens tackled the character of Prince Charlie or of King James themselves, choosing instead to focus on minor actors in revolutions and rebellions. Through this short story, Stevenson demonstrates that a king would not look very royal rolling in the heather like Alan Breck, and would be obnoxious if he was constantly defending his rights to the crown.

The last major rebellion novel that Stevenson wrote was *David Balfour*. It focuses on David's adventures during his attempts to clear James Stewart's name by attempting to testify on his behalf. He is prevented by William Grant of Prestongrange, Lord Advocate of Scotland, who kidnaps him and maroons him on an island with a group of Highlanders until the trial is over. The English publisher's title for the novel, *Catriona*, encourages the genre confusion that surrounds these novels. The last couple of movements in the novel, after Stewart's fate is sealed, shift to a description of the relationship between David and two girls: Miss Grant, the advocate's daughter, and Catriona Drummond Macgregor, the daughter of Rob Roy's oldest son, James More. James makes a deal with the government and escapes from his holding cell in Edinburgh Castle in order to avoid execution for the Appin murder. Similarly to the radically political female love interests in Scott's novels, Catriona was "the only lady of the clan that" came out during the '45 Jacobite rebellion, inspiring Glengyle to kiss her on the face for her Scottish patriotism.[55] David confesses early on that he eventually married Catriona, so the reader keeps her in mind as David kisses and shops with Miss Grant. The plot of *Balfour* makes a major blunder of having too many movements that focus on David's love interests after the rebellion plot comes to a screeching halt with an execution that's barely mentioned. In reality, the love theme is only a repetitive background; the assassination and its aftermath are at the forefront of these novels. Stevenson downplayed the assassination and instead stressed the political kidnappings that David suffered. Since David is kidnapped in *Kidnapped* and also in *Balfour*, it might have been a more fitting title to name the second book, "Kidnapped ... Again." In contrast to *Balfour*, "There is no love-making in 'Kidnapped,'" and, with one exception, no woman takes any share in the action,"[56] or, as another early critic writes, "There is no love in the story, which will perhaps make it the more popular with boys."[57] Stevenson repeatedly acknowledged that he was not good at portraying women or love in fiction, and typically tried to stick to adventure. But, at the end of his life, he felt compelled to make love a driving force for the last Jacobite story, despite the primary rebellion theme.

Stevenson followed his own path by choosing not to split all of his plots in two as Dickens did, and not writing solely about Jacobite rebellions as Scott did. As Menikoff writes, Stevenson was "an inveterate experimenter in fictional form."[58] Ignoring the pro-rebellion nature of these works has led critics to misinterpretations or an inability to place them within a fitting genre. Kiely wrote: "Both *Kidnapped* and *David Balfour* are essentially amoral novels, aimless, hectic, and almost totally devoid of characters complex enough to experience the pleasures or pains of maturity."[59] The plot of the novels only becomes highly structured across these six works when one defines them as rebellion novels, and then the five movements repeat throughout, with a few exceptions of Stevenson's incomplete or unpublished works that stray a bit from the finished rebellion novel's plot formula.

A brief comparison of Scott and Stevenson's formulas might help readers to see how the genre changed across the century. Stevenson's dual purpose was identical to Scott's — to sell books to the populace and to promote Scottish nationalism. The endings of Stevenson's rebellion novels occasionally diverge from Scott's model, as some protagonists, such as the dynamiter, lose or die at the end, while other rebellious protagonists, such as David Balfour, win a fortune and a great marriage. Love is also an inconstant presence in Stevenson's novels, as it doesn't appear in *Kidnapped* but has a strong presence in *Balfour*. Some elements remained constant across the century, as both Scott and Stevenson send their characters on perilous journeys, which are typically full of adventure, and the rebellions are typically an adventurous endeavor. Stevenson's modernist absurdity and detachment is the reason some of his rebellious antagonists die, as the excess violence from increased quantities of dynamiter and other violent schemes made people desensitized to violence in fiction. This allowed Stevenson the freedom to show the death of the protagonist and still retain readers, who might have been repelled by such a violent end for the character they cared the most about at the beginning of the century. Boys preferred reading about adventure, so the love element became secondary for Stevenson. The changes in the rebellion novel genre from 1814 to the middle of the century and then towards its end are primarily the result of the changes in literary tastes from Scott's historical and romantic (nationalism) fiction, to Dickens' realist and socialist fiction, and to Stevenson's absurdist and modernist fiction. The progression was a smooth one across the century. Scott was near the end of the romantic wave, and Stevenson came just before the crust of absurdity, but these categorical shifts help to explain some of the big changes the genre saw during the century.

Time

Similarly to Scott, Stevenson was also preoccupied with eighteenth-century Jacobite rebellions, setting three out of his six novels in the eigh-

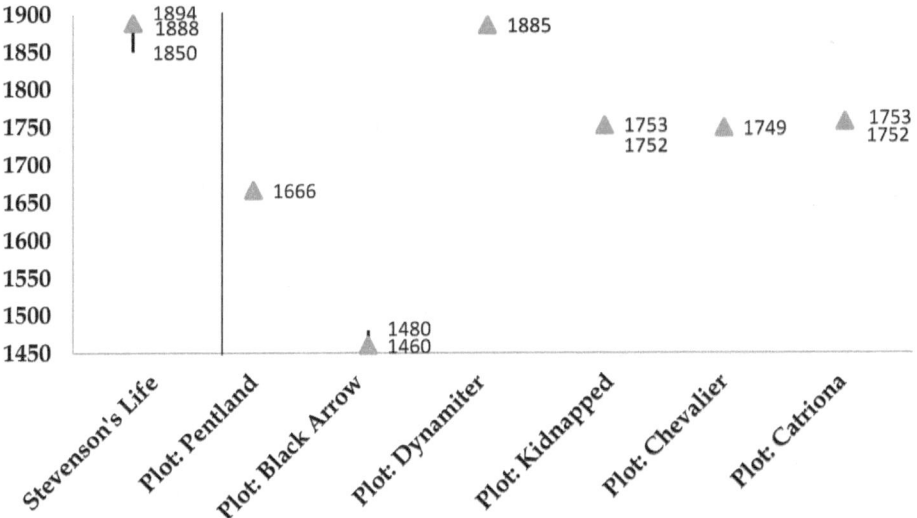

Figure 35. Comparative Times of Stevenson's Rebellion Novels

teenth century. Also like Scott, he placed the rest of his rebellion novels in a variety of different centuries: the fifteenth, seventeenth, and nineteenth centuries.

With a few exceptions, Stevenson broke the timing rules set by Scott and Dickens, by setting many of his plots not in the middle or the beginning of a rebellion but rather after the peak of the main rebellion, or in times of mild unrest. For example, *The Black Arrow* does not have the typical time setting of most of Scott's or Dickens' rebellion novels because there are two rebellions going on, a major war and a minor rising by a band of assassins. The novel opens in May 1460. The War of the Roses began in 1455, "when Henry VI regained his sanity."[60] The eight months in the novel are a period when the war was at its peak. The two rebellions are the War of the Roses and the rebellion by the Black Arrow against aristocratic oppressors. Thus, while the novel fully explores the Black Arrow's rebellion, it does not catch most of the rebellious warfare that raged during the entire War of the Roses. One of the reasons Stevenson might have written mostly works about minor parts of rebellions, or about minor rebellions, is that there were so many historical rebellion novels published during the century that it became difficult to pick a rebellion history that was not yet covered by another fiction writer. As Stevenson wrote about *Pentland Rising's* 1666 time period, "I find it a most picturesque period, and wonder Scott let it escape."[61] Stevenson was anxiously grabbing the periods that were left over.

Stevenson mostly followed Scott's rules on setting the actions in the historic past. One of the exceptions was a recent dynamiter incident that Stevenson covers in *The Dynamiter*. On the other hand, *Kidnapped* and all of the other novels are set at least sixty years into the past. All of Stevenson's works are in part historical, or historically researched: "His novels and stories, with relatively few exceptions, take place in time past — the Middle Ages, the Renaissance, most often the eighteenth century, and usually not later in the nineteenth century than 1820, a safe thirty years before he was born,"[62] or sixty years into the past, as Scott and Dickens prescribed.

Place

Once again, Stevenson typically mimicked Scott's preference and set the location of his novels in Scotland. Sutherland argues that the setting for the *Black Arrow*, East Anglia, is unusual for Stevenson, who usually described Scotland, the South Seas and other peripheries.[63] Indeed, only two of these novels are set in England, and the other four are primarily set in Scotland.

	Pentland Rising	Black Arrow	Dynamiter	Kidnapped	Young Chevalier	Catriona
Locations:	Edinburgh	East Anglia	London	Scotland, sea	Scotland (City of Avignon)	Scotland

Figure 36. Comparative Places of Stevenson's Rebellion Novels

Characters

The characters in Stevenson's rebellion novels belong in diverse categories. The rebellions are against preachers, aristocrats, anti–Jacobites, and the people of London. The rebels are frequently Jacobites, but can also be terrorists, farmers, assassin gang members or princes. This diversity of character types makes Stevenson's novels entertaining to read.

One of the main differences in the characters between Scott and Dickens and Stevenson, is that the latter portrayed the "insanity" of the mob with absurdist horror. With the development of Freudian psychoanalysis in the 1890s and other psychological innovations shortly before this point, the "madness" of a rebellious mob became a form of clinical "insanity," a term that suggested that the mob was now ill, as opposed to "evil." In a book on gothic elements in English fiction, Linda Dryden writes about the intermingling of immorality and insanity in the vision of 19th-century writers. She asserts that the fear of mob violence that all rebellion novels play off was a hysteria that the majority of the English population shared. "In the *Dynamiter* one of the three main protagonists, Somerset, threatens Zero, the urban terrorist, with the mob evoking in the latter a fear that prefigures Le Bon's point: 'The brutal mob, the savage passions ... Somerset, for God's sake, a public house! (*MNAN* [*More New Arabian Nights*], 294). By the 1890s, this horror of the mob had become hysteria."[64]

The strongest element in *Kidnapped* and the weakest in *Balfour* are the characters that Stevenson built. Stevenson explains the difference between the

	Pentland Rising	Black Arrow	Dynamiter	Kidnapped	Young Chevalier	Catriona
Characters:	Rebels vs. Preachers	Black Arrow rebels vs. aristocrats	Irish terrorists vs. London people	Jacobite rebels & kidnapping victim vs. oppressors	Prince Charlie (Jacobite), French gentleman, Scots	Jacobites/ rebels vs. Lord Advocate & Scottish Law

Figure 37. Comparative Characters of Stevenson's Rebellion Novels

two in a letter written from Vailima on May 18, 1892, a couple of years before his death, to Sidney Colvin:

> If I have got to kill a man, I kill him good; and if my characters have to go to bed to each other — well, I want them to go.... However there's David Balfour's love affair.... The difficulty in a love yarn, which dwells at all on love, is the dwelling on one string ... I am a realist and a prosaist, and a most fanatical lover of plain physical sensations plainly and expressly rendered; hence my peril. To do love in the same spirit as I did (for instance) D. Balfour's fatigue in the heather; my dear sir, there were grossness ready made!... If ever I do a rape, which may the almighty God forfend! You would hear a noise about my rape.[65]

Stevenson's problem in *Balfour* was the "sentimental," "romantic" focus on the relationship between Catriona and David Balfour. Neither *Kidnapped* nor *Barnaby Rudge* includes an enduring love story. *Kidnapped* does not have any major female characters and the closest thing to a love interest in it is the "friendship" between David and Alan, but an aside into hints of homosexuality in Stevenson would be lengthy and would not reflect an element of the rebellion novel genre as a whole. In *Balfour*, there are two love interests, so they cancel each other out — the reader's emotions are negated. Stevenson also faced the problem of being tongue-tied when he was trying to write about love, similarly to how David exclaims, "Catriona!" and then cannot think of what to say next: "It seemed that was the first and last word of my eloquence."[66] Stevenson challenged himself to the task of writing a love yarn, but realized that the love depends on having Catriona repeatedly and without due cause denying Balfour's advances until the very end of the novel. This delay meant that in the meantime the two repeat very similar dialogues about their feelings for each other and there is barely any action or adventures like the action scenes of vigorous running in *Kidnapped*. This time David runs with Catriona, only briefly meeting up with Alan Breck, and Catriona isn't made for prolonged runs in the heather. Of course, David fainted frequently and needed alcohol to jump from a height in *Kidnapped*, but the situation is not as threatening as *Balfour* and the couple walks, rather than runs, during their escape. Because David is resigned to his lot and doesn't run, David is successfully kidnapped, imprisoned and cast out of his home country to Holland, instead of successfully escaping in *Kidnapped* with the streetwise Alan Breck. At the end, the characters in both *Kidnapped* and *Balfour* are believable, even if in the latter they are sentimental.

Stevenson's great failure with Catriona was not realizing before finishing fifteen chapters of a novel that scenes of courtly love are boring because they are repetitive. In addition, Stevenson was hardly a feminist, and had a flat view of women. While he writes that he thinks his lord advocate is a "strong sketch," he refers to Catriona and Miss Grant in one gasp as the "two girls," and states that he thought they were "very pleasing creatures."[67] A rape would have been exciting, as he suggests in the above-quoted letter, but it just was not done in the 19th century — at least not by Dickens or Scott, who focused on murderous violence in their rebellions and only made hints at the rapes that might have taken place during the chaos of a rebellion or a revolution.

Stevenson is known as a great modern experimenter in fiction because he took chances like this one with his characters. As usual, some experiments work out better than others. Stevenson comments on the doomed nature of his "sentimental" *Balfour* experiment, writing, "I wonder whether twenty-five years of life spent in trying the one thing," meaning swift adventure stories, "will not make it impossible for me to succeed in the other."[68] This "one thing" for Stevenson was the rebellion novel genre, and by trying it over six times, Stevenson improved on his structural formulaic tricks until he created novels that are still studied by literary critics.

Stevenson's Novelistic Method

Because this book is about formulaic fiction, and speed and method of execution are key to all formulaic fiction, it is important to consider the details of Stevenson's creative process and writing method. Like Dickens, Stevenson began his novels by "writing out a list of chapters" and creating maps and outlines for the whole project.[69] As Robson writes, in Stevenson, "The topography is carefully worked out" based on "the countryside he knew from his youth."[70] Stevenson wrote steadily, also like Dickens and Scott, "at the rate of a chapter a day." He used an "almanac," a "map of the country, and the plan of every house" to avoid embarrassing miscalculations. It is obvious that Stevenson has read every page of *Rob Roy* with a calculating eye from the fact that he explains that in *Rob Roy*, Scott makes the mistake of having "two horsemen, journeying on a most urgent affair" take more time to reach their destination than would be logical from studying a map of the terrain that they traveled across.[71] Stevenson was a workaholic writer like Scott and Dickens, one who "recast[ed] and revise[d] and reject[ed]."[72]

Stevenson's greatest adversary and challenge as a fiction writer was the clock. He was painfully conscious, or rather made "sick," by the fact that Scott needed "three weeks" to finish *Guy Mannering*. His head was "spinning" from finishing seven pages. He was so overwhelmed that he projected the blame on others, exclaiming, "Weakling generation."[73] In a letter to George Iles on October 29, 1887, as well as in his essay, "My First Book," he explains that *Treasure Island* was written "in two bursts of about fifteen days each, my quickest piece of work. *Kidnapped* was all written at Bournemouth, inside of a year: probably five months actual writing, and one of these months entirely over the last chapter which had to be put together, without interest or inspiration, almost word by word, for I was entirely worked out."[74] For a writer who preferred brevity and speedy conclusions to projects, it is miraculous that Stevenson stuck it out to the end of *Balfour*.

He makes over a dozen comments in letters to friends and family that *Balfour* was dragging by and that while only the last chapter of *Kidnapped* was "work," it seems that only the first 15 chapters of *Balfour* were play, until Stevenson went back to edit and read them and found major structural problems with the book. "David Balfour is skelping along,"[75] he writes on March 9, 1892. Then Stevenson begins to count off the pages: 79 on the ninth, 100 on the twelfth. The first part is in the press on August 9, 1892. He believes that he has finished on September 26, but he returns to the book again when his editor asks him to make corrections. Stevenson soon writes to the editor to confess that the mistakes in the work are "inherent," and he wouldn't be able to fix most of them. Throughout, Stevenson keeps complaining to relations, "I was rather tired of it." A bit later he feels the book is "like a hundred and twenty sermons on end."[76] Stevenson is struggling with a monumental task despite ill health and unlikely financial results, and such struggles are typically driven by political or social reasons rather than solely personal reasons.

The second reason he was doggedly determined to finish *Balfour* despite setbacks was to avert a "financial catastrophe for the year." Stevenson ended up traveling across the world and living in exotic countries in his last couple of years because he struggled through 1892 and completed several projects on deadlines that were as tight as the schedules that Dickens kept throughout his editing and writing career. "We shall all probably make a little trip to Tahiti in October. But *D.B.* must be finished first,"[77] he wrote. These and other quotations from Stevenson, and the sensationalism and high adventure in his publications, have led to several critics calling him a "commercial hack."[78] Writer's fiscal situation usually has an enormous impact on their writing method. If Stevenson was not constantly ill and impoverished, he would have had a very different writing methodology, for better or for worse.

Another striking characteristic of Stevenson's method is that he did more reading in preparation for a fictional book than writing. As I discussed in the chapters on Dickens and Scott, both of these authors did heavy research for their projects. In contrast, Stevenson did an extraordinary quantity of research; so much so that Barry Menikoff has published an entire scholarly book— *Narrating Scotland: The Imagination of Robert Louis Stevenson* (2005)— that describes the various sources that Stevenson read in order to write *Kidnapped* and *Balfour*. While the introductions to Scott's and Dickens' historical novels go up to fifty pages per introduction, Stevenson avoided writing introductions to his histories, choosing to make them appear to be fun adventure stories for boys. Meanwhile, he slaved to make the research behind them fitting for his application for a professorship in history, which he didn't win. He did write at least three introductions: one was discussed earlier, a second to *Treasure Island*, which he published in a magazine. The third was a "Note to *Kidnapped*," where he explains that his intention was to describe the 1715 and 1745 rebellions, "the collapse of the clan system, and the causes and growth of existing discontents." The term "existing" clearly proves that Stevenson knew of current discontents; Stevenson stresses that he was among those who were discontented with the union with England.

Kidnapped was "inspired" by the "printed trial" for the Appin murder.[79] Stevenson's primary research began as early as 1880, when he visited Appin.[80] Stevenson read most of the Edinburgh Advocates' Library collection between 1875 and 1885, focusing on various types of mostly primary materials on the Appin case. Also around the year 1880, around the time when his application for the professorship was rejected, Stevenson purchased the first of these primary sources, *The Trials of James Stewart for the Murder of Colin Campbell* (1753). He later read such works as: Edmund Burt's *Letters from a Gentleman in the North of Scotland to His Friend in London* (1754), David Stewart's *Sketches of the Character, Manners, and Present State of the Highlands of Scotland*, and the *Trials of Three Sons of Rob Roy*.[81]

All this research and work paid off. Many prior critics have concluded that Stevenson achieved something original and innovative with his political novels. Menikoff even finds that Stevenson might have invented a "new genre."[82] While it is more likely that Scott invented the new rebellion genre and Stevenson mimicked his predecessors, it is still clear that Stevenson wrote masterpiece rebellion novels that deserve to stand next to their predecessors.

15

Stevenson's Linguistic Features

Stevenson's Linguistic Formula

Writing in a letter about *Kidnapped*, right after its publication in July 1886, Edmund Gosse admires Stevenson's linguistic style: "The language is exceedingly pure and true, sometimes the answers crack like a whip. I feel sure that you have never done such good dialogue before."[1]

What are the elements that make Stevenson's linguistics crisp and appealing to readers? Here are the comparative linguistic rebellion novel formulas for the focal writers:

> Scott's Linguistic Formula = Epic Imagery and Techniques + Scots/Gaelic Language and Allusions + Middle English and Renaissance Borrowings
>
> Dickens' Linguistic Formula = Epic Imagery and Techniques + English Regional and Class Dialects + Religious Allusions + Slogans + Idiolects or Invented Individualized Speech + French/ Foreign Expressions

Stevenson borrows most of the above elements, and his formula can be summarized as:

> Stevenson's Linguistic Formula: Epic Meter + Scots/Gaelic Language and Allusions + Middle English and Renaissance Borrowings

Stevenson's linguistic formula is closer to Scott's than to Dickens.' He primarily mimicked Scott, and made only a few imitations of Dickens' rebellion novels. There are two significant changes between Scott's and Stevenson's linguistic formulas. First, Stevenson's novels were shorter and focused on less epic plotlines, so it's only the meter that is epic. There is less epic imagery and techniques in Stevenson than in Scott. Secondly, Scots and Gaelic became less popular at the end of the nineteenth century, so Stevenson is less familiar with both of these languages than Scott, and makes frequent linguistic mistakes. These glitches have meant that few linguists have dug into Stevenson's linguistics, as doing so would be at the peril of pointing out that he makes grammatical and stylistic mistakes in his Gaelic and Scots. Still, there are many interesting elements of Stevenson's linguistics, which reflect his own time and national origin, so they need to be examined for a fuller picture of the rebellion novel during the nineteenth century.

Variety of Discourse: Adjectives, and Epic Meter

Adjectives

One of the elements that distinguishes Stevenson from his predecessors is that he avoided a heavy use of description or adjectives. A year before Stevenson's death, in 1893, Stevenson replied to a letter he received from Henry James, saying that he objects to James' remark "on the starving of the visual sense" in *Catriona* because he wrote it with two aims in mind for his fiction:

> 1st. War to the adjective.
> 2nd. Death to the optic nerve.[2]

Stevenson was interested in the adventurous actions around the rebellions, rather than in describing the scenery. Of course, there are divergences from this rule, as, for example, *Kidnapped* includes many detailed descriptions. It is likely that Henry James pointed out the "starvation of the visual sense" because he was expecting the same quantity of visual descriptions in the second part of the Kidnapped series, *Catriona*, as in the first novel, *Kidnapped*.

Epic Meter

The following negative criticism should be prefaced with a quotation from Stevenson's friend W. E. Henley, who wrote in a review of *Prince Otto* in the *Athenaeum* that Stevenson has "a constant respect for the principles of art."[3] When reviewing a draft of *Prince Otto* that Stevenson sent to him, W. E. Henley writes that the dialogue is too iambic:

> Of the dialogue I am not (as yet) so greatly taken. It beats too often with the iambic pulse; it feels too often a little Stevensonian, a little mannered and dry. The iambic pulse, by the way, is more audible all over the shop than I like to remember: e.g.
>
> > In a few white-hot words he bade adieu.
> > Dubbed desperation by the name of love,

> And called his wrath forgiveness; cast one look
> Of leave taking upon the place that was
> No longer to be his and hurried forth,
> Love's prisoner or pride's![4]

Stevenson took this criticism to heart and deleted the iambic meter from this and other passages before publication. If Scott took pride in his use of meter and musical language, we can see here that by the end of the nineteenth century, the same linguistic techniques were out of vogue, and were negative elements to be deleted.

Stevenson confessed many times that for him the musical linguistic style in his writing is essential to his work. *Kidnapped* and *Balfour* are full of not only "Jacobite toasts and Gaelic songs," or Alan's "whistling of many tunes, warlike, merry, plaintive,"[5] but every word in the novels is musically pleasing. "On Some Technical Elements of Style in Literature" was first published by Robert Stevenson in the *Contemporary Review* in April 1885. In this work Stevenson shows his learned knowledge of the "the elements of style" in fiction writing. In the popular book by William Strunk, Jr., and E. B. White, *The Elements of Style*, the authors divides style into the categories of: usage or grammar, principles of composition (voice, needless words), form (hyphens, quotations), and rules about commonly used words and expressions (its/it's). Stevenson skips over basic grammar and begins with a dissection of the necessity of musical rhythm not only in poetry but also in prose. He suggests that the meter has to be constantly varied in order to keep surprising readers.[6] Stevenson explains the art of writing symbolically, as a trick that the writer has to learn by first juggling two, then three, then four oranges. He points out that Dickens' "earlier attempts to be impressive" as well as most other bad writings "fall at once into the production of bad blank verse."[7] The writer speaks to the ear of the reader with meter as well as sound in alliteration and assonance, as well as to the eye that sees the words on the page. Stevenson looks so closely at language that he notices a repetition of the sounds *PVF* in random passages from Shakespeare, Coleridge and Macaulay, pointing out that the trick made him feel a bit crazed at first.[8] He ends his theory that the best writers in English all use the repetition of the sounds *PVF*, by finding a passage with an overwhelming quantity of repeating *K*'s. Stevenson concludes that bad novel writers do not deliberately go out of their way to repeat the same sounds, but only "upon a rare occasion," use a "patch of assonance or a momentary jingle of alliteration." These bad writers leave behind a "cacophony supreme, the rattle of incongruous consonants only relieved by the jaw-breaking hiatus, and whole phrases not to be articulated by the powers of men."[9] Stevenson's prose is highly musical and metrically formed, and this is one of the reasons he is now considered as a classical, and not only as a hack, children's author.

Multilingual Elements: Archaic Languages, Scots, and Gaelic

The influence that gave Stevenson his Scots language and knowledge of Scottish linguistics is his nurse, Cummy. Cummy's "bed was kept in Louis's night nursery until he was almost ten years old ... Cummy sang him ballads and psalms, read to him from the Bible and Bunyan (particularly during the long, still Edinburgh Sabbath), and told him 'blood-curdling tales of the Covenanters and their struggles...' Cummy read well and without affectation, she gave him a link with the Scots tongue, which was then dying out in the better parts of the city, especially in the New Town."[10] Stevenson picked up on the contrast between Cummy's speech and the more standard variety of English that his parents used. The Covenanters was a Scottish Presbyterian movement that participated in the Glorious Revolution and in the Jacobite rebellions. It was a religious sect that was in frequent conflict with both Protestants and Catholics. Having a nanny who recited rebellious religious doctrine as children's stories must have also affected Stevenson's early political and religious development.

Another influence that affected Stevenson's Scottish linguistic development was his stays at the Swanson Cottage for fourteen summer vacations in his youth.

> Swanson was important ... for tuning his ear to the speech of the countryside, the old speech of the Lothians that was to give him his version of Scots.... The shepherd John Todd, recalled in the essay "Pastoral" that first appeared in Longman's Magazine in 1887: "He spoke in the richest dialect of Scots I every heard; the words in themselves were a pleasure and often a surprise to me, so that I often came back from one of our patrols with new acquisitions; and this vocabulary he would handle like a master, stalking a little before me, 'beard on shoulder,' the plaid hanging loosely about him, the yellow staff clapped under his arm ... I might count him with the best talkers; only that talking Scots and talking English seem incomparable acts." Todd's speech survived, if nowhere else, in *Weir of Hermiston*, but there were many more like him around Swanston.[11]

Stevenson used class dialects, idiolects and some archaic dialects. The most repeated and relevant to the rebellion genre feature of Stevenson's linguistics is his use of Scots and Gaelic languages, a trick or a nationalistic habit that he acquired from not only his nurse and country friends but primarily from Scott. In Stevenson's novels, naturally, poor characters have slightly different linguistic quirks from wealthy characters; however, these distinctions do not stand out as much as in Dickens or in Scott. In addition, Stevenson's use of Gaelic and Scots is closer linked to his rebellion novel formula because his rebellion novels frequently touch on nationalist Scottish rebellions.

At the beginning of the eighteenth century, Gaelic was the language that was commonly used in the Scottish Highlands. Scots was more popular in the south of Scotland, closer to the border with England. In contrast, today Scotland's official language is Scottish Standard English, not Gaelic or Scots. While Gaelic is now an archaic language for all but 1 percent of Scotland, Scots is still used by 80 percent of the Lowland Scotland region. The opposite was true before the Jacobite risings, starting in the tenth century, when Gaelic was the commonly used language across Scotland. Both Scott and Stevenson primarily used Scots in their novels, only sprinkling in a few Gaelic expressions or ballads because Gaelic is impossible for an English reader to understand, while Scots is similar enough to English for it to be mildly comprehensible. The Scots and Gaelic languages began to wane in popularity starting with the Reformation, when the available Bibles were only in the English language. Scots was also dramatically affected by the fact that James VI or James I, the Scottish king who took the English throne, "adopted" the English language, instead of bringing Scots to England, and as a result Scottish nobility followed his example. The most dramatic blow to the Scottish languages, both Scots and Gaelic, was the suppression of these languages by English laws against them, after the unsuccessful, though destructive, Jacobite rebellions in the eighteenth century. This is the cultural colonialism that Scott harshly criticized in most of his novels, and especially in his novels about Jacobite rebellions.[12]

Scottish nationalists since Scott and Stevenson have used the Scots and Gaelic languages in their works to support the idea that these languages are not "common slang," or "'bad' English," but rather "'guid' Scots." Hodgart points out several current regional varieties of Scottish: Lowland Scots, Lallans, and Doric or Patter.[13] In general, there are many variations in the different Scottish languages and dialects. The nationalist concerns for the survival of the dying Gaelic language, and for the acceptance of Scots as a national language rather than a "slang" variety of the English language, are heated issues to this day, especially since Scotland was granted its own Parliament in 1999. A discussion of the use of Scots and Gaelic in Scott and Stevenson's novels is a very relevant topic to modern Scottish politics.

In his history of Scotland, Fitzroy MacLean summarizes that "there were in Scotland no signs of any fresh national revival in the arts or in literature, comparable to that earlier flowering," referring to the progress made decades earlier by Sir Walter Scott. In contrast, MacLean calls Stevenson an individual, who made a name for himself.[14] While Scott is used as an icon of Scottish linguistic nationalism, Stevenson is used as an example of innovations and changes in the Scots language throughout the nineteenth century by critics like Joan Beal and Graham Tulloch, especially in their chapters of *The Edinburgh History of the Scots Language*.

Stevenson's use of Scots is erratic and is based on a variety of earlier traditions, including Scott, Middle English, innovations made during his time, and his own edits to the language, which he himself has admitted he did not fully know as a native tongue, having spoken and written mostly in English as a child. An example of Stevenson following the trends in Scots in his lifetime is when he makes the common Scots substitution of using the pronoun *us* or the shortened *'s*, instead of "me," which was a common innovation of the "Central Scots urban working-class speech" in the late nineteenth century. Here is an example of Stevenson's use of the *'s* pronoun in *Weir of Hermiston's* Chapter 6: "'Will ye no gie*'s* [my italics] a kiss?' she said."[15] Stevenson also used a "recent" Scots innovation when he used the "possessive mines," which was "an analogical formation on the patter of Standard English yours." In *Weir of Hermiston's* Chapter 5, Stevenson writes, "*Mines* [my italics] is no to be mentioned wi' it." "Mines" does not appear in Scott's or other earlier Scottish writers' works,[16] so it is clear that Stevenson was aware of the changes in the Scots language during his own time and did not solely rely on previously published books. However, due to Stevenson's heavily English upbringing, he does not make some of the other common Scots substitutions, such as the rule that in Scots, "the indirect object pronoun" is placed "before the direct object, as in *give me it*." But in Stevenson's novels, for example, once again in *Weir of Hermiston*, in Chapter 5, the direct object comes first: "I'll show *it ye* [my italics] some of thir days if ye're good."[17] Stevenson breaks a Scots variation that many of the other Scottish speakers and writers of his day used heavily. Joan Beal concludes, based on the evidence that Stevenson did not use the reversed position for the direct object, that "Stevenson's representation of Scots is less than authentic."[18]

Stevenson picked up Scott's use of "archaic language" from Middle and Renaissance English, adopting older versions of English, using them besides Scottishisms, to give their historical fiction an "archaic flavor."[19] For example, in *The Black Arrow*, the language throughout is Middle English, or a shade of northern English, with words like *fynde, knight, unkind, fro*, and *ye*, used in a letter from Richard Shelton to Sir Daniel Brackley.[20]

Several critics and biographers have noticed subversive strains in Stevenson's use of the Scottish language. Harman points out that Stevenson was writing a bilingual book of poems simultaneously with *Kidnapped*, titled *Underwoods*, where, similarly to Scott's duality, when Stevenson is writing in English, the poems are "personal ... mostly addressed to friends," but when he writes in the second half of the book in Scots, the "style and tone" changes into "bracing lyrics and ballads."[21] There are notes of Scottish nationalism, and anti-unionist and anti–English sentiments in these "bracing" lyrics. Similarly to Scott's revivalism, in the preface to *Underwoods*, Stevenson also fears that, "The day draws near when this illustrious and malleable tongue [specifically his Lothian Scottish dialect] shall be quite forgotten.... Till then I would love to have my hour as a native Maker, and be read by my own countryfolk in our own dying language."[22] When Stevenson expresses a wish to be a "native Maker," he is referring to the fact that Scott is credited for partially creating some of the "native" traditions that Scotland became popularly known for, such as the kilts, because King George IV wore a kilt during his visit to Scotland and due to the popularity of Scott's vision of "native" Scotland. Even if Stevenson's linguistic shortfalls prevented him from expressing the same level of anti–English subversion in Scottish, he at least made an effort to develop his writing in this direction. Archaic English and the Scottish linguistic variations that Stevenson invents or improvises are read as genuinely Scottish by non–Scottish readers.

> Perhaps a non–Scottish reader has not as sensitive an ear for dialogue in Scots as someone brought up in Stevenson's native Edinburgh, but I must confess that I always find Stevenson's dialogue most convincing and most firmly wrought into the fabric of the novel [*Weir of Hermiston*] when he is handling the Scots tongue. The careful balance between Archie's English speech and his father's almost belligerent Doric sets a ground swell going throughout the work, and it is the rise and fall of this swell which carries the whole emotional burden. It is all done with a perfect ear, a fine gearing of vocabulary to character, and a profound dramatic use of language.... Notice the rise and fall of the dialogue, the deft alternation of Scots and English, corresponding to the contrast between Weir's savage irony and Archie's penitent meekness.[23]

Regardless of whether a Scots language teacher would approve of Stevenson's linguistic inconsistencies, Daiches argues that Stevenson's musical language is artistically beautiful to the ear, and achieves literary merit, without a need for grammarian precision. While Stevenson spent his youth in Scotland, he learned rudimentary Gaelic only later in life.[24] Stevenson knew Scots from Cummy and other poor Scottish neighbors. He did not learn either of these languages in formal schooling, so he was not familiar with enough grammatical and spelling standards in either Scots or Gaelic to use it fluently in his novels.

> [In *Kidnapped*,] language ... becomes a symbol of alienation. David has no Gaelic. On the other hand there are those Highlanders who will speak English only at a price; on the other, those who courteously insist, at some cost to themselves, that only English shall be spoken in his presence. He finds himself a stranger in what he had assumed to be his own country, speaking a language which his supposed countrymen regard as foreign.[25]

The characters are awakened or dimmed through the style of their dialogue. Stevenson wrote, "A photographic exactitude in dialogue is now the exclusive fashion."²⁶ Stevenson pinpoints the problem with his own *David Balfour* when he writes, "Our little passionate story drowns in a deep sea of descriptive eloquence or slipshod talk."²⁷ The Scottish dialect is too difficult for non–Scots to comprehend, and the descriptions, while eloquent, are too slippery and non-concrete to keep the readers on their toes.

In 1879 in a letter to Edmund Gosse, claiming that it is from Stevenson's *Handy Cyclopedia*, Stevenson gave the following definition of the English: "A dull people, incapable of comprehending the Scottish tongue. Their history is so intimately connected with that of Scotland, that we must refer our readers to that heading. Their literature is principally the work of venal Scots."²⁸ This must have been humorous given Stevenson's own difficulties with Gaelic. The truth was that "times had changed so rapidly in Scotland that in his late teens Stevenson knew no one of his own generation (certainly not of his class) whose primary language was Scots."²⁹ Stevenson was aware that his Scots was impure when he wrote, "'If it be not pure, what matters it?'"³⁰ Despite Stevenson's vernacular shortfalls, his novels (and especially *Kidnapped* and *Catriona*), "did almost as much to promote and perpetuate the Scottish myth in the twentieth century as his great forerunner Walter Scott had done in the nineteenth."³¹ Many critics point out that because Scots wasn't commonly spoken around Stevenson, he only "discovered himself to be a Scot" after his temporary exile in California in 1880, while hunting for his future wife.³² Soon after his return to Scotland, Stevenson also realized that he wouldn't be able to stay there because the climate was destroying his health. When he came to the realization that he was going to be in exile from Scotland for the rest of his life, Stevenson began a book about the "Act of Union between England and Scotland in 1707." "He only became a writer of Scotland ... when he gave up the idea of residing there,"³³ Harman wrote. He gushes over *Catriona* as "probably his most Scots book, most notably in the quantity and variety of Scots language used in it," referring to David's "soft Lowland dialect" and Catriona's "Highland phraseology." Harman also stresses "Black Andie's power of vernacular," and especially "Andie's tale, told in broad Scots," as well as the "Gaelic-speaker" who interrupts this tale.³⁴ Not just one Scottish language but half a dozen different dialects of Scottish are represented in *Catriona*. Stevenson initially hoped to write a grand epic history of Scotland from the union through the rebellions and their aftermath in *Kidnapped*, but soon discovered that he was not equal to the task, primarily because, "I was myself debarred by the difficulties of the Gaelic language." He attempted to learn it late in life, after mastering French and Latin.³⁵

Stevenson confesses his shortcomings in Gaelic through David's voice, saying that he had "no Gaelic." As David listens to a Scot talk, he begins to "suspect he thought he was talking English," thus stressing the incomprehensible nature of the mixture of Gaelic and English and his own difficulties with the language of the Scottish people.³⁶

Like Scott and Dickens, Stevenson occasionally uses some common linguistic tricks to indicate his Scottish characters' accents without overwhelming the reader, such as when he writes *Palfour* instead of "Balfour," or *wass* instead of "was" in "The Bravo" chapter of *Balfour*,³⁷ changing only a letter or two in the English instead of using Gaelic words and phrases. After using some of these slight modifications in David and Catriona's speech, Stevenson gives a summary of the linguistic techniques that he has been utilizing: "I had the Low Country tongue and dwelled upon my words; she had a hill voice, spoke with something of an English accent, only far more delightful and was scarce quite fit to be called a deacon in the craft of talking English grammar."³⁸

Stevenson's attempts at using Gaelic despite the fact that he was really a native English speaker show a rebellious spirit that surpasses Scott's. At least Scott knew some Gaelic from reading Gaelic ballads and other works in his youth. Stevenson's mimicry of Scott's Gaelic and archaic words also shows the enormous effort that Stevenson put into his mimicries. If he wanted to take an easy road to quick money, he would have avoided attempts at creating musical prose and especially attempts at the Gaelic tongue. But instead Stevenson marched bravely into this difficult linguistic field. This nationalist spirit shows the heart and passion behind Stevenson's radical socialism and nationalism. Stevenson and Scott's rebellions were against cultural colonialism of Scotland, and the best way to make this protest in the nineteenth century was by using the Gaelic and Scots languages, which were suppressed by the English empire.

Linguistic Evidence of Socialist Radicalism

The absurdist detachment from the violence of rebellions in Stevenson's works can be seen by comparing the heartfelt Gaelic and Scottish songs in Scott's rebellion novels, with a short rhyme sung by M'Guire shortly before his death in *The Dynamiter*:

> I care for nobody, no, not I,
> And nobody cares for me...³⁹

In comparison, here is a piece from "Scottish Popular Rhymes on a Bad Inn" from Scott's *Rob Roy*:

> Baron of Bucklivie,
> May the four fiend drive ye,
> And a' to pieces rive ye,

> For building sic a town,
> Where there's neither horse meat, nor man's meat,
> Nor a chair to sit down.[40]

The latter piece by Scott makes a sentimental appeal for the well-being of the Scottish people, who are in want, but the rhyme by Stevenson is flat and devoid of passion and sentimentality. It is not only the content of these rhymes that makes one modernist and the other romantic but also the fact that Scott uses the Scottish language to give an added dimension to the text and to make the words more sympathetic to readers, while Stevenson uses flat language that is more common in absurdist theater, where only minimalist words are used to describe only basic emotions.

Stevenson is slightly less absurdist and has a bit more heart in his song in *The Black Arrow*, when he retreats to the far past in East Anglia, as opposed to his present time in London. "Jon Amend-All of the Green Wood,/And his jolly fellaweship." The rebels of the Black Arrow send the following propagandistic sing-song letter to explain whom they are fighting against,

> I had four black arrows under my belt,
> Four for the greefs that I have felt,
> Four for the number of ill menne
> That have oppressed me now and then.[41]

The rhyme goes on to give the names of the four people who are the intended victims of the rebels, and explains why those people are being targeted for their evil deeds. The reader is inspired with sympathy for the rebels of the Black Arrow due to the national color of this poem, which inspires ideas of home and native belonging. In fact, Stevenson introduces the letter by writing that the lines were in a "very rugged doggerel, hardly even rhyming, written in a gross character and most uncouthly spelt." In fact, the spelling is so bad, Stevenson wrote that he "bettered" it before reprinting the text.[42] Typically, characters who are "rugged," and who spell poorly inspire more sympathy due to their supposed simplicity and in turn relative innocence than rich characters who write letters that are perfectly spelled and rhymed.

Stevenson does something very similar to the linguistics in the above *Black Arrow* letter in *Kidnapped*, also stressing that he is "translating" the text and including heartfelt rebel songs.

> This is the song of the sword of Alan;...
> Come to me from the hills of heather,
> Come from the isles of the sea.
> O far-beholding eagles,
> Here is your meat.[43]

Alan frequently sings this song in Gaelic, and David Balfour translates it for his readers in the book into "king's English," explaining that he does not translate it in verse because he has "no skill" for verse.⁴⁴ It is a mystery how David managed to translate this song from Gaelic, as across the entire length of the novel he keeps repeating things like, "I told him I had no Gaelic; and at this he became very angry, and I began to suspect he thought he was talking English."⁴⁵ The narrator, David Balfour, keeps explaining that he has "no Gaelic," whenever one of the Highlanders tries to communicate with him in this language. This insistence that the narrator is lacking something because he does not know Gaelic helps to stress the richness of the language and the relative lack of Scottish national culture for those who try to integrate into the Highland environment without learning this essential linguistic tool. David Balfour is an outsider and has difficulty communicating with the Highlanders. He needs Alan to translate his wants and needs to the Highlanders. The Scottish nation is put by Stevenson in a higher regard through these explanations of the value of its language and culture. Stevenson, like Scott, is expressing his strong Scottish nationalism by enriching his Jacobite rebellion novels with the languages and culture of Scotland.

Stevenson expresses a similar pro–Jacobite Scottish nationalism in *David Balfour*, where he relates several tragic "songs" that were created upon the news that Stewart was found to be guilty of the Appin murder, despite his actual innocence. Here are two of the songs Stevenson quotes from popular folklore:

> It fell on a day when Argyle was on the bench,
> That they served him a Stewart for his denner.
>
> Then up and spak the Duke, and flyted on his cook,
>   I regaird it as a sensible aspersion,
>   That I would sup ava', an' satiate my maw,
>   With the bluid of ony clan of my aversion.⁴⁶

These songs speak about the disputes within Scotland between the clans, and specifically between clans that supported the union and integration and clans that were for separation from the union or at least for the return to power of the Jacobites, and a shifting of English power towards favoring Scottish rights.

As a last note on Stevenson's Scottish songs and linguistic style, here is a quotation from one of the last chapters in *Balfour*: "Then he [Catriona's father, James] would sing again, and translate to me pieces of the song, with a great deal of boggling and much expressed contempt against the English language."⁴⁷ The "contempt" for the English language furthers Stevenson's campaign of supporting the validity and beauty of the Scots and Gaelic languages. By downplaying and ridiculing English and by showing how in Scotland, Gaelic and Scots are more useful than English, Stevenson expresses a nationalist pride in the Scottish nation and culture, and this was a radical idea in the nineteenth century.

Conclusion

The rebellion novel genre was a subversive and direct form of communication for nineteenth century British authors who held anti-imperial and anti-monarchic views. There is substantial proof that both Scott and Stevenson were Scottish nationalists; Dickens was a radical socialist; and Stevenson was also a radical socialist and an anticolonialist. These three radical writers, and other participants in the rebellion novel genre, wrote works that sympathetically portrayed the rebellious struggles of the poor, of the periphery and of the disenfranchised. The nineteenth-century public was eager to politically rebel against slavery, unfair wages, tyranny and other wrongs, but it was not as violent as its eighteenth century predecessors. McCord and Perdue wrote: "Nothing in the nineteenth century approached in the scale the Gordon Riots of June 1780."[1] Most of the uprisings that Scott, Dickens and Stevenson covered happened in the eighteenth century because that was when most of the violent British uprisings occurred. These great authors also strategically chose to focus on the eighteenth century to write freely about past, instead of current, disagreements between the government and the people. Supporting ongoing rebellions and revolutions against England could have been considered a treasonous act at the beginning of the nineteenth century, and publishers were hesitant to publish books of pro-rebellion propaganda throughout the nineteenth century. Thus, the rebellion novel genre is a subgenre of the historical novel, and all rebellion novels that meet the set criteria are also historical novels, as opposed to novels about current or imaginative events.

The English mob fought for their rights in the streets. Politicians in the nineteenth century mostly won their battles in Parliament and in the courts. And political novelists typically fought their political battles with stories of past historical clashes, only occasionally making direct orations for a specific political cause, or publishing histories or treatises on specific radical political issues. The rebellion novelists discussed in this book occasionally used their rebellious characters and narrators to make direct pro-rebellion statements and at other times enclosed these ideas in subversive or hidden messages that were not obvious to either their publishers or to a censor who might have read these rebellion novels. Scott received direct patronage in the form of a barony and money from King George IV, and both Dickens and Stevenson relied on their wealthy aristocratic patrons. These authors could not write anti-monarchic political pamphlets or they would lose the primary source of their livelihood. Occasionally, they had to use foreign accents and distant settings (indirectly supporting the rights to a national or a regional identity of the Scottish or of the impoverished English people) to simultaneously give the public what it wanted to buy — stories about attempts to overthrow corrupt governments — and what the aristocracy wanted to support — great British fiction.

Rebellion novels can be labeled as a separate genre because they have repeating features, just as there are repeating properties in gothic, historical, nationalist or political novels. There is a correlation between popularity or sales of a nineteenth century novelist and their publication of at least one rebellion novel. Two of the main authors discussed in this book are classically known as the pioneering best-selling writers who paved the way for the current publishing climate: Charles Dickens and Sir Walter Scott. Rebellion novels sold well, so many later novelists, including Robert Stevenson and Benjamin Disraeli, mimicked the characteristics and the theme of classics like *Waverley* and *A Tale of Two Cities*. Mimicry of previously used rebellion novel techniques and features created linguistic and structural parallels across dozens of rebellion novels that were published from the beginning to the end of the nineteenth century.

While earlier researchers addressed the nature of rebellious or revolutionary themes in these rebellion novels, there has been no previous study that united these works into a dynamic and simultaneously formulaic genre. These findings shed light on the pro-rebellion political purposes of some of the most influential and widely read novelists of the nineteenth century. The novelists' purposes and their writing techniques in rebellion novels overlap. Scott, Stevenson and Dickens used national and regional dialects as well as class lexicon and pronunciations to convey their social purposes. Therefore, both a linguistic and a structural analysis were needed to prove the *reasons* for the existence and the *existence* of the rebellion genre. The nineteenth century saw the first nearly universally literate society, which primarily borrowed cheap novels from circulating libraries. Because of this enlarged reading public, for the first time in British history, a novelist could affect and convince the minds of the populace with the themes and arguments expressed in popularly read novels. It is telling that some of the best-read and best-received novels had rebellious themes. Rebellion novels played a major role in British publishing, culture, society and history.

Furthermore, the findings point to a gap in genre studies research. There is a need to step away from postmodern speculations about the theory of genre and to instead edit the previously used categories for genre division. In a perfectly logical genre theory, all texts would fall into a clearly defined genre subcategory. There would be a mathematical and logical formula that would allow a critic to calculate the percentage of linguistic and structural features that identify a work with others like it. Current literary criticism is too romantic for such pure logic. Modern bookstores primarily sell genre fiction, such as romance novels, mystery novels, and fantasy novels. Thus, divisions for current fiction are specifically defined because of the need to shelve new books in a logical order that a consumer can easily understand. However, there are extreme differences between modern and nineteenth-century romance novels. Modern readers would benefit from a genre theory that includes a taxonomic breakdown that explains genre relationships on a historic timeline, as well as in linguistic and structural dimensions of genre development and mutation. Genre has to be studied with linguistic and structural statistics and logic that requires mathematical formulas, rather than literary theory alone, to define a category as a unique genre. Linguistic studies focus primarily on speech or nonfiction patterns of communication, as Vijay K. Bhatia does in *Analysing Genre: Language in Professional Settings*. I hope that in the future the same variety of linguistic logic will be turned to more in-depth novel-genre analyses.

In addition to a more logical genre classification system, there is a need to welcome researchers to examine patterns in literature for unidentified or unclassified genres and to incorporate new findings into earlier taxonomic divisions. Logical genre studies will not only help readers to understand the relationships between different kinds of novels, they will also help novelists decide on a subgenre that best fits the goals they have for a new writing project. In general, studying the elements of genre can make stronger future novelists. Therefore, if genre techniques were explored in serious academic studies, and not primarily in popular reference books like *The Screenwriter's Bible*, the quality of the fiction produced by publishers would significantly improve.

Rebellion novels prove that there are patterns between them that form a rebellion novel genre. Rebellion novels center on a rebellion theme: a revolution, an uprising, an assassination, or another revolt against an established government or the mother country. The characters, plots and settings frequently have similar structures. The writers use subversive linguistic techniques to communicate anti-empire, anti-union or socialist messages. Hundreds of nineteenth-century novelists wrote the occasional rebellion novel, including popular works like: *Mutiny on the Bounty* (1831), *Sybil, the Two Nations* (1845), *The Virginians: A Tale of the Last Century* (1857-59), and *Felix Holt, The Radical* (1866). For the three focal novelists, political reform through political and, primarily, rebellion novels dominated their literary careers. Both Robert Louis Stevenson and Sir Walter Scott wrote more than six rebellion novels each. Even Charles Dickens' *A Christmas Carol* has a radical political purpose. He broke into popular literature with the help of radical Tories and he stuck to social themes, especially when he became independent and had near total control over the publishing process of his novels. His novel about the French Revolution, *A Tale of Two Cities*, and another novel about the notorious Gordon Riots from the same period, *Barnaby Rudge*, fit perfectly into the rebellion novel genre's pattern of construction.

Scott, Stevenson and Dickens all had family members who were impoverished and exploited by the empire, or who were Tory, Jacobite or otherwise anti-empiric political rebels. At the same time, all three benefited from wealthy aristocratic patrons in the form of their publishers, investors in their journals, or direct funding through family or regional connections. Scott's first historical rebellion novels were rooted in the writing techniques and plotlines of Irish national tales, the adventure of scandal fiction, as well as in antiestablishment fiction of the great periphery satirists, like Jonathan Swift. Because Scott was the first commercially successful novelist in the history of British publishing, Dickens, Stevenson and many other writers mimicked not only the historical novel genre that he founded, but also the themes, characters, settings and linguistic tricks that he used.

The structural patterns in rebellion novels grow parallel to the prevalent rebellion theme. There are a few exceptions to every generalization that can be made about the rebellion novel, as many of these novelists use techniques to distinguish their works from previous rebellion novels. Generalizing repeating patterns in most rebellion novels based on the statistical repetitions of similar elements in a significant percentage of rebellion novels forms formulas that are helpful to understanding the essential elements in their construction. The similarities spring from the fact that certain characters, situations and linguistic features are necessary for a novelist to depict a story about a rebellion. Scott, Dickens and Stevenson used reappearing epic, Homeric or mythic character types in the rebellion novels: the wild rebel (frequently a robber or someone who is committing criminal acts), the authority figure, the waverer, the strong-minded and armed rebellious woman, and the returning heir.

The rebellion theme also forms the arch of a rebellion plot. A rise in the action begins when the hero travels to the periphery (Scotland), or, in reverse, from the countryside to London, or even further, from London to Paris. The constant element is that the main character changes locations and enters an unfamiliar setting. Because the location is unfamiliar to the traveler, the narrator is motivated to closely describe the manners, language and habits of the "natives" of Scotland or of the poor neighborhood where he ends up; thereby promoting the national heritage of the region. Being arrested, running from the law, or witnessing a close friend executed for rebellion is another common plot pattern. The rebels typically lose or fail in their goal of overthrowing the English empire, or of winning independence for their country, or in winning rights due to the workers. The loss is frequently tragic and elicits sympathy for the rebels in the readers.

A typical rebellion novel's plot comprises five movements: a description of the setting and of the character's political and social background; the main character faces social or political problems with the establishment; a rebellion occurs and sweeps up the main character in its actions; the main character flies away from the heat of the rebellion; lastly, the hero recovers an inheritance and/or marries, while the brute rebels are executed or dispersed.

The time setting of the discussed rebellion novels is important because of a trick Scott originated when he chose to write about the 1740s, and later about the 1760s: they were approximately sixty years before Scott began writing the novels. Dickens mimicked this timeline, focusing on the 1780s through 1800, also sixty years before his time. However, by the time Stevenson wrote his rebellion novels, he would have had to write about the 1848 revolutions if he focused on events that happened about sixty years earlier. Instead, Stevenson chose to focus primarily on the same eighteenth-century Scottish or Jacobite uprisings that Scott chose, following Scott's example but breaking his sixty-year rule.

Stevenson broke many other rules set by Scott and Dickens, such as the fact that he wrote a political pamphlet about the Samoan Civil War that occurred while he resided in Samoa. This is one of the best examples of how the rebellion novel naturally evolved during the nineteenth century as censorship laws changed, the publishing industry mutated, and nonviolent reform came into vogue. Scott wrote his rebellion novels under an assumed name and worked to look like a loyalist by orchestrating a visit from the king to Edinburgh. Dickens was also tamer about expressing his rebellious leanings. On the other hand, at the end of the nineteenth century, a popular novelist like Stevenson was not convicted for treason despite participating in or writing about Irish nationalists, French commune dwellers, the Samoan Civil War and other revolutionary and rebellious movements.

Rebellion novels are notoriously difficult for literary critics to categorize because if one ignores the prevalence of the rebellion theme, one is hard-pressed to guess which other single genre they might fall into. Most rebellion novels have features of the gothic, mystery, historic, political, social, comedic, epic, satiric, mythic, national, sensational and many other genres. Occasionally ghosts float by, and at other times the story sticks to the historical records from the period, and at yet other times the narrator and the characters slip into political propaganda. The rebellion theme unifies these different features, which partially exist in order to subversively hide the violent uprisings under the guise of structural innovations and beautiful technical maneuvers by a given novel's skillful author.

Dickens confessed to greatly admiring Scott. Stevenson confessed that he adored both Scott and Dickens. Thus, the parallels between Scott's linguistic and stylistic techniques and those used by Dickens and Stevenson are natural derivations. If one looks closely at the linguistic and stylistic features of rebellion novels by Dickens, Scott and Stevenson, one is amazed at the intricate complexity and multiple levels in their design. These three writers are among the best-known for their stylistic skill.

Scott uses extensive figurative imagery, epithets, gnomic wisdom, proverbs, and other tricks he mimics from classical authors like Homer; James Macpherson (better known under the name of his narrator, Ossian, as Ossian poetry); and even from biblical proverbs. Scott's language was saturated with borrowings from Middle English, Cant terms, foreign words, quotations from classics, and imitations of "real" Scottish regional speech. The complexity of the language meant that many of the original British readers could not understand anti–British passages written in Scottish or with embellishments that were foreign to an average nineteenth-century reader.

Dickens mimicked many of Scott's stylistic tricks, also using proverbs, psalms, songs, and religious and mythic allusions. Dickens was not as lucky as Scott when it came to the ability to speak in subversively foreign languages in his fiction — his French was nearly as weak as his Scottish. Therefore, Dickens focused on using class dialects in the form of substandard speech, vulgarisms, regional British dialects, and even made-up words and phrases in order to enrich the texture of his writing. Using class dialects showed Dickens' sympathy with the poor and with their rebellious and revolutionary acts.

Stevenson mimics Scott's use of Scottish because of their similar national origins. The musical quality of rebellion novels is something that few of the other novelists discussed. Stevenson describes in detail how he carefully measured the musical linguistic style of his novels. The music is present not only in the Jacobite toasts, Gaelic songs, and Alan's whistling but in the rhythm of the narrative. Stevenson believed that not only poetry but also prose had to be metrically measured and sounded for alliterations and assonance. Stevenson edited his writing to avoid the antimusical cacophony that bad writers leave behind. This close attention to the details of the language is what separates Scott, Dickens and Stevenson into a league of the most meticulous and skillful writers of the nineteenth century. Stevenson's use of beautiful musical linguistics is used to show the musical beauty of the Scottish national identity as well as the beauty of the language of the Jacobite rebels and other rebellious characters.

Rebellion novels were written to be sold to a wide popular audience primarily with financial profits in mind. It is absurd to say that rebellion novels were written with the purpose of overthrowing the English empire. But it is clear that Scott's, Dickens' and Stevenson's rebellion novels echo the writers' anti–Empire, anticolonial and anticorruption views. Even if all three writers were anticolonial socialists, they did not write outright socialist manifestos, unlike Karl Marx. Scott wanted Scottish independence. Dickens supported the Chartist worker uprisings. Stevenson wrote a manifesto history for Samoan freedom from colonialism, and books about Scottish and Irish independence. However, none of the three allowed themselves the luxury of voicing outright, extensive proclamations for their chosen causes in their commercial rebellion novels. Propaganda just didn't sell well in the nineteenth century; sensational and mysterious rebellion stories did. Rebellion novels are interesting because of the complexity of the genre techniques that Scott, Dickens and Stevenson developed. Rebellion novelists were waging a "literary battle with England," not a violent guerrilla attack on the monarchy. The monarchy and capitalism paid the writers' artistic bills. Despite censorship limitations, the ideas Scott, Dickens and Stevenson expressed in their rebellion novels influenced later socialists and the public opinion of the populace and policy-makers during their own time.

Chapter Notes

Introduction

1. Louis Cazamian, *The Social Novel in England 1830–1850: Dickens, Disraeli, Mrs. Gaskell, Kingsley* (1903) (New York: Routledge, 1973).
2. Edwin Pugh, *Charles Dickens: The Apostle of the People* (1908) (New York: AMS Press, 1975).
3. T. A. Jackson, *Charles Dickens: The Progress of a Radical* (1937) (New York: Haskell, 1971).
4. George Orwell, *Dickens, Dali & Others* (1946) (San Diego: Harcourt Brace Jovanovich, 1973).
5. Graham Law, *Serializing Fiction in the Victorian Press* (New York: Palgrave, 2000), 196.
6. William Black, *Donald Ross of Heimra* (London: Harper, 1894. Google Books. Accessed May 11, 2011), 233.
7. Ibid., 8.
8. Ibid.
9. Ibid., 44.
10. Ibid., 46.
11. Ibid., 77.
12. Peter J. Manning, "Wordsworth in the *Keepsake*, 1829," *Literature in the Marketplace: Nineteenth-Century English Publishing and Reading Practices*, John O. Jordan and Robert L. Patten, eds. (Cambridge: Cambridge University Press, 1996. 44–73), 48.
13. William Harrison Ainsworth, *Sir John Chiverton: A Romance*, 2nd ed. (London: John Ebers, 1827, Google Books).
14. *Old Mortality*, 346–47.
15. John Sutherland, *Victorian Fiction:* *Writers, Publishers, Readers* (New York: Macmillan, 2006), 169.
16. "Aunt Margaret."

Part I: Chapter 1

1. Nicholas Rance, *The Historical Novel and Popular Politics in Nineteenth-Century England* (New York: Barnes and Noble, 1975), 73.
2. Norman McCord and Bill Purdue, *English History: 1815–1914*, 2nd ed. (Oxford: Oxford University Press, 2007), 28.
3. Ibid., 150.
4. Ibid., 158.
5. Robert McNamara, "England's Disastrous Retreat from Kabul: The 1842 Afghanistan Massacre, Only One English Soldier Survived" About Guide: 19th-Century History (Accessed March 17, 2011).
6. McCord, *English History*, 41.
7. "Reform Bill." *Encyclopaedia Britannica Online* (Accessed March 17, 2011).
8. McCord, *English History*, 43.

Chapter 2

1. Alan Sandison, "A World Made for Liars: Stevenson's *Dynamiter* and the Death of the Real." *Robert Louis Stevenson Reconsidered: New Critical Perspectives* (Jefferson, N.C.: McFarland, 2003), 140–62.
2. John P. Farrell, *Revolution as Tragedy: The Dilemma of the Moderate from Scott to Arnold* (New York: Cornell University Press, 1980).

3. Linda K. Hughes and Michael Lund, *The Victorian Serial* (Charlottesville: University Press of Virginia, 1991), 61.
4. Karl Marx, *Karl Marx: Selected Writings*, 2nd ed. (Oxford: Oxford University Press, 2005).
5. Morris E. Speare, The *Political Novel: Its Development in England and in America* (New York: Russell & Russell, 1966), ix.
6. George Orwell, "Politics and the English Language," *All Art Is Propaganda: Critical Essays* (Orlando, Fla.: Harcourt, 2008), 286.
7. Aristotle, "Poetics," *The Rhetoric and the Poetics of Aristotle* (New York: Modern Library, 1984), 219–66.
8. John Frow, *Genre* (New York: Routledge, 2006), 1–5.
9. Gerard Genette, "The Architext," *Modern Genre Theory* (Essex: Pearson, 2000).
10. Ireneusz Opacki, "Royal Genres," *Modern Genre Theory* (Essex: Pearson, 2000), 119–120.
11. Tzvetan Todorov, "The Origin of Genres," *Modern Genre Theory* (Essex: Pearson, 2000), 197–198.
12. Genette, *Modern Genre Theory*, 213.
13. Alastair Fowler, "Transformation of Genre," *Modern Genre Theory* (Essex: Pearson, 2000), 232–245.
14. Benedetto Croce, *History, Its Theory and Practice* (New York: Russell & Russell, 1960), 8.

Chapter 3

1. Grace Moore, *Dickens and Empire: Discourse of Class, Race and Colonialism in the Works of Charles Dickens* (Aldershot, U.K.: Ashgate, 2004), 141.
2. Thomas More, *Utopia* (Rockville, Md.: Arc Manor, 2008. Google Books).
3. Jonathan Swift, *Gulliver's Travels* (Chicago: Rand McNally & Company, 1912. Google Books).
4. Harrison Ainsworth, *Historical Romances of William Harrison Ainsworth: Guy Fawkes, Volume XIX* (1840) (LaVergne, Tn.: Kessinger Press, 2010), 5.
5. Avrom Fleishman, *The English Historical Novel: Walter Scott to Virginia Woolf* (Baltimore: Johns Hopkins University Press, 1971).
6. Morris E. Speare, *The Political Novel: Its Development in England and in America* (New York: Russell & Russell, 1966).
7. Caroline McCracken-Flesher, "Thinking Nationally/Writing Colonially? Scott, Stevenson, and England," *NOVEL: A Forum on Fiction* (Vol. 24, No. 3, Spring 1991). Durham: Duke University Press. JSTOR. 296–318) 296.
8. Edwin M. Eigner, *Robert Louis Stevenson and Romantic Tradition* (Princeton: Princeton University Press, 1966), 40.
9. William Harrison Ainsworth, *Sir John Chiverton: A Romance*, 2nd ed. (London: John Ebers, 1827, Google Books).
10. Horace Smith, *Brambletye House, or, Cavaliers and Roundheads* (1826) (London: G. Dearborn, 1837, Google Books).
11. John Hayden, *Scott: The Critical Heritage* (New York: Barnes & Noble, 1970), 299–301.
12. John G. Lockhart and Sir Walter Scott, *Memoirs of the Life of Sir Walter Scott, Volume I, Collection of Ancient and Modern English Authors*, Vol. CLXXV (Paris: Baudry's European Library, 1838, Google Books).
13. Charles Knight, "Sir John Chiverton," *The Monthly Review: From September to December Inclusive, 1826, Volume III* (Hurst, Robinson, 1826), 439.
14. Horace Smith, *Brambletye House*, 56.

Chapter 4

1. E. P. Thompson, *The Making of the English Working Class* (New York: Vintage Books, 1966), 712.
2. Benjamin Disraeli, *Coningsby: Or the New Generation* (Leipzig: Berhn. Tauchnitz June 1844, Google Books).
3. Ian St. John, *Disraeli and the Art of Victorian Politics* (London: Anthem Press, 2005), 105.
4. Ibid., 111.
5. Ibid., 120.
6. Ibid., 159.
7. Benjamin Disraeli, *The Young Duke* (1831). *The Works of Benjamin Disraeli: The Young Duke, V. 1* (M. W. Dunne, 1904, Google Books).
8. John Sutherland, *Victorian Fiction: Writers, Publishers, Readers* (New York: Macmillan, 2006), 10.
9. Benjamin Disraeli, *Endymion* (1880) (Longmans, Green, 1920, Google Books).

10. *Sybil*, 24.
11. Ibid., 29.
12. Ibid., 46.
13. Jonathan Rose, "How Historians Study Reader Response: Or, What Did Jo Think of *Bleak House*?" *Literature in the Marketplace: Nineteenth-Century English Publishing and Reading Practices* (John O. Jordan and Robert L. Patten, eds., Cambridge: Cambridge University Press, 1996, 195–212), 207.
14. Ibid., 196.
15. Sutherland, *Victorian Fiction*, 166–167.
16. Ibid., 55.
17. Lee Erickson, *The Economy of Literary Form: English Literature and the Industrialization of Publishing, 1800–1850* (Baltimore: Johns Hopkins University Press, 1996), 148–149.
18. Sutherland, *Victorian Fiction*, 10.
19. Sir Walter Scott, *Ivanhoe: A Romance* (1820) (London: Baudry's European Library, 1835, Google Books).
20. John Jordon, *The Cambridge Companion to Charles Dickens* (New York: Cambridge University Press, 2001), 196–200.
21. Richard Altick, *The English Common Reader: A Social History of the Mass Reading Public, 1800–1900*. 2nd ed. (1957) (Columbus: Ohio State University Press, 1998), 2.
22. Sutherland, *Victorian Fiction*, 5.
23. Rose, *Literature in the Marketplace*, 208.

Chapter 5

1. Robert Justin Goldstein, *Political Censorship of the Arts and the Press in Nineteenth-Century Europe* (New York: St. Martin's Press, 1989), 40.
2. Ibid., 44.
3. Ibid., 52.
4. E. P. Thompson, *The Making of the English Working Class* (New York: Vintage Books, 1966), 720.
5. Ibid., 728.
6. Ibid., 729.
7. Ibid., 732.
8. Sir Walter Scott, Chapter 28, *Rob Roy* (1817) (New York: Penguin, 2007).
9. John Feather, *A History of English Publishing*, 2nd ed. (New York: Routledge, 2004), 63.
10. Ibid., 55.
11. Ibid., 56.
12. Ibid., 133.
13. Thomas Paine, *Common Sense* (1776) (P. Eckler, 1918, Google Books).
14. Feather, *A History*, 92.
15. Gilbert Wakefield, *A Reply to Some Parts of the Bishop Llandaff's Address to the People of Great Britain*, 2nd ed. (London: Johnson, 1798, Google Books), 6.
16. William Blake, *The Complete Poetry & Prose of William Blake* (David V. Erdman, ed., New York: Anchor Books), 1988.
17. Gilbert Keith Chesterton, *William Blake* (New York: Cosimo, 2005, Google Books), 41.
18. Thompson, *The Making*, 721.
19. Ibid., 725.
20. Ibid.
21. Thomas Paine, *Age of Reason: Being an Investigation of True and Fabulous Theology* (1794, 1795, 1807) (New York: Truth Seeker Company, 1898, Google Books).
22. Thompson, *The Making*, 721.
23. Ibid., 721.
24. Ibid., 721.
25. Ibid., 722.
26. Ibid., 722.
27. Richard Carlile, ed., *The Republican, Volume 9* (London: R. Carlile, 1824, Google Books).
28. William Hone and George Cruikshank, *Right Divine of Kings to Govern Wrong. Facetiae and Miscellanies*, 2nd ed. (London: Hunt and Clarke, 1827, Google Books).
29. William Hone, *The Queen's Matrimonial Ladder: A National Toy, with fourteen step scences; and illustrations in verse, with eighteen other cuts* (London: William Hone, 1820, Google Books).
30. Queen Caroline, *Non Mi Ricordo. The Important and Eventful Trial of Queen Caroline, Consort of George IV for "Adulterous Intercourse" with Bartolomo Bergami, Parts 1–2* (London: Geo. Smeeton, 1820, Google Books).
31. William Hone, George Canning, and George Cruikshank, *The Man in the Moon*, 2nd ed. (London: William Hone, 1820, Google Books).
32. Thompson, *The Making*, 722.
33. Caroline, *Non Mi Ricordo*.
34. Thomas Jonathan Wooler, ed., *The Black Dwarf, Volume 6* (London: T. J. Wooler, 1821, Google Books).
35. Ngugi wa Thiong'o, and Ngugi wa Mirii, *I Will Marry When I Want* (Oxford: Heinemann, 1988), 116.

36. Thompson, *The Making*, 808.
37. Ibid., 808–809.
38. Karl Marx, "On Violent Revolution," *Karl Marx: Selected Writings*, 2nd ed., McLellan, David, ed. (Oxford: Oxford University Press, 2005), 642–643.
39. Thompson, *The Making*, 829.
40. Ibid., 809.
41. Frank Ferdinand Rosenblatt, *The Chartist Movement in Its Social and Economic Aspects. Issues 171–173: Columbia Studies in the Social Sciences* (New York: Columbia University, 1916).
42. Thompson, *The Making*, 818.
43. Kate Flint, *The Woman Reader: 1837–1914* (Oxford: Clarendon Press, 1994), 221.
44. John Sutherland, *Victorian Fiction: Writers, Publishers, Readers* (New York: Macmillan, 2006), 170.
45. Ibid., 170.
46. Feather, *A History*, 108.
47. Ibid., 121.
48. Ibid., 119.
49. Ibid., 123.
50. Sutherland, *Victorian Fiction*, 169.
51. Ibid., 169.
52. Allan C. Dooley, *Author and Printer in Victorian England* (Charlottesville: University Press of Virginia, 1992), 150.
53. Elizabeth Morrison, "Serial Fiction in Australian Colonial Newspapers," *Literature in the Marketplace: Nineteenth-Century English Publishing and Reading Practices* (John O. Jordan and Robert L. Patten, eds. Cambridge: Cambridge University Press, 1996, 306–324), 314.
54. Lee Erickson, *The Economy of Literary Form: English Literature and the Industrialization of Publishing, 1800–1850* (Baltimore: Johns Hopkins University Press, 1996), 155–156.

Chapter 6

1. Paul M. Handley, *The King Never Smiles: A Biography of Thailand's Bhumibol Adulyadej* (New Haven: Yale University Press, 2006).
2. Todd Pitman, and Sinfah Tunsarawuth, "Thailand Arrests American for Alleged King Insult" (Associated Press, 27 May 2011).
3. William Hone and George Cruikshank, *Right Divine of Kings to Govern Wrong. Facetiæ and Miscellanies*, 2nd ed. (London: Hunt and Clarke, 1827, Google Books).
4. Aviva Freedman and Peter Medway, *Genre and the New Rhetoric* (New York: Taylor & Francis, 2003), viii.
5. Jack G. Voller, "Joseph Sheridan LeFanu," *The Literary Gothic* (22 June 2012).
6. Avrom Fleishman, *The English Historical Novel: Walter Scott to Virginia Woolf* (Baltimore: Johns Hopkins University Press, 1971).
7. Josephine M. Guy, *The Victorian Social-Problem Novel: The Market, the Individual, and Communal Life* (London: Macmillan, 1996).
8. *Colonel Torlogh*, 8.
9. Nicholas Rance, *The Historical Novel and Popular Politics in Nineteenth-Century England* (New York: Barnes and Noble, 1975), 14.
10. Mikhail Bakhtin, "Epic and Novel: Toward a Methodology for the Study of the Novel," *Modern Genre Theory* (Essex: Pearson, 2000), 71.
11. Ibid., 72.
12. *Hereward*, 1–2.
13. Ibid., 13, 18.
14. *White Hoods*, 67–69.
15. *Sybil*, 85.
16. Terry Eagleton, *The English Novel* (Malden: Blackwell, 2005), 104.
17. Ibid., 149.
18. Ibid., 150.
19. E. P. Thompson, *The Making of the English Working Class* (New York: Vintage Books, 1966), 714.
20. Eagleton, *The English Novel*, 147.
21. *Barnaby Rudge*, 503.
22. Patricia Poussa, "Dickens as Sociolinguist: Dialect in *David Copperfield*," *Writing in Nonstandard English* (Irma Taavitsainen, Gunnel Melchers and Paivi Pahta, eds. Philadelphia: John Benjamins, 1999, 27–44), 28.
23. Miriam Meyerhoff, *Introducing Sociolinguistics* (New York: Routledge, 2006), 12.
24. D'Arcy, 22.
25. Ibid., 37.
26. Ibid., 42.
27. Horace Walpole, *The Castle of Otranto: A Gothic Story... Last Edition Adorned with Cuts* (London: C. F. Himbourg, 1794. Google Books, 22 June 2012).
28. Fleishman, *English Historical Novel*, 20–23.
29. *Colonel Torlogh*, 12–13.
30. *White Hoods*, 165.

31. *Felix Holt*, 229–30.
32. *Virginians*, 9.

Part II: Chapter 7

1. Peter Garside, "Popular Fiction and National Tale: Hidden Origins of Scott's *Waverly*," *Nineteenth-Century Literature* (1991 June; 46 (1): 30–53. JSTOR), 53.
2. Sir Walter Scott, *Letters of Sir Walter Scott*, ed. H. J. C. Greirson, Volume III (London: Parker, 1932), 302.
3. Ina Ferris, *The Romantic National Tale and the Question of Ireland* (Cambridge: Cambridge University Press, 2002), 129.
4. "The Ballantyne Brothers," Walter Scott Digital Archive (Edinburgh: Edinburgh University Library).
5. John Sutherland, *Victorian Fiction: Writers, Publishers, Readers* (New York: Macmillan, 2006), 71.
6. *Waverley*, 57.
7. Sutherland, *Victorian Fiction*, 107.
8. Nicholas Rance, *The Historical Novel and Popular Politics in Nineteenth-Century England* (New York: Barnes and Noble, 1975), 21.
9. D'Arcy, 28–29.
10. John Prebble, *The King's Jaunt: George IV in Scotland, August 1822 "One and Twenty Daft Days"* (1988) (London: Birlinn, 2000).
11. Michael Leapman, *Great England: Eyewitness Travel* (London: DK, 2010), 492.
12. "Obituary: Sir Walter Scott, Bart," *The Gentleman's Magazine*, Volume 152 (1832), 377.
13. Ibid., 378.
14. Edwin Muir, *Scott and Scotland: The Predicament of the Scottish Writer* (1936) (Edinburgh: Polygon, 1982).
15. David Daiches, *Literary Essays* (1956) (Edinburgh: Oliver and Boyd, 1966).
16. Moray McLaren, *Sir Walter Scott: The Man and Patriot* (Edinburgh: Morrison & Gibb, 1970), 108, 110.
17. *Mid-Lothian*, 10.
18. D'Arcy, 230.
19. Ibid., 139.
20. Thomas Carlyle, "On Sir Walter Scott (1771–1832)" (1838) (Internet Modern History Sourcebook).
21. Lockhart, 2–3.
22. Carlyle, "On Sir Walter Scott."
23. Lockhart, 4.
24. Sutherland, *Victorian Fiction*, 159.
25. Lockhart, 7.
26. Sutherland, *Victorian Fiction*, 173.
27. Sir James Knowles, *The Nineteenth Century, Volume 26* (London: Henry S. King, 1889, Google Books), 438.
28. Sutherland, *Victorian Fiction*, 47.
29. Lockhart, 17.
30. Ibid., 263.
31. Leapman, *Great England*, 482.
32. William Anderson, *The Scottish Nation; or, the Surnames, Families, Literature, Honours, and Biographical History of the People of Scotland*, Volume III (Edinburgh: Fullarton, 1867, Google Books), 416.
33. Ibid., 577.

Chapter 8

1. Miguel Cervantes Saavedra, *The Ingenious Gentleman Don Quixote de la Mancha* (1605, 1615) (Trans: Samuel Putnam, New York: Viking Press, 1949).
2. Vasco Lobeira, *Amadis of Gaul, Volume 1: Library of Old Authors* (Trans. Robert Southey, London: J. R. Smith, 1872, Google Books).
3. Sir Walter Scott, *Essays on Chivalry, Romance and the Drama* (1834) (Freeport, N.Y.: Books for Libraries Press, 1972), 226.
4. Katie Trumpener, "National Character, National Plots: National Tale and Historical Novel in the Age of Waverly, 1806–1830," *ELH*, Vol. 60, No. 3 (Autumn 1993) (JSTOR, 685–731), 708–709.
5. Ibid., 708–709.
6. Thomas Carlyle, "On Sir Walter Scott (1771–1832)" (1838) (Internet Modern History Sourcebook).
7. Sir Walter Scott, *Critical and Miscellaneous Essays*, Volume I (Philadelphia: Carey & Hart, 1841), 245–246.
8. Lockhart, 270–273.
9. John P. Farrell, *Revolution as Tragedy: The Dilemma of the Moderate from Scott to Arnold* (New York: Cornell University Press, 1980).
10. Joanna Baillie, "Rayner: A Tragedy in Five Acts." *Miscellaneous Plays*, 2nd ed. (London: Longman, Hurst, Rees and Orme, 1805, Google Books), i–vi.
11. Peter M. Darling, *The Romance of the Highlands*, Volume I (Edinburgh: George Ramsay, 1810, Google Books).
12. Peter Garside, "Popular Fiction and

National Tale: Hidden Origins of Scott's *Waverly*," *Nineteenth-Century Literature* (1991 June; 46 (1): 30–53. JSTOR), 46.
13. Ibid., 49.
14. Ibid., 51.
15. John Sutherland, *Victorian Fiction: Writers, Publishers, Readers* (New York: Macmillan, 2006), 159.
16. Trumpener, "National Character, National Plots," 692.
17. T. S. Surr, *A Winter in London; Or Sketches of Fashion: A Novel* (London: Richard Phillips, 1806, Google Books), 2.
18. Ibid., 12.
19. Ibid., 14.
20. Trumpener, "National Character, National Plots," 693.
21. Ibid., 697.
22. Lockhart, 22, 29.
23. Black Dwarf, 8.
24. D'Arcy, 89.
25. William Cadbury, "The Two Structures of *Rob Roy*," *Modern Language Quarterly* (Seattle, Wash.: 1968; 29: 42–60, EBSCO), 56.
26. Ibid., 56.
27. Ibid., 56–60.
28. *Black Dwarf*, 371.
29. *Waverley*, 453.
30. *Rob Roy*, 56.
31. *Old Mortality*, 35.
32. Ibid., 35.
33. Ibid., 14.
34. Ibid., 29.
35. *Waverley*, 174.
36. Ibid., 81.
37. Ibid., 157.
38. Christabel F. Fiske, *Epic Suggestion in the Imagery of the Waverley Novels* (New Haven: Yale University Press, 1940), 1.
39. *Black Dwarf*, 372.
40. Ibid., 14.
41. Ibid., 15.
42. *Waverley*, 167.
43. *Black Dwarf*, 15.
44. *Mid-Lothian*, 13.
45. Ibid., 25.
46. Ibid., 319.

Chapter 9

1. Christabel F. Fiske, *Epic Suggestion in the Imagery of the Waverley Novels* (New Haven: Yale University Press, 1940), 47.
2. *Rob Roy*, 172.
3. Graham Tulloch, *The Language of Walter Scott: A Study of His Scottish and Period Language* (London: Andre Deutsch, 1980), 135.
4. Ibid., 183.
5. Ibid., 186.
6. Anne McKim, ed., "The Wallace: Introduction," *The Wallace: Selections* (1471–1479), Blind Harry, author (Kalamazoo, Mich.: Medieval Institute Publications, 2003, Medieval Institute Publications Online Store).
7. John Barbour, *The Bruce; or, The History of Robert I, King of Scotland: Written in Scotish Verse, Volumes 1–3* (London: H. Hughs for G. Nicol, Bookseller to His Majesty, 1790, Google Books).
8. Ibid., 12.
9. McKim, *The Wallace*, 136.
10. David Murison, "1: The Historical Background," *Languages of Scotland* (The Association for Scottish Literary Studies Occasional Paper Number 4. A. J. Aitken and Tom McArthur, eds., Edinburgh: W & R Chambers, 1979), 9.
11. Ibid., 9.
12. William Forbes Skene, *The Dean of Lismore's Book: a selection of ancient Gaelic poetry from a manuscript collection made by Sir James M'Gregor, dean of Lismore, in the beginning of the sixteenth century* (Thomas Maclauchlan, ed, Edinburgh: Edmonston and Douglas, 1862).
13. Murison, *Languages of Scotland*, 10.
14. Sir Walter Scott, *The Lady of the Lake* (Boston: 1883, Project Gutenberg).
15. Murison, *Languages of Scotland*, 11.
16. David Hume, "Scotticisms," *The Philosophical Works of David Hume*, Volume 1 (London: A. Black and W. Tait, 1826, cxxv–cxxix, Google Books).
17. Deborah Chirrey, "12: Edinburgh: Descriptive Materials," *Urban Voices: Accent Studies in the British Isles* (Paul Foulkes and Gerard J. Docherty, eds., London: Arnold, 1999), 223.
18. Ibid., 224.
19. Ibid., 225.
20. Lockhart, 270–273.
21. Ibid.
22. Derick McLure, *Scott and His Influence: The Papers of the Aberdeen Scott Conference, 1982: Issue 6 of Occasional Papers* (Association for Scottish Literary Studies, John

H. Alexander and David Hewitt, eds., Edinburgh: Association for Scottish Literary Studies, 1983), 129–35, 138–39.
23. D'Arcy, 133.
24. Sir Walter Scott, *Life of Swift. The Miscellaneous Prose Works of Sir Walter Scott, Bart* (Edinburgh: Cadell, 1827, Google Books).
25. Jonathan Swift, *Gulliver's Travels* (Chicago: Rand McNally & Company, 1912. Google Books).
26. Colm Toibin, ed., *The Penguin Book of Irish Fiction* (New York: Penguin, 1999), 9–11.
27. Ibid., 14.
28. Ibid., 20.
29. George Orwell, "Politics vs. Literature: An Examination of *Gulliver's Travels,*" *All Art Is Propaganda: Critical Essays* (Orlando, Fla.: Harcourt, 2008), 306.
30. Tulloch, *The Language of Walter Scott.*
31. Ibid., 9.
32. Sir Walter Scott, *Critical and Miscellaneous Essays*, Volume I (Philadelphia: Carey & Hart, 1841), 245–246.
33. Tulloch, *The Language of Walter Scott,* 30.
34. *Waverley,* 99.
35. John Sinclair, *Observations on the Scottish Dialect* (London: Strahan and T. Cadell, 1782, Google Books).
36. *Waverley,* 104.
37. Ibid., 110.
38. Ibid., 111.
39. Sinclair, *Observations on the Scottish Dialect,* 85.
40. Ibid., 88.
41. *Waverley,* 112.
42. Sinclair, *Observations on the Scottish Dialect,* 15.
43. Ibid., 22.
44. Ibid., 23.
45. Ibid., 26.
46. D'Arcy, 33.
47. Tulloch, *The Language of Walter Scott,* 92.
48. Ibid., 135.
49. Ibid., 138.
50. Edwin Muir, *Scott and Scotland: The Predicament of the Scottish Writer* (1936) (Edinburgh: Polygon, 1982), 4, 6.
51. Andrew Lincoln, "Scott and Empire: The Case of *Rob Roy,*" (*Studies in the Novel,* 2002 Spring; 34 (1): 43–59), 51.
52. *Waverley,* 98.

53. Moray McLaren, *Sir Walter Scott: The Man and Patriot* (Edinburgh: Morrison & Gibb, 1970), ix.
54. Lockhart, 12.
55. Fiske, *Epic Suggestion,* xxiii, 5, 47.
56. Ibid., 47–77.
57. Thomas Carlyle, "On Sir Walter Scott (1771–1832)" (1838) (Internet Modern History Sourcebook).
58. Bruce K. Waltke, *The Book of Proverbs: Chapters 1–15,* Volume I (Cambridge: William Eerdmans, 2004), 38–50.
59. Lockhart, 20–21.

Chapter 10

1. T. A. Jackson, *Charles Dickens: The Progress of a Radical* (1937) (New York: Haskell, 1971).
2. Edwin Pugh, *Charles Dickens: The Apostle of the People* (1908) (New York: AMS Press, 1975).
3. Louis Cazamian, *The Social Novel in England 1830–1850: Dickens, Disraeli, Mrs. Gaskell, Kingsley* (1903) (New York: Routledge, 1973).
4. Ibid., 167.
5. Rev. Charles Kingsley, "Chapter X. How Folks Turn Chartists," *Alton Locke, Tailor and Poet, An Autobiography* (1850) (Project Gutenberg).
6. Pugh, *Charles Dickens,* 235.
7. Ibid., 297.
8. Ibid., 281–5.
9. Bernard Shaw, *Shaw on Dickens* (Dan H. Laurence and Martin Quinn, eds., New York: Frederick Ungar Press, 1985), 111.
10. Ibid., 102.
11. Jackson, *Charles Dickens,* 28.
12. Ibid., 29.
13. Ibid., 29–30.
14. Ibid., 32.
15. George Orwell, *All Art Is Propaganda: Critical Essays* (Orlando, Fla.: Harcourt, 2008), 2.
16. Ibid., 4.
17. Ibid., 3.
18. Ibid., 4.
19. Ibid.
20. Ibid., 5.
21. Ibid.
22. Ibid., 7.
23. Ibid., 12.
24. Ibid., 13.

25. Ibid., 31.
26. Ibid., 46.
27. Ibid., 59.
28. Ibid., 5.
29. Ibid., 8.
30. Ibid.
31. Ibid., 62.
32. Ibid., 31.
33. Ibid., 47.
34. Ibid., 48.
35. Ibid., 60.
36. Ibid., 2.
37. Ibid., 18.
38. Ibid., 6.
39. Philip Collins, *Dickens: The Critical Heritage* (New York: Barnes & Noble, 1971), 104.
40. Ibid., 588.
41. Ibid., 618.
42. Ibid., 101–102.
43. *Barnaby Rudge*, 477.
44. Collins, *Dickens*, 409.
45. Ibid., 421.
46. Anthony O'Brien, "Benevolence and Insurrection: The Conflicts of Form and Purpose in *Barnaby Rudge*," *Dickens Studies* (Cambridge: Cambridge University Press, 1969; 5: 26–44), 28.
47. *Tale*, 278.
48. *Barnaby*, 357.
49. *Tale*, 282.
50. Ibid., 292.
51. Jackson, *Charles Dickens*, 11–12.
52. C. Baldridge, "Alternatives to Bourgeois Individualism in *A Tale of Two Cities*," *Studies in English Literature (Rice)* (30.4 (1990): 633, Academic Search Complete, EBSCO), 634.
53. *Barnaby*, 351.
54. Ibid., 356.
55. Ibid., 393.
56. Ibid., 420.
57. Ibid., 442.
58. Ibid., 501.
59. Ibid., 393.
60. Ibid., 477.
61. Ibid., 547.
62. Ibid., 488.
63. Jackson, *Charles Dickens*, 170.
64. Karl Marx, *Karl Marx: Selected Writings*, 2nd ed. (Oxford: Oxford University Press, 2005), 263.
65. Ibid., 271.
66. Ibid., 642–643.
67. Ibid., 257.
68. Ibid., 263.
69. Jackson, *Charles Dickens*, 10.
70. Deborah Wynne, "Scenes of 'Incredible Outrage': Dickens, Ireland and *A Tale of Two Cities*," *Dickens Studies Annual: Essays on Victorian Fiction* (2006; 37: 51–64), 51–52.
71. John Forster, *The Life of Charles Dickens: Volume II, 1847–1870. The Works of Charles Dickens*, Volume 36 (London: Chapman & Hall, 1899, Google Books), 478.
72. Monroe Engel, "The Politics of Dickens' Novels," *PMLA* (December 1956; 71: 945–974), 950.
73. Michael Goldberg, "From Bentham to Carlyle: Dickens' Political Development," *Journal of the History of Ideas*, Vol. 33, No. 1 (January–March, 1972) (University of Pennsylvania Press, JSTOR, 61–76), 62.
74. Engel, "The Politics of Dickens' Novels," 947.
75. Ibid., 954–955.
76. Goldberg, "From Bentham to Carlyle," 62.
77. Ibid., 65.
78. Jeremy Bentham, *Canada. Emancipate Your Colonies! An Unpublished Argument* (London: Effingham Wilson, 1838, Google Books), iii.
79. Ibid., 2.
80. Thomas Carlyle, *Chartism*, 2nd ed. (London: Chapman and Hall, Strand, 1842, Google Books), 1.
81. Ibid., 3.
82. Thomas Hobbes, *Leviathan: Or the Matter, Forme & Power of a Commonwealth, Ecclesiasticall and Civill* (1651) (Cambridge: Cambridge University Press, 1904, Google Books), 149.
83. Grace Moore, *Dickens and Empire: Discourse of Class, Race and Colonialism in the Works of Charles Dickens* (Aldershot, U.K.: Ashgate, 2004), 105.
84. Ibid., 80.
85. Ibid., 5.
86. Dickens, *Letters, Volume 7*, 443–4.
87. Moore, *Dickens and Empire*, 81.
88. Ibid., 86.
89. Ibid., 87.
90. Ibid., 113.
91. Ibid., 126.
92. Ibid., 129.
93. Ibid., 153.
94. Ibid., 129.
95. Ibid., 146.

Chapter 11

1. Aristotle, "Poetics," *The Rhetoric and the Poetics of Aristotle* (New York: Modern Library, 1984. 219–266), 229.
2. Mark Willis, "Charles Dickens and the Fictions of the Crowd," *Dickens Quarterly* (23.2 (2006): 85–107, Academic Search Complete, EBSCO), 103.
3. *Barnaby*, 10.
4. Iain Crawford, "Dickens, Classical Myth, and Representation of Social Order in *Barnaby Rudge*," *Dickensian* (1997 Winter; 93: 3 [443]: 185–87), 188.
5. Ibid., 190.
6. Philip Collins, *Dickens: The Critical Heritage* (New York: Barnes & Noble, 1971), 488.
7. Anthony O'Brien, "Benevolence and Insurrection: The Conflicts of Form and Purpose in *Barnaby Rudge*," *Dickens Studies* (Cambridge: Cambridge University Press, 1969; 5: 26–44), 29.
8. Collins, *Dickens*, 105–112.
9. *Barnaby*, 372.
10. Ibid., 371.
11. Ibid., 404.
12. Ibid., 491.
13. Ibid., 442.
14. Ibid., 451.
15. Ibid., 485.
16. Nicholas Rance, *The Historical Novel and Popular Politics in Nineteenth-Century England* (New York: Barnes and Noble, 1975), 49.
17. Angus Wilson, *The World of Charles Dickens* (New York: Viking Press, 1970), 105.
18. Ibid., 105.
19. Ibid., 147.
20. Ibid., 147.
21. *Tale*, 3.
22. Thomas Carlyle, *The French Revolution: A History* (1837) (New York: Modern Library, 2002), 774–775.
23. *Tale*, 385–386.
24. Gareth Stedman Jones, "The Redemptive Power of Violence?: Carlyle, Marx and Dickens," *History Workshop Journal* (2008 Spring; 65: 1–22), 3.
25. *Barnaby*, ix.
26. Charles Dickens, *American Notes* (1842) (New York: Penguin, 2004), 114.
27. Ibid., 296–297.
28. Aristotle, "Poetics," 234.
29. Ibid., 234.
30. Ibid., 230.
31. Collins, *Critical*, 109–111.
32. Humphry House, *The Dickens World*, 2nd ed. (London: Oxford University Press, 1961), 204.
33. Thomas Carlyle, *Cruthers and Jonson; Or the Outskirts of Life: A True Story* (1831) *Critical and Miscellaneous Essays: In Five Volumes*, Volume V (London: Chapman and Hall, 1899, Google Books, 168–198), 181.
34. David D. Marcus, "The Carlylean Vision of *A Tale of Two Cities*," *Studies in the Novel* (8.1 (1976): 56, Academic Search Complete, EBSCO), 56.
35. Jones, "The Redemptive Power of Violence?" 3.
36. Ibid., 3.
37. *Barnaby*, 464.
38. Ibid., 483.
39. Ibid., 536.
40. Ibid., 502.
41. Crawford, "Dickens," 187.
42. *Barnaby*, 9.
43. *Waverley*, 7.
44. Scott Dransfield, "Reading the Gordon Riots in 1841: Social Violence and Moral Management in *Barnaby Rudge*" (*Dickens Studies Annual: Essays on Victorian Fiction*. 1998; 27: 69–95), 69–90.
45. "Lear." *Encyclopaedia Britannica Online*. 2011.
46. *Barnaby*, 375.
47. Ibid., 388.
48. Ibid., 426.
49. Ibid., 390.
50. Ibid., 660.
51. Michael Slater, *Charles Dickens* (New Haven: Yale University Press, 2009), 412–413.
52. Ibid., 605.
53. Ibid.

Chapter 12

1. Stanley Gerson, *Sound and Symbol in the Dialogue of the Works of Charles Dickens* (Stockholm: Almqvist & Wiksell, 1967), xvii, xix.
2. *Barnaby*, 421.
3. Ibid., 448.
4. Ibid., 386.
5. Ibid., 374.
6. Ibid., 455.
7. Ibid., 465.

8. Ibid., 444.
9. *Tale*, 282.
10. Ibid., 19.
11. G. L. Brook, *The Language of Dickens* (London: Andre Deutsch, 1970), 200.
12. Ibid., 200.
13. *Barnaby*, 151–152.
14. Brook, *The Language of Dickens*, 216–7.
15. Ibid., 187.
16. *Barnaby*, Ch. 9.
17. *Tale*, 11.
18. *Barnaby*, 409.
19. *Barnaby*, Ch. 8; Brook, *The Language of Dickens*, 89.
20. *Barnaby*, Ch. 27; Brook, *The Language of Dickens*, 59.
21. Brook, *The Language of Dickens*, 81.
22. *Barnaby*, Ch. 37.
23. Brook, *The Language of Dickens*, 109
24. Ibid., 112.
25. *Barnaby*, 447.
26. Brook, *The Language of Dickens*, 112.
27. Gerson, *Sound and Symbol*, 357–359, 64.
28. Brook, *The Language of Dickens*, 138.
29. Ibid., 143.
30. *Barnaby*, 503.
31. Brook, *The Language of Dickens*, 117.
32. *Tale*, 13.
33. Copperfield, 9.
34. Elizabeth Cleghorn Gaskell, *Mary Barton* (1815) (London: Century Company, 1906, Google Books), 31.
35. *Hard Times*, 43.
36. Ibid., 176.
37. Ibid.
38. *Barnaby*, Ch. 41.
39. Ibid., Ch. 7.
40. Ibid., Ch. 22.
41. Ibid., Ch. 39.
42. Ibid., Ch. 37.
43. Gareth Stedman Jones, "The Redemptive Power of Violence?: Carlyle, Marx and Dickens," *History Workshop Journal* (2008 Spring; 65: 1–22), 3.
44. *Tale*, 267.
45. Ibid., 284.
46. Jones, "The Redemptive Power of Violence?" 4.
47. Ibid., 8.
48. Charles Dickens, *The Letters of Charles Dickens*, The Pilgrim Edition, Volume 5; Volume 7 (Oxford: Oxford University Press, 1981), 256.
49. Philip Collins, *Dickens: The Critical Heritage* (New York: Barnes & Noble, 1971), 111.
50. *Tale*, 276.
51. Anthony O'Brien, "Benevolence and Insurrection: The Conflicts of Form and Purpose in *Barnaby Rudge*," *Dickens Studies* (Cambridge: Cambridge University Press, 1969; 5: 26–44), 38–39.
52. *Tale*, 278.

Part IV: Chapter 13

1. Ian Bell, *Dreams of Exile: Robert Louis Stevenson: A Biography* (New York: Henry Holt, 1992), 70–71.
2. Loraine Fletcher, "Long John Silver, Karl Marx and the Ship of State: Robert Louis Stevenson's Novel *Treasure Island*" (New York: Critical Survey, 1 May 2007, Highbeam Business).
3. Christopher Harvie, "The Politics of Stevenson," *Stevenson and Victorian Scotland* (Edinburgh: Edinburgh University Press, 1981), 112–121.
4. Barry Menikoff, *Narrating Scotland: The Imagination of Robert Louis Stevenson* (Columbia: University of South Carolina Press, 2005),
5. Robert L. Stevenson, *Essays in the Art of Writing* (London: Chatto & Windus, 1920), 92.
6. Ibid., 92–93.
7. Claire Harman, *Myself and the Other Fellow: A Life of Robert Louis Stevenson* (New York: HarperCollins, 2005), 323.
8. Robert L. Stevenson, *Across the Plains: With Other Memories and Essays* (London: Nelson, 1892), 281.
9. Ibid., 281–282.
10. Caroline McCracken-Flesher, "Thinking Nationally/Writing Colonially? Scott, Stevenson, and England," *NOVEL: A Forum on Fiction* (Vol. 24, No. 3 (Spring, 1991). Durham: Duke University Press. JSTOR. 296–318), 299.
11. Robert L. Stevenson, *Selected Letters of Robert Louis Stevenson*, Ernest Mehew, ed. (New Haven: Yale University Press, 1998), 99.
12. Ibid., 116.
13. Harman, *Myself and the Other Fellow*, 321.
14. Ibid., 313.

15. Ibid., 318.
16. Robert L. Stevenson, *Selected Letters*, 319.
17. Michael Balfour, "The First Biography," *Stevenson and Victorian Scotland* (Edinburgh: Edinburgh University Press, 1981, 33–47), 33.
18. Fitzroy MacLean, *Scotland: A Concise History* (London: Thames & Hudson, 2000), 108–109.
19. Ibid., 133.
20. Ibid., 157.
21. Ibid., 157.
22. Ibid., 190.
23. Harvie, *Stevenson and Victorian Scotland*, 112–121.
24. Ibid., 112–121.
25. Alan Sandison, "A World Made for Liars: Stevenson's *Dynamiter* and the Death of the Real," *Robert Louis Stevenson Reconsidered: New Critical Perspectives*, William B. Jones, Jr., ed. (Jefferson, N.C.: McFarland, 2003, 140–162), 143.
26. Kenneth O. Morgan, *The Oxford History of England*, rev. ed. (Oxford: Oxford University Press, 2010), 555–557.
27. Harman, *Myself and the Other Fellow*, 319.
28. Ibid., 319.
29. Ibid., 320.
30. Ibid., 319.
31. Ibid., 423.
32. Ibid., 393–394.
33. Ibid., 441.
34. Ibid.
35. Ibid., 442.
36. J. C. Furnas, "Stevenson and Exile," *Stevenson and Victorian Scotland* (Edinburgh: Edinburgh University Press, 1981), 126.
37. Caroline McCracken-Flesher, "Thinking Nationally/Writing Colonially? Scott, Stevenson, and England," *NOVEL: A Forum on Fiction* (Vol. 24, No. 3, Spring 1991), Durham: Duke University Press, JSTOR, 296–318), 310.
38. *Kidnapped*, 99, 129, 137, 200.
39. Ibid., 138.
40. *Footnote*, 6.
41. Ibid., 2.
42. Ibid., 21.
43. Ibid., 22.
44. Oliver S. Buckton, *Cruising with Robert Louis Stevenson: Travel, Narrative, and the Colonial Body* (Athens: Ohio University Press, 2007), 182.
45. *Footnote*, 322.
46. Sandison, "A World Made for Liars," 140–41.
47. Ibid., 142.
48. Ibid., 149.
49. Ibid., 152.
50. Ibid., 155.
51. Ibid., 157.
52. Ibid.
53. Oscar Wilde, *Vera; Or, the Nihilists* (London: Privately Printed, 1902, Project Gutenberg), 11.
54. Ibid., 28.
55. Ibid., 33.
56. Ibid., 43.
57. *Dynamiter*, 120.
58. Ibid., 120.
59. Ibid., 122.
60. Ibid., 126.
61. Ibid., 124.
62. Ibid.
63. *Kidnapped*, 58.
64. Ibid., 71.
65. *Kidnapped*, 100.
66. *Balfour*, 182.
67. Ibid., 186.
68. Ibid., 196.
69. *Pentland*, 378.

Chapter 14

1. Paul Maixner, *Robert Louis Stevenson: The Critical Heritage* (London: Routledge & Kegan Paul, 1981), 176.
2. W. W. Robson, "On *Kidnapped*," *Stevenson and Victorian Scotland* (Edinburgh: Edinburgh University Press, 1981, 88–106), 92.
3. Susan R. Gannon, "Repetition and Meaning in Stevenson's David Balfour Novels," *Studies in the Literary Imagination* (1985 Fall; 18 (2): 21–33), 21.
4. Robson, "On Kidnapped," 92.
5. Ibid., 106.
6. Claire Harman, *Myself and the Other Fellow: A Life of Robert Louis Stevenson* (New York: HarperCollins, 2005), 9.
7. Robert L. Stevenson, *Essays in the Art of Writing* (London: Chatto & Windus, 1920), 108.
8. Ibid., 117.
9. *Kidnapped*, 114.
10. Stevenson, *Essays in the Art of Writing*, 125–26.

11. Maixner, *Robert Louis Stevenson*, 233–34.
12. Ibid., 238.
13. Ibid., 241.
14. Ibid., 319.
15. Ibid., 330.
16. David Daiches, *Literary Essays* (1956) (Edinburgh: Oliver and Boyd, 1966), 11.
17. Edwin Eigner, *Robert Louis Stevenson and Romantic Tradition* (Princeton: Princeton University Press, 1966), viii.
18. Ibid., 85.
19. Ibid., 84.
20. Ibid., 165.
21. Ibid., 26.
22. Ibid., 113.
23. Henry James, "Preface to Volume 5 of the New York Edition of *Princess Casamassima*." (1908). The Ladder: A Henry James Website. Adrian Dover, ed. Google Books.
24. Hilary J. Beattie, "'The Interest of the Attraction Exercised by the Great RLS of Those Days': Robert Louis Stevenson, Henry James and the Influence of Friendship," *Journal of Stevenson Studies*, Volume 4 (Wiltshire: The Center for Scottish Studies, University of Stirling, 2007, 91–113), 95.
25. Ibid., 94.
26. Karen Davidson, ed., "Introduction: *Kidnapped*: Robert Louis Stevenson's 'Highest Point,'" *Kidnapped*, Robert Stevenson (New York: Pocket Books, 2007), viii.
27. Stevenson, *Essays in the Art of Writing*, 98.
28. Ibid., 100.
29. Robson, "On Kidnapped," 93.
30. Ibid., 89.
31. Robert L. Stevenson, *Selected Letters of Robert Louis Stevenson*, Ernest Mehew, ed. (New Haven: Yale University Press, 1998), 321.
32. *Pentland*, 377–78.
33. Ibid., 381–82.
34. Ibid., 400.
35. Ibid., 396–97.
36. Harman, *Myself and the Other Fellow*, 253.
37. *Black Arrow*, 85.
38. Maixner, *Robert Louis Stevenson*, 322.
39. Ibid., xxxvii.
40. Ibid., xxxix.
41. Ibid., xxxix.
42. *Black Arrow*, 136.
43. Ibid., 159.
44. Ibid., 186.
45. Ibid., 187.
46. Ibid., 192.
47. Ibid., 250.
48. *Dynamiter*, v.
49. Ibid., 128.
50. *Kidnapped*, 73.
51. Ibid., 1.
52. Stevenson, *Selected Letters*, 515.
53. Ibid., 515.
54. "Young Chevalier," 7.
55. *Balfour*, 244.
56. Maixner, *Robert Louis Stevenson*, 234.
57. Ibid., 240.
58. Barry Menikoff, *Narrating Scotland: The Imagination of Robert Louis Stevenson* (Columbia: University of South Carolina Press, 2005), 125.
59. Robert Kiely, *Robert Louis Stevenson and the Fiction of Adventure* (Cambridge: Harvard University Press, 1964), 82.
60. *Black Arrow*, xxv.
61. Stevenson, *Selected Letters*, 303.
62. Kiely, *Robert Louis Stevenson*, 64.
63. John Sutherland, *Victorian Fiction: Writers, Publishers, Readers* (New York: Macmillan, 2006), xx.
64. Linda Dryden, *The Modern Gothic and Literary Doubles: Stevenson, Wilde and Wells* (New York: Palgrave Macmillan, 2003), 77.
65. Stevenson, *Selected Letters*, 489–490.
66. *Balfour*, 239.
67. Stevenson, *Selected Letters*, 530.
68. Stevenson, *Selected Letters*, 498.
69. Stevenson, *Essays in the Art of Writing*, 123.
70. Robson, "On Kidnapped," 91.
71. Stevenson, *Essays in the Art of Writing*, 130–136.
72. Robert L. Stevenson, *Across the Plains: With Other Memories and Essays* (London: Nelson, 1892), 279.
73. Stevenson, *Selected Letters*, 483.
74. Ibid., 349.
75. Ibid., 483.
76. Ibid., 491, 511.
77. Ibid., 496–97.
78. Kiely, *Robert Louis Stevenson*, 66.
79. Menikoff, *Narrating Scotland*, xi.
80. Robert L. Stevenson, *Kidnapped; or, The Lad with the Silver Button*, Barry Menikoff, ed. (New York: Random House, 2001), 241.
81. Menikoff, *Narrating Scotland*, 4.
82. Ibid., 3.

Chapter 15

1. Paul Maixner, *Robert Louis Stevenson: The Critical Heritage* (London: Routledge & Kegan Paul, 1981), 232–233.
2. Ibid., 441.
3. Ibid., 187.
4. Ibid., 179.
5. *Kidnapped*, 127, 177.
6. Robert Stevenson, "On Some Technical Elements of Style in Literature," *Contemporary Review*, April 1885, 27.
7. Ibid., 28.
8. Ibid., 39.
9. Robert L. Stevenson, *Essays in the Art of Writing* (London: Chatto & Windus, 1920), 42.
10. Ian Bell, *Dreams of Exile: Robert Louis Stevenson: A Biography* (New York: Henry Holt, 1992), 25–26.
11. Ibid., 25–26.
12. John Sutherland, *Victorian Fiction: Writers, Publishers, Readers* (New York: Macmillan, 2006), 58–60.
13. John Hodgart, "Chapter 5: The Scots Language in the Schuil," *Teaching Scottish Literature: Curriculum and Classroom Applications. Scottish Language and Literature, Volume 3*, Alan MacGillivray, ed. (Edinburgh: Edinburgh University Press, 1997, 84–96), 84–85.
14. Fitzroy MacLean, *Scotland: A Concise History* (London: Thames & Hudson, 2000), 209.
15. Joan Beal, "Chapter 9: Syntax and Morphology," *The Edinburgh History of the Scots Language*, Charles Jones, ed. (Edinburgh: Edinburgh University Press, 1997, 335–77), 344.
16. Ibid., 347.
17. Ibid., 364.
18. Ibid., 365.
19. Graham Tulloch, *The Language of Walter Scott: A Study of His Scottish and Period Language* (London: Andre Deutsch, 1980), 414.
20. *Black Arrow*, 115.
21. Claire Harman, *Myself and the Other Fellow: A Life of Robert Louis Stevenson* (New York: HarperCollins, 2005), 316.
22. Ibid., 316.
23. David Daiches, *Literary Essays* (1956) (Edinburgh: Oliver and Boyd, 1966), 17–18.
24. Barry Menikoff, *Narrating Scotland: The Imagination of Robert Louis Stevenson* (Columbia: University of South Carolina Press, 2005), 20.
25. Mary Lascelles, *The Story-Teller Retrieves the Past: Historical Fiction and Fictitious History in the Art of Scott, Stevenson, Kipling, and Some Others* (Oxford: Clarendon Press, 1980), 48.
26. Stevenson, *Essays in the Art of Writing*, 101.
27. Ibid., 108.
28. Robert L. Stevenson, *Selected Letters of Robert Louis Stevenson*, Ernest Mehew, ed. (New Haven: Yale University Press, 1998), 144.
29. Harman, *Myself and the Other Fellow*, 41.
30. Ibid., 42.
31. Ibid.
32. Ibid., 201.
33. Ibid., 202–3.
34. Ibid., 435.
35. Menikoff, *Narrating Scotland*, 126.
36. *Kidnapped*, 121.
37. *Balfour*, 84.
38. Ibid., 273.
39. *Dynamiter*, 126.
40. *Rob Roy*, Chapter 28.
41. *Black Arrow*, "Jon Amend-All of the Green Wood."
42. Ibid., 18.
43. *Kidnapped*, 85.
44. Ibid.
45. Ibid., 121.
46. *Balfour*, 197.
47. Ibid., 305.

Conclusion

1. Norman McCord and Bill Purdue, *English History: 1815–1914*, 2nd ed. (Oxford: Oxford University Press, 2007), 125.

Bibliography

Ainsworth, William Harrison. *Historical Romances of William Harrison Ainsworth: Guy Fawkes, Volume XIX* (1840) (Philadelphia: Barrie, 1901. LaVergne, Tenn.: Kessinger Press, 2010).

———. *Sir John Chiverton: A Romance*, 2nd ed. (London: John Ebers, 1827, Google Books).

Altick, Richard. *The English Common Reader: A Social History of the Mass Reading Public, 1800–1900.* 2nd ed. (1957) (Columbus: Ohio State University Press, 1998).

Anderson, William. *The Scottish Nation; or, the Surnames, Families, Literature, Honours, and Biographical History of the People of Scotland*, Volume III (Edinburgh: Fullarton, 1867, Google Books).

Aristotle, "Poetics," *The Rhetoric and the Poetics of Aristotle* (New York: Modern Library, 1984).

Baillie, Joanna. "Rayner: A Tragedy in Five Acts." *Miscellaneous Plays*, 2nd ed. (London: Longman, Hurst, Rees and Orme, 1805, Google Books).

Bakhtin, Mikhail. "Epic and Novel: Toward a Methodology for the Study of the Novel," *Modern Genre Theory* (Essex: Pearson, 2000).

Baldridge, C. "Alternatives to Bourgeois Individualism in *A Tale of Two Cities*," *Studies in English Literature (Rice)* (30.4 (1990): 633, *Academic Search Complete*, EBSCO).

Balfour, Michael. "The First Biography," *Stevenson and Victorian Scotland* (Edinburgh: Edinburgh University Press, 1981, 33–47).

"The Ballantyne Brothers," Walter Scott Digital Archive (Edinburgh: Edinburgh University Library).

Barbour, John. *The Bruce; or, The History of Robert I, King of Scotland: Written in Scotish Verse, Volumes 1–3* (London: H. Hughs for G. Nicol, Bookseller to His Majesty, 1790, Google Books).

Barrow, Sir John. *A Description of Pitcairn's Island and Its Inhabitants with an Authentic Account of the Mutiny of the Ship Bounty and the Subsequent Fortunes of the Mutineers* (1831) (New York: Haskell, 1972).

Beal, Joan. "Syntax and Morphology," *The Edinburgh History of the Scots Language*, Charles Jones, ed. (Edinburgh: Edinburgh University Press, 1997, 335–77).

Beattie, Hilary J. "'The Interest of the Attraction Exercised by the Great RLS of Those Days': Robert Louis Stevenson, Henry James and the Influence of Friendship," *Journal of Stevenson Studies*, Volume 4 (Wiltshire: The Center for Scottish Studies, University of Stirling, 2007, 91–113).

Bell, Ian. *Dreams of Exile: Robert Louis Stevenson: A Biography* (New York: Henry Holt, 1992).

Bentham, Jeremy. *Canada. Emancipate Your Colonies! An Unpublished Argument* (London: Effingham Wilson, 1838, Google Books).

Black, William. *Donald Ross of Heimra* (London: Harper, 1894. Google Books. Accessed May 11, 2011).

Blake, William. *The Complete Poetry & Prose of William Blake* (David V. Erdman, ed., New York: Anchor Books, 1988).

Bray, Anna E. *The White Hoods: An Historical Romance* (1828) (BiblioBazaar, 2009).
Brook, G. L. *The Language of Dickens* (London: Andre Deutsch, 1970).
Buckton, Oliver S. *Cruising with Robert Louis Stevenson: Travel, Narrative, and the Colonial Body* (Athens: Ohio University Press, 2007).
Cadbury, William. "The Two Structures of Rob Roy," *Modern Language Quarterly* (Seattle, Wash.: 1968; 29: 42–60, EBSCO).
Carlile, Richard, ed. *The Republican, Volume 9* (London: R. Carlile, 1824, Google Books).
Carlyle, Thomas. *Chartism*, 2nd ed. (London: Chapman and Hall, Strand, 1842, Google Books).
_____. *Cruthers and Jonson; Or the Outskirts of Life: A True Story* (1831) *Critical and Miscellaneous Essays: In Five Volumes*, Volume V (London: Chapman and Hall, 1899, Google Books, 168–198).
_____. *The French Revolution: A History* (1837) (New York: Modern Library, 2002).
_____. "On Sir Walter Scott (1771–1832)" (1838) (Internet Modern History Sourcebook).
Queen Caroline, *Non Mi Ricordo. The Important and Eventful Trial of Queen Caroline, Consort of George IV for "Adulterous Intercourse" with Bartolomo Bergami, Parts 1–2* (London: Geo. Smeeton, 1820, Google Books).
Cazamian, Louis. *The Social Novel in England 1830–1850: Dickens, Disraeli, Mrs. Gaskell, Kingsley* (1903) (New York: Routledge, 1973).
Cervantes Saavedra, Miguel. *The Ingenious Gentleman Don Quixote de la Mancha* (1605, 1615) (Trans. Samuel Putnam, New York: Viking Press, 1949).
Chesterton, Gilbert Keith. *William Blake* (New York: Cosimo, 2005, Google Books).
Chirrey, Deborah. "12: Edinburgh: Descriptive Materials," *Urban Voices: Accent Studies in the British Isles* (Paul Foulkes and Gerard J. Docherty, eds., London: Arnold, 1999).
Collins, Philip. *Dickens: The Critical Heritage* (New York: Barnes & Noble, 1971).
Crawford, Iain. "Dickens, Classical Myth, and Representation of Social Order in *Barnaby Rudge*," *Dickensian* (1997 Winter; 93: 3 [443]: 185–87).
Croce, Benedetto. *History, Its Theory and Practice* (New York: Russell & Russell, 1960).
Daiches, David. *Literary Essays* (1956) (Edinburgh: Oliver and Boyd, 1966).

D'Arcy, Julian Meldon. *Subversive Scott: The Waverley Novels and Scottish Nationalism* (Hagatorgi: University of Iceland Press, 2005).
Darling, Peter M. *The Romance of the Highlands*, Volume I (Edinburgh: George Ramsay, 1810, Google Books).
Davidson, Karen, ed. "Introduction: *Kidnapped*: Robert Louis Stevenson's 'Highest Point,'" *Kidnapped*, Robert Stevenson (New York: Pocket Books, 2007).
Dickens, Charles. *American Notes* (1842) (New York: Penguin, 2004).
_____. *Barnaby Rudge* (1841) (Oxford: Oxford University Press, 2008).
_____. *Bleak House* (1852) (New York: Bantam, 1985).
_____. *Hard Times: For These Times* (1854) (London: Bradbury & Evans, 1854, Google Books).
_____. *The Letters of Charles Dickens*, The Pilgrim Edition, Volume 5; Volume 7 (Oxford: Oxford University Press, 1981).
_____. *Little Dorrit* (1855), *The Writings of Charles Dickens* (Boston: Houghton, Mifflin, 1894, Google Books).
_____. *The Personal History of David Copperfield* (1849) (London: Bradbury & Evans, 1850, Google Books).
_____. *A Tale of Two Cities* (1859) (New York: Signet, 2007).
Disraeli, Benjamin. *Coningsby: Or the New Generation* (Leipzig: Berhn. Tauchnitz, June 1844, Google Books).
_____. *Endymion* (1880) (Longmans, Green, 1920, Google Books).
_____. *Sybil, the Two Nations* (1845) (London: Oxford University Press, 1925).
_____. *The Young Duke, The Works of Benjamin Disraeli: The Young Duke, V. 1* (1831) (M. W. Dunne, 1904, Google Books).
Dooley, Allan C. *Author and Printer in Victorian England* (Charlottesville: University Press of Virginia, 1992).
Dransfield, Scott. "Reading the Gordon Riots in 1841: Social Violence and Moral Management in *Barnaby Rudge*" (*Dickens Studies Annual: Essays on Victorian Fiction*. 1998; 27: 69–95).
Dryden, Linda. *The Modern Gothic and Literary Doubles: Stevenson, Wilde and Wells* (New York: Palgrave Macmillan, 2003).
Eagleton, Terry. *The English Novel* (Malden: Blackwell, 2005).
Eigner, Edwin M. *Robert Louis Stevenson and*

Romantic Tradition (Princeton: Princeton University Press, 1966).

Eliot, George. *Felix Holt, The Radical* (1866) (Orchard Park, N.Y.: Broadview Press, 2000).

Engel, Monroe. "The Politics of Dickens' Novels," *PMLA* (December, 1956; 71: 945–974).

Erickson, Lee. *The Economy of Literary Form: English Literature and the Industrialization of Publishing, 1800–1850* (Baltimore: Johns Hopkins University Press, 1996).

Farrell, John P. *Revolution as Tragedy: The Dilemma of the Moderate from Scott to Arnold* (New York: Cornell University Press, 1980).

Feather, John. *A History of English Publishing*, 2nd ed. (New York: Routledge, 2004).

Ferris, Ina. *The Romantic National Tale and the Question of Ireland* (Cambridge: Cambridge University Press, 2002).

Fiske, Christabel F. *Epic Suggestion in the Imagery of the Waverley Novels* (New Haven: Yale University Press, 1940).

Fleishman, Avrom. *The English Historical Novel: Walter Scott to Virginia Woolf* (Baltimore: Johns Hopkins University Press, 1971).

Fletcher, Loraine. "Long John Silver, Karl Marx and the Ship of State: Robert Louis Stevenson's Novel *Treasure Island*" (New York: Critical Survey, 1 May 2007, *Highbeam Business*).

Flint, Kate. *The Woman Reader: 1837–1914* (Oxford: Clarendon Press, 1994).

Forster, John. *The Life of Charles Dickens: Volume II, 1847–1870. The Works of Charles Dickens*, Volume 36 (London: Chapman & Hall, 1899, Google Books).

Fowler, Alastair. "Transformation of Genre," *Modern Genre Theory* (Essex: Pearson, 2000).

Freedman, Aviva, and Peter Medway, *Genre and the New Rhetoric* (New York: Taylor & Francis, 2003).

Frow, John. *Genre* (New York: Routledge, 2006).

Furnas, J. C. "Stevenson and Exile," *Stevenson and Victorian Scotland* (Edinburgh: Edinburgh University Press, 1981).

Gannon, Susan R. "Repetition and Meaning in Stevenson's David Balfour Novels," *Studies in the Literary Imagination* (1985 Fall; 18 (2): 21–33).

Garside, Peter. "Popular Fiction and National Tale: Hidden Origins of Scott's *Waverly*," *Nineteenth-Century Literature* (1991 June; 46 (1): 30–53. JSTOR).

Gaskell, Elizabeth Cleghorn. *Mary Barton* (1815) (London: Century Company, 1906, Google Books).

Genette, Gerard. "The Architext," *Modern Genre Theory* (Essex: Pearson, 2000).

Gerson, Stanley. *Sound and Symbol in the Dialogue of the Works of Charles Dickens* (Stockholm: Almqvist & Wiksell, 1967).

Goldberg, Michael. "From Bentham to Carlyle: Dickens' Political Development," *Journal of the History of Ideas*, Vol. 33, No. 1 (January–March, 1972) (University of Pennsylvania Press, JSTOR, 61–76).

Goldstein, Robert Justin. *Political Censorship of the Arts and the Press in Nineteenth-Century Europe* (New York: St. Martin's Press, 1989).

Guy, Josephine M. *The Victorian Social-Problem Novel: The Market, the Individual, and Communal Life* (London: Macmillan, 1996).

Handley, Paul M. *The King Never Smiles: A Biography of Thailand's Bhumibol Adulyadej* (New Haven: Yale University Press, 2006).

Harman, Claire. *Myself and the Other Fellow: A Life of Robert Louis Stevenson* (New York: HarperCollins, 2005).

Harvie, Christopher. "The Politics of Stevenson," *Stevenson and Victorian Scotland* (Edinburgh: Edinburgh University Press, 1981).

Hayden, John. *Scott: The Critical Heritage* (New York: Barnes & Noble, 1970).

Hobbes, Thomas. *Leviathan: Or the Matter, Forme & Power of a Commonwealth, Ecclesiasticall and Civill* (1651) (Cambridge: Cambridge University Press, 1904, Google Books).

Hodgart, John. "Chapter 5: The Scots Language in the Schuil," *Teaching Scottish Literature: Curriculum and Classroom Applications. Scottish Language and Literature, Volume 3*, Alan MacGillivray, ed. (Edinburgh: Edinburgh University Press, 1997, 84–96).

Hone, William. *The Queen's Matrimonial Ladder: A National Toy, with fourteen step scences; and illustrations in verse, with eighteen other cuts* (London: William Hone, 1820, Google Books).

Hone, William, George Canning, and George Cruikshank, *The Man in the Moon*, 2nd ed. (London: William Hone, 1820, Google Books).

Hone, William, and George Cruikshank, *Right Divine of Kings to Govern Wrong. Facetiae and Miscellanies*, 2nd ed. (London: Hunt and Clarke, 1827, Google Books).

House, Humphry. *The Dickens World*, 2nd ed. (London: Oxford University Press, 1961).

Hughes, Linda K., and Michael Lund, *The Victorian Serial* (Charlottesville: University Press of Virginia, 1991).

Jackson, T. A. *Charles Dickens: The Progress of a Radical* (1937) (New York: Haskell, 1971).

James, Henry. "Preface to Volume 5 of the New York Edition of *Princess Casamassima*." (1908). *The Ladder: A Henry James Website*. Adrian Dover, ed. Google Books.

Jones, Gareth Stedman. "The Redemptive Power of Violence?: Carlyle, Marx and Dickens," *History Workshop Journal* (2008 Spring; 65: 1–22).

Jordon, John. *The Cambridge Companion to Charles Dickens* (New York: Cambridge University Press, 2001).

Kiely, Robert. *Robert Louis Stevenson and the Fiction of Adventure* (Cambridge: Harvard University Press, 1964).

Kingsley, Charles, Rev. "Chapter X. How Folks Turn Chartists," *Alton Locke, Tailor and Poet, An Autobiography* (1850) (Project Gutenberg).

_____. *Hereward the Wake* (1865) (New York: Dutton, 1961).

Knight, Charles. "Sir John Chiverton," *The Monthly Review: From September to December Inclusive, 1826, Volume III* (Hurst, Robinson, 1826).

Knowles, Sir James. *The Nineteenth Century, Volume 26* (London: Henry S. King, 1889, Google Books).

Lascelles, Mary. *The Story-Teller Retrieves the Past: Historical Fiction and Fictitious History in the Art of Scott, Stevenson, Kipling, and Some Others* (Oxford: Clarendon Press, 1980).

Law, Graham. *Serializing Fiction in the Victorian Press* (New York: Palgrave, 2000).

Leapman, Michael. *Great England: Eyewitness Travel* (London: DK, 2010).

"Lear." Encyclopaedia Britannica Online. Encyclopaedia Britannica, 2011.

Le Fanu, Sheridan. *The Fortunes of Colonel Torlogh O'Brien: A Tale of the Wars of King James* (1847) (India: Nabu Press, 2010).

Lincoln, Andrew. "Scott and Empire: The Case of *Rob Roy*," (*Studies in the Novel*, 2002 Spring; 34 (1): 43–59).

Lobeira, Vasco. *Amadis of Gaul, Volume I: Library of Old Authors* (Trans. Robert Southey, London: J. R. Smith, 1872, Google Books).

Lockhart, John G., and Sir Walter Scott, *Memoirs of the Life of Sir Walter Scott*, Volume I, *Collection of Ancient and Modern English Authors*, Vol. CLXXV (Paris: Baudry's European Library, 1838, Google Books).

MacLean, Fitzroy. *Scotland: A Concise History* (London: Thames & Hudson, 2000).

Maixner, Paul. *Robert Louis Stevenson: The Critical Heritage* (London: Routledge & Kegan Paul, 1981).

Manning, Peter J. "Wordsworth in the *Keepsake*, 1829," *Literature in the Marketplace: Nineteenth-Century English Publishing and Reading Practices*, John O. Jordan and Robert L. Patten, eds. (Cambridge: Cambridge University Press, 1996. 44–73).

Marcus, David D. "The Carlylean Vision of *A Tale of Two Cities*," *Studies in the Novel* (8.1 (1976): 56, Academic Search Complete, EBSCO).

Marx, Karl. *Karl Marx: Selected Writings*, 2nd ed. (Oxford: Oxford University Press, 2005).

_____. "On Violent Revolution," *Karl Marx: Selected Writings*, 2nd ed., McLellan, David, ed. (Oxford: Oxford University Press, 2005).

McCord, Norman, and Bill Purdue. *English History: 1815–1914*, 2nd ed. (Oxford: Oxford University Press, 2007).

McCracken-Flesher, Caroline. "Thinking Nationally/Writing Colonially? Scott, Stevenson, and England," *NOVEL: A Forum on Fiction* (Vol. 24, No. 3, Spring 1991). Durham: Duke University Press. JSTOR).

McKim, Anne, ed., "The Wallace: Introduction," *The Wallace: Selections* (1471–1479), Blind Harry, author (Kalamazoo, Mich.: Medieval Institute Publications, 2003, Medieval Institute Publications Online Store).

McLaren, Moray. *Sir Walter Scott: The Man and Patriot* (Edinburgh: Morrison & Gibb, 1970).

McLure, Derick. *Scott and His Influence: The Papers of the Aberdeen Scott Conference, 1982: Issue 6 of Occasional Papers*, (Association for Scottish Literary Studies, John H. Alexander and David Hewitt, eds., Edinburgh: Association for Scottish Literary Studies, 1983).

McNamara, Robert. "England's Disastrous Retreat from Kabul: The 1842 Afghanistan Massacre, Only One English Soldier Survived" About Guide: 19th-Century History (Accessed March 17, 2011).

Menikoff, Barry. *Narrating Scotland: The Imagination of Robert Louis Stevenson* (Columbia: University of South Carolina Press, 2005).

Meyerhoff, Miriam. *Introducing Sociolinguistics* (New York: Routledge, 2006).

Moore, Grace. *Dickens and Empire: Discourse of Class, Race and Colonialism in the Works of Charles Dickens* (Aldershot, U.K.: Ashgate, 2004).

More, Thomas. *Utopia* (Rockville, Md.: Arc Manor, 2008. Google Books).

Morgan, Kenneth O. *The Oxford History of England*, rev. ed. (Oxford: Oxford University Press, 2010).

Morrison, Elizabeth. "Serial Fiction in Australian Colonial Newspapers," *Literature in the Marketplace: Nineteenth-Century English Publishing and Reading Practices* (John O. Jordan and Robert L. Patten, eds. Cambridge: Cambridge University Press, 1996, 306–24).

Muir, Edwin. *Scott and Scotland: The Predicament of the Scottish Writer* (1936) (Edinburgh: Polygon, 1982).

Murison, David. "1: The Historical Background," *Languages of Scotland* (The Association for Scottish Literary Studies Occasional Paper Number 4. A. J. Aitken and Tom McArthur, eds., Edinburgh: W & R Chambers, 1979).

Ngugi wa Thiong'o and Ngugi wa Mirii, *I Will Marry When I Want* (Oxford: Heinemann, 1988).

"Obituary: Sir Walter Scott, Bart," *The Gentleman's Magazine*, Volume 152 (1832).

O'Brien, Anthony. "Benevolence and Insurrection: The Conflicts of Form and Purpose in *Barnaby Rudge*," *Dickens Studies* (Cambridge: Cambridge University Press, 1969; 5: 26–44).

Opacki, Ireneusz. "Royal Genres," *Modern Genre Theory* (Essex: Pearson, 2000).

Orwell, George. *All Art Is Propaganda: Critical Essays* (Orlando, Fla.: Harcourt, 2008).

_____. *Dickens, Dali & Others* (1946) (San Diego: Harcourt Brace Jovanovich, 1973).

_____. "Politics and the English Language," *All Art Is Propaganda: Critical Essays* (Orlando, Fla.: Harcourt, 2008).

_____. "Politics vs. Literature: An Examination of *Gulliver's Travels*," *All Art Is Propaganda: Critical Essays* (Orlando, Fla.: Harcourt, 2008).

Paine, Thomas. *Age of Reason: Being an Investigation of True and Fabulous Theology* (1794, 1795, 1807) (New York: Truth Seeker Company, 1898, Google Books).

_____. *Common Sense* (1776) (P. Eckler, 1918, Google Books).

Pitman, Todd, and Sinfah Tunsarawuth. "Thailand Arrests American for Alleged King Insult" (Associated Press, 27 May 2011).

Poussa, Patricia. "Dickens as Sociolinguist: Dialect in *David Copperfield*," *Writing in Nonstandard English* (Irma Taavitsainen, Gunnel Melchers and Paivi Pahta, eds. Philadelphia: John Benjamins, 1999, 27–44).

Prebble, John. *The King's Jaunt: George IV in Scotland, August 1822 "One and Twenty Daft Days"* (1988) (London: Birlinn, 2000).

Pugh, Edwin. *Charles Dickens: The Apostle of the People* (1908) (New York: AMS Press, 1975).

Rance, Nicholas. *The Historical Novel and Popular Politics in Nineteenth-Century England* (New York: Barnes and Noble, 1975).

"Reform Bill." *Encyclopaedia Britannica Online* (Accessed March 17, 2011).

Robson, W. W. "On *Kidnapped*," *Stevenson and Victorian Scotland* (Edinburgh: Edinburgh University Press, 1981, 88–106).

Rose, Jonathan. "How Historians Study Reader Response: Or, What Did Jo Think of *Bleak House*?" *Literature in the Marketplace: Nineteenth-Century English Publishing and Reading Practices* (John O. Jordan and Robert L. Patten, eds., Cambridge: Cambridge University Press, 1996, 195–212).

Rosenblatt, Frank Ferdinand. *The Chartist Movement in Its Social and Economic Aspects. Issues 171–173: Columbia Studies in the Social Sciences* (New York: Columbia University, 1916).

Sandison, Alan. "A World Made for Liars: Stevenson's *Dynamiter* and the Death of the Real." *Robert Louis Stevenson Reconsid-*

ered: New Critical Perspectives (Jefferson, N.C.: McFarland, 2003).
Scott, Sir Walter. *The Black Dwarf* (1816) (Edinburgh: Edinburgh University Press, 1993).
_____.*Critical and Miscellaneous Essays*, Volume I (Philadelphia: Carey & Hart, 1841).
_____.*Essays on Chivalry, Romance and the Drama* (1834) (Freeport, N.Y.: Books for Libraries Press, 1972).
_____.*The Heart of Mid-Lothian* (1818). *Tales of My Landlord, Second Series, Collected and Arranged by Jedediah Cleishbotham, in Four Volumes*, Vol. II (Edinburgh: Constable, 1818. Google Books. Accessed May 29, 2011).
_____.*Ivanhoe: A Romance* (1820) (London: Baudry's European Library, 1835, Google Books).
_____.*The Lady of the Lake* (Boston: 1883, Project Gutenberg Ebook).
_____.*Letters of Sir Walter Scott*, ed. H. J. C. Greirson, Volume III (London: Parker, 1932).
_____.*Life of Swift. The Miscellaneous Prose Works of Sir Walter Scott, Bart* (Edinburgh: Cadell, 1827, Google Book).
_____. "My Aunt Margaret's Mirror" (London: *The Keepsake Annual* (Volume I), 1828. Project Gutenberg. Accessed May 27, 2011).
_____.*Redgauntlet* (1824) (New York: Penguin, 2000).
_____.*Rob Roy* (1817) (New York: Penguin, 2007).
_____.*The Tale of Old Mortality* (1816) (New York: Penguin, 1999).
_____.*Waverley* (1814) (New York: Penguin, 1994).
Scott, Sir Walter, and John G. Lockhart. *Memoirs of the Life of Sir Walter Scott*, Volume I. *Collection of Ancient and Modern English Authors*, Vol. CLXXV (Paris: Baudry's European Library, 1838. Google Book. Accessed November 15, 2010).
Shaw, Bernard. *Shaw on Dickens* (Dan H. Laurence and Martin Quinn, eds., New York: Frederick Ungar Press, 1985).
Sinclair, John. *Observations on the Scottish Dialect* (London: Strahan and T. Cadell, 1782, Google Books).
Skene, William Forbes. *The Dean of Lismore's Book: a selection of ancient Gaelic poetry from a manuscript collection made by Sir James M'Gregor, dean of Lismore, in the beginning of the sixteenth century* (Thomas Maclauchlan, ed., Edinburgh: Edmonston and Douglas, 1862).
Slater, Michael. *Charles Dickens* (New Haven: Yale University Press, 2009).
Smith, Horace. *Brambletye House, or, Cavaliers and Roundheads (1826)* (London: G. Dearborn, 1837, Google Books).
Speare, Morris E. *The Political Novel: Its Development in England and in America* (New York: Russell & Russell, 1966).
Stevenson, Robert. "On Some Technical Elements of Style in Literature," *Contemporary Review*, April 1885.
Stevenson, Robert L. *Across the Plains: With Other Memories and Essays* (London: Nelson, 1892).
_____. *The Black Arrow: A Tale of the Two Roses* (1888) (New York: Penguin, 2007).
_____. *David Balfour: Being Memoirs of the Further Adventures of David Balfour at Home and Abroad* (1893) (New York: Charles Scribner's Sons, 1994).
_____. *Essays in the Art of Writing* (London: Chatto & Windus, 1920).
_____. *A Footnote to History: Eight Years of Trouble in Samoa* (New York: Charles Scribner's Sons, 1895).
_____. *Kidnapped* (1886) (New York: Pocket Books, 2007).
_____. *The Pentland Rising. The Novels and Tales of Robert Louis Stevenson, Volume 14* (New York: Charles Scribner's Sons, 1895. Google Books. Accessed November 15, 2010).
_____. *Prince Otto: A Romance* (London: Chatto & Windus, Piccadilly, 1885. Google Books. Accessed November 15, 2010).
_____. *Selected Letters of Robert Louis Stevenson*, Ernest Mehew, ed. (New Haven: Yale University Press, 1998).
_____. "The Young Chevalier" (1892) (Unpublished. Accessed November 15, 2010).
_____, and Fanny Van de Grift Stevenson, *The Dynamiter* (London: Longmans, Green, and Co., 1885. Google Books. Accessed November 15, 2010).
St. John, Ian. *Disraeli and the Art of Victorian Politics* (London: Anthem Press, 2005).
Surr, T. S. *A Winter in London; Or Sketches of Fashion: A Novel* (London: Richard Phillips, 1806, Google Books).
Sutherland, John. *Victorian Fiction: Writers, Publishers, Readers* (New York: Macmillan, 2006).

Swift, Jonathan. *Gulliver's Travels* (Chicago: Rand McNally & Company, 1912. Google Books).

Thackeray, W. M. *The Complete Works of William M. Thackery: The Virginians: A Tale of the Last Century,* Volume 7 (1857–59) (New York: Thomas Crowell, 1881).

Thompson, E. P. *The Making of the English Working Class* (New York: Vintage Books, 1966).

Todorov, Tzvetan. "The Origin of Genres," *Modern Genre Theory* (Essex: Pearson, 2000).

Toibin, Colm, ed. *The Penguin Book of Irish Fiction* (New York: Penguin, 1999).

Trumpener, Katie. "National Character, National Plots: National Tale and Historical Novel in the Age of Waverly, 1806–1830," *ELH*, Vol. 60, No. 3 (Autumn 1993) (JSTOR, 685–731).

Tulloch, Graham. *The Language of Walter Scott: A Study of His Scottish and Period Language* (London: Andre Deutsch, 1980).

Voller, Jack G. "Joseph Sheridan LeFanu," *The Literary Gothic* (22 June 2012).

Wakefield, Gilbert. *A Reply to Some Parts of the Bishop Llandaff's Address to the People of Great Britain,* 2nd ed. (London: Johnson, 1798, Google Books).

Walpole, Horace. *The Castle of Otranto: A Gothic Story ... Last Edition Adorned with Cuts* (London: C. F. Himbourg, 1794. Google Books, 22 June 2012).

Waltke, Bruce K. *The Book of Proverbs: Chapters 1–15,* Volume I (Cambridge: William Eerdmans, 2004).

Wilde, Oscar. *Vera; Or, the Nihilists* (London: Privately Printed, 1902, Project Guterberg eBook).

Willis, Mark. "Charles Dickens and the Fictions of the Crowd," *Dickens Quarterly* (23.2 (2006): 85–107, *Academic Search Complete,* EBSCO).

Wilson, Angus. *The World of Charles Dickens* (New York: Viking Press, 1970).

Wooler, Thomas Jonathan, ed. *The Black Dwarf, Volume 6* (London: T. J. Wooler, 1821, Google Books).

Wynne, Deborah. "Scenes of 'Incredible Outrage': Dickens, Ireland and *A Tale of Two Cities,*" *Dickens Studies Annual: Essays on Victorian Fiction* (2006; 37: 51–64).

Index

Acts of Union 38
Afghan Uprising 13
Age of Reason 41, 229, 244
Ainsworth, Harrison 5–6, 27, 29–30, 45, 139–40, 143, 227–28, 240
American Revolution 12, 19, 39, 46, 54, 74
Annual Keepsake 5
archaic language 155, 159, 211–13
Aristotle 20, 143, 149, 228, 235, 240
"Aunt Margaret" 5–6, 69, 227, 245

Ballantyne 34–35, 66–67, 70, 73, 139, 231, 240
Barnaby Rudge 12, 28, 32, 40, 47, 57, 113, 116, 118, 121, 123–24, 137–40, 142, 145, 150, 156, 167, 180, 204, 222, 230, 234–36, 241, 244
Black Arrow 47, 165, 190–91, 197, 202, 213, 217, 238–39, 245
Black Dwarf 28, 42, 83, 90, 92, 95, 229, 232, 245–46
Bleak House 28, 113, 117, 128, 159, 229, 241, 244
Bruce 82, 99, 102, 222, 232–33, 240, 246

Capital 125
Carlile, Richard 41–42, 229, 241
Carlyle, Thomas 36, 49, 72–73, 81, 110, 116, 124, 130–31, 135, 140–49, 162, 231, 233–36, 241–43
Cato Street conspiracy 12, 65, 69
Chartism 131, 234, 241
class dialect 56–58, 152–53, 155–56, 158, 164, 208, 211, 224
Cold War 2–3, 113–15, 117, 125–26, 134
Colonel Torlogh 49, 60, 230, 243
Communist Manifesto 13, 92, 113, 125, 129

Condition of England 31, 36, 48, 131, 134
Crimean War 132
Cruthers and Jonson 144, 235, 241

D'Arcy, Julian M. 2–3, 18, 59, 69, 72, 76, 88, 90–91, 104, 107, 109, 230–33, 241
David Balfour 17, 28, 55, 119, 165, 167, 171, 177–78, 181–85, 189, 193, 198–201, 203–7, 210, 215–18, 237–40, 242, 245
Dynamiter 29, 165, 173, 179, 181–83, 193–95, 198, 202–3, 216, 227, 237–39, 244–45

1848 Revolutions 13, 49, 92, 113, 125, 128, 129, 223
Eliot, George 1, 12, 46, 60, 242
Elizabeth I, Queen 140
Emmet, Robert 12
Endymion 32, 36, 228, 241

Farrell, John 2, 17, 82–83, 227, 231, 242
Felix Holt 1, 222, 231, 242
Fenian Rebellion 13
Footnote to History 176–78, 245
Fowler, Alastair 22, 228, 242
French Revolution 1, 3, 12, 18, 27, 40, 49, 74–75, 116, 119, 122, 124, 127, 131, 137, 140–41, 145–47, 149, 156, 162, 222, 235, 241

Gaelic 4, 6, 76, 97–98, 102–3, 105, 108, 111, 208–12, 214–18, 224, 232, 245
Gaskel, Elizabeth 12, 58, 114–15, 141, 144, 160–61, 227, 233, 236, 241–42
Genette, Gerard 20, 228, 242
George IV, King 11, 14, 35, 42, 67, 69, 71, 105, 127, 214, 220, 229, 231, 241, 244

Glorious Revolution 10, 211
Gordon Riots 12, 27, 40, 116, 119, 135–38, 140, 143, 145–47, 156–57, 162, 164, 219, 222, 235, 241
gothic 2, 15, 48–49, 136, 138, 141–42, 179, 187, 198, 203, 220, 223, 230, 238, 241, 246
Gulliver's Travels 26, 105, 228, 233, 244, 246
Guy Fawkes 6, 228, 240

Hard Times 28, 113–14, 117, 159–61, 236, 241
Heart of Mid-Lothian 28, 41, 44, 57, 69, 72, 83, 88, 90, 96, 140, 142, 192, 231–32, 245
Heimra 3, 227, 240
Hereward the Wake 52–53, 230, 243
historical novel 2–3, 11, 15–17, 19–21, 24, 26–27, 29–30, 35, 48, 59, 63, 69, 71, 78–80, 82, 84–85, 88, 138–42, 147, 165, 187, 207, 219, 222, 227–28, 230–31, 235, 242, 244, 246
Hobbes, Thomas 131–32, 149, 234, 242
Hogarth, George 113, 139–40
Homer 82, 94, 102, 110, 222, 224

idiolect 145, 152–53, 155, 157–58, 164, 208, 211
Indian Mutiny 25, 132, 134–35
Industrial Revolution 173

Jackson, T.A. 3, 114, 116–17, 125, 227, 233–34, 243
Jacobite 1, 5–6, 11, 18, 26–28, 36, 38, 53, 65, 67, 69, 71–73, 76–77, 84, 86–87, 90, 92–95, 102, 104, 138, 140, 142, 144, 147, 162, 164, 171–72, 180–81, 183–85, 189–90, 192, 194, 198–201, 203, 210–12, 218, 222–25
James, Henry 192–93, 209, 238, 240, 243

Kidnapped 28–29, 83, 119, 165, 167, 171, 177, 179, 181–85, 187–90, 192–93, 195, 198, 200–4, 206–10, 213–15, 217, 237–39, 241, 244–45

literary battle 29, 61, 92, 116, 122, 124, 126–30, 225
literary warfare 37, 116
Little Dorrit 28, 113, 116–17, 134, 241
Lloyd's Weekly 3–4
Lockhart, John G. 29, 66, 75–76, 142, 228, 231–33, 243, 245

Marx, Karl 13, 18, 28, 43, 92, 113, 115, 120, 122, 125, 127–29, 157, 166–67, 170, 177–78, 181, 225, 228, 230, 234–36, 242–43
Meredith, George 12
Middle English 59, 97–99, 108, 152, 159, 161, 208, 213, 224
Mutiny on the Bounty 222, 240

Napoleon Bonaparte 12
Napoleonic Wars 74–75
national tale 15, 23, 50, 65, 77, 83–88, 109–10, 147, 222, 231–32, 242, 246
Ngugi, Thiongo 42–43, 229, 244

Old English 59, 98–99, 108, 111, 155, 160
Oliver Twist 117, 140, 160
Orwell, George 3, 19, 106, 117–22, 227–28, 233, 244
Ossian 82, 100, 102–3, 110, 224

Pentland Rising 28, 165, 185, 195–96, 202, 237–38, 245
Pentrich Revolution 12
Peterloo Massacre 69
Potato famine 14, 28, 132, 174
Prince Charlie 199
Prince Otto 26, 29, 179, 187, 193, 198, 209, 245
propaganda 5, 19–20, 35–37, 61, 86, 106, 120, 125–26, 142, 164, 185, 194, 219, 224–25, 228, 233, 244
Pugh, Edwin 2, 114–16, 227, 233, 244

Redgauntlet 6, 28, 189, 192, 245
Reform Acts 13–14, 130
regional dialect 60, 99, 153, 159, 164, 220
Rob Roy 28–29, 38, 55, 57, 69, 73, 75, 78–80, 83, 85, 87, 89, 91, 94–95, 98, 103–4, 106–8, 184, 189–90, 192–93, 199, 205, 207, 216, 229, 232–33, 239, 241, 243, 245

Scottish Insurrection 5–6, 12, 35, 65, 69–70, 73, 92
Shakespeare, William 38, 57, 81, 98, 107–8, 110, 149, 210
Six Acts 41, 69
Sketches by Boz 139–40
Speare, Morris E. 19, 27, 228, 245
standard English 56, 59, 98–99, 101, 105–7, 111, 119, 157–58, 164, 212–13, 230, 244
Sutherland, John 36, 66, 70, 74, 202, 227–32, 238–39, 245
Sybil, the Two Nations 1, 31–33, 55, 115, 144, 196, 222, 229–30, 241

Tale of Old Mortality 5, 28, 69, 83, 88, 227, 232, 245
Tale of Two Cities 1, 18, 28–29, 113, 115–16, 118, 121, 131–32, 135, 142, 145, 192, 196, 199, 220, 222, 234–35, 240–41, 243, 246
Todorov, Tsvetan 22, 228, 246

Virginians 32, 54, 222, 231, 246

Wallace, William 99–100, 102, 162, 232, 243

Waverley 2, 9, 11–12, 14, 21–22, 28, 34, 36, 42, 50, 54–55, 57, 59, 66–67, 69–72, 74–79, 81, 83, 85, 87–89, 91–95, 99, 102, 105–6, 109–10, 138, 141, 144–45, 147, 152, 180, 183–84, 188–89, 191–92, 220, 231–33, 235, 241–42, 245
White Hoods 54, 60, 230, 241, 246
Wilde, Oscar 179–81, 237–38, 241, 246

Young Chevalier 28, 165, 199, 238, 245

www.ingramcontent.com/pod-product-compliance
Lightning Source LLC
Chambersburg PA
CBHW051216300426
44116CB00006B/594